One-to-One
A Practical Guide to Learning at Home
Age 0-11

About the Authors:
Gareth Lewis has taught Mathematics and Science in state schools and Steiner schools and has worked as a private tutor for children with special needs. For the past twelve years he has home educated his three children with his wife Lin.

The family moved to Brittany, France in 1994 where they have a smallholding from which they operate an independent publishing company, Nezert Books.

The illustrations in One-to-One are by Bethan, Wendy and Samuel Lewis - self-taught artists following the principles laid out in the book.

Gareth is the editor of the Freedom-in-Education website and the Freedom-in-Education newsletter.

One-to-One

A Practical Guide to Learning At Home
Age 0 - 11

Gareth Lewis
Lin Lewis

Illustrations
Bethan, Wendy and Samuel Lewis

Nezert Books
Nezert, 22160 Duault, France

First Published 2001
This book was first published under the pen-name Martin Williams. ISBN: 095227051X

Revised, Second Edition 2003
Reprinted 2003

Published by Nezert Books
Nezert, 22160 Duault, France

Copyright © 2001, 2003 Nezert Books

British Library Cataloguing-in-Publication Data
A catalogue record for this book is available from the British Library
ISBN: 0952270560

Printed and bound in Great Britain by
Antony Rowe Ltd, Chippenham, Wiltshire

Special thanks to Rose Elliot for giving permission to use recipes from The Classic Vegetarian Cookbook
pub. 1994 Dorling Kindersley: Fantail roast potatoes p. 216; Bombay potatoes p. 217; and from The Bean
Book pub. 1982 Fontana/Collins: Tofu and carrot salad with raisins p.215 (known as Bean curd, carrot and
sultana salad) now published by Thorsons.

Contents

The School Boy

I love to rise in a summer morn
When the birds sing on every tree;
The distant huntsman winds his horn
And the sky-lark sings with me.
O! what sweet company.

But to go to school in a summer morn,
O! it drives all joy away;
Under a cruel eye outworn,
The little ones spend the day
In sighing and dismay.

Ah! then at times I drooping sit,
And spend many an anxious hour,
Nor in my book can I take delight,
Nor sit in learning's bower,
Worn thro' with the dreary shower.

How can the bird that is born for joy
Sit in a cage and sing?
How can a child, when fears annoy,
But droop his tender wing,
And forget his youthful spring.

O! father and mother, if buds are nip'd
And blossoms blown away,
And if the tender plants are strip'd
Of their joy in the springing day,
By sorrow and care's dismay,

How shall the summer arise in joy,
Or the summer fruits appear?
Or how shall we gather what griefs destroy,
Or bless the mellowing year,
When the blasts of winter appear?

William Blake

Introduction

This book aims to be of practical use to parents who are taking an active interest in their child's education. It contains sections on a more enlightened approach to the teaching of reading, writing and arithmetic and also has extensive sections on gardening, cooking, crafts and art: activities that everyone can pursue with their children and which provide a welcome antidote to the stress and pressure associated with school work.

It should be a useful resource both for parents who are teaching their children at home, and for those who want to make better use of the time that they spend with their children after school and in the holidays.

It covers the first eleven years of a child's life – because this is the time when it is of the greatest importance to them to be in a secure home environment: as children get older they become more outward-looking, and are better able to cope with an education that takes place away from their home.

An Overview

Parents receive very little good advice on how to educate their young children. There is an almost unquestioned assumption that children should go to nursery school and from there to full-time primary school and from there to secondary school and, if possible, from there to University.

This desire for success has tended to obscure the simple fact that a child's overriding requirement is to be brought up in a loving family atmosphere, and that it is from within the security provided by that family that they are able to learn and to develop into well-balanced adults.

When education takes a child away from their home for too much of the time, problems are bound to result. In addition to emotional and health problems, too much early schooling can have a detrimental effect upon a child's education.

When children are playing on their own or interacting with an adult or another child one-to-one, they are learning all the time: a young child's whole waking day is made up of useful activity and their desire to learn and to understand the world around them propels them from one subject to the next with remorseless intensity. This means that they can come to terms with all the various aspects of their environment at their own pace and in their own time and that they develop in a balanced way.

If a child is made to spend too much time in a school-type environment, however, the situation is radically different. They have to learn subjects such as reading and writing, not when it is appropriate for them, but when it fits into the school curriculum. A school can never be flexible enough to meet the real needs of each individual child, and the frustration and boredom that children inevitably experience at school has a negative impact upon their ability to learn.

These points are simply a matter of common sense – more or less everyone knows that a young child is more likely to be happy at home, if they are being well cared for, than in any other situation and that everyone, children included, learns best in a one-to-one situation.

In addition, few people would doubt that the majority of today's parents are more than capable of teaching their children to read, write and do simple sums.

However, the obvious conclusion, that parents should be encouraged to take over the major role in children's primary education, is seldom drawn. Instead, it is the school system that is being constantly developed and expanded and it is left to individual parents to try to find a sensible balance between the demands of the education system and the needs of their own children.

The situation that exists today is roughly as follows:

0 to 3-Year-Olds

This is the age at which human beings learn most rapidly and, fortunately, children of this age are not generally drawn into the education system.

The more time that you can spend with your children when they are of this age the better, because there isn't anything that can give you a better insight into how people learn. If you develop a good relationship with your child at this stage, you will be less likely to fall into the trap, later on, of trying to 'teach' them things instead of letting them learn things for themselves.

3 to 4-Year-Olds

Organised education starts to enter many children's lives, through the medium of nursery schools, when they are about three or four years old.

Taken in conjunction with childminders, crèches and other childcare arrangements, nursery schools mark the beginning of confusion for many children.

Having to deal with a succession of different adults, each with their own agenda and set of objectives, puts a large amount of stress onto a young child.

Many children of this age start to experience a conflict between their own desire to learn and their teachers' desire to teach them. This can result in their spending hours each day doing nothing at all: a very bad habit to develop at a young age.

5 to 11-Year-Olds

Full-time school attendance starts at the age of five for most children and it is at this time that problems can begin to become serious.

Children lose control of the learning process and simply become things that are being taught. Schools now have a curriculum which they apply to every child irrespective of their individual talents. They are then tested on their ability to repeat what they have been told, and their success in these tests is the sole criterion by which they are judged.

A child could probably adapt to spending a few months in the stifling atmosphere of a school and still manage to retain their enthusiasm and sense of purpose – but the six years that most children spend in primary schools is too long for anyone to survive unscathed, and the people who emerge from the primary school system at the age of eleven are not the same as those who entered it at the age of five.

As adults, we tend to think that this change is an inevitable part of growing up, but it would be foolish to imagine that the dulling influence that school exercises upon children day in, day out has no long-term effect upon those who attend.

Parents have it within their power to do something about this and can mitigate some of the worst aspects of school simply by adopting a common-sense approach to their children's education.

11+

Once children reach the age of eleven, they are more able to look after themselves and if they are helped to negotiate their first eleven years safely, they should be able to make their own, better-informed, decisions about what form of secondary education they wish to pursue.

Very Young Children

Babies and toddlers do not fall into the normal remit of education, but they do provide a very clear picture of how children learn and also of how modern society is letting children down in general.

No one doubts that children of this age have a motivation that comes from within, which makes them want to acquire the basic skills necessary for human life. They do, however, need assistance from adults. A stimulating environment and a secure home are their basic requirements.

A Stimulating Environment

Children learn through their senses – looking, listening, touching, tasting and smelling things. The more varied their environment, the more they will learn.

The environment that we now provide for our children is generally not sufficiently stimulating. Most small children spend much of their time indoors, which is bound to be less stimulating than being out of doors, and even the outdoors experience that children do have is often lacking in much of the diversity that is present in a really natural, unspoilt environment. They may be hemmed in by buildings, the ground may be covered in tarmac and there may be a complete absence of wildlife.

A child born into a society that is closely connected to nature would have a more varied experience. They would see the sun rising and setting every day and the moon and stars in the night sky; their days would be full of the sights and sounds of nature – bird song, the trees rustling in the wind, the buzzing of insects and the clouds moving across the sky.

Nature is a world in which everything moves, everything has its own feel, its own taste and its own sound: a modern, western home is a very dull environment when compared to this natural kaleidoscope of experience.

Parents have to recognise this fact and make their homes more interesting – the provision of suitable toys can make a substantial difference.

A Secure Home

A baby is totally dependent on adults for every aspect of life and this dependency lasts for many years, while they gradually acquire the skills necessary for survival.

This learning process is made easier when a child feels safe and secure in their home and when they feel that that home is going to provide them with the care and shelter that they need until they are old enough to fend for themselves.

Children who do not have this sense of security become disturbed. It is not surprising that they cannot concentrate on their 'education' but, instead, worry about their personal situation.

A child's sense of security comes not from places but from people. Children can cope with moving from place to place providing that it is the same adults who are always looking after them – for most children this will be their parents.

This means that the importance placed upon employment in our society actually works against the well-being of children who now, increasingly, do not have a parent at home to look after them for much of the time.

Many children are put in the care of childminders from an early age and they often experience being looked after by a succession of different adults. This is bound to make them feel insecure and it is hard to see how they *could* come to terms with what is happening to them.

From the child's point of view they are being cared for by one person who then leaves and is replaced by someone else; they develop a relationship with the new person and then that person leaves and so on – it is like a series of bereavements.

This cannot help but be a deeply unsettling experience for a young child.

The solution is for parents to spend as much time with their young children as they possibly can. Sometimes financial imperatives make it impossible to 'stay at home' and it is certainly true that the system is stacked against parents who want to spend a reasonable amount of time with their children. However, it is worth making considerable sacrifices to give your child a good start in life, and being at home with them for the first years must be the main priority – otherwise, why have children?

Bunnies go to Nursery School continued on page 15

Play

'Play' is not often given the respect that it deserves. For many people it conjures up an idea of wasting time and not being involved in constructive activity.

In reality, play is *the* means by which children learn. When children are playing they engage all their faculties in what they are doing and it is in this way that they discover things about themselves and the world around them.

This is obvious for very young children – one can actually see their skills and understanding develop as they play with objects that fall within their grasp.

The significance of play as a means of learning is, however, undervalued for older children. Adults sometimes consider play to be frivolous and try to direct children towards more 'educational' activities. This is a mistake. Nothing is more educational than playing and, rather than obstructing it, parents should constantly be looking for ways to give their children more opportunities to play.

The Importance of Toys

An important aspect of play is toys. Parents who want to encourage their children to play have to think carefully about what sort of toys they provide for them.

Toys have a special significance because they are the part of the child's environment that has been provided specifically for their use.

The wrong sort of toys will fail to hold the child's interest and will not encourage play.

The Problem With Modern Toys

The main problem with modern toys is that they are produced by an industry that is not driven by a desire to meet the long-term needs of children.

Instead, the commercial toy industry is motivated purely by the search for profits. Toy manufacturers have to exhaust every means at their disposal to produce toys as cheaply as possible and to sell them for as much as possible.

In order to do this, they exploit children's innocence and naivety. Children are especially vulnerable to the influence of television, and toy manufacturers have found that they can sell almost anything if it is promoted with the right sort of advertisements.

Bright colours, enticing soundtracks, fast-moving images and carefully-crafted propaganda are combined to con children into wanting toys that are cheaply produced and that have no intrinsic value.

Children are invariably disappointed with these toys, and most households have cupboards full of useless plastic junk that has hardly ever been played with and which nobody wants.

Who is to Blame?

It is clearly parents who must accept responsibility for this state of affairs. Children are the victims and simply respond to the stimulation that they are given. A child who is sat down in front of a television screen for several hours per day is obviously going to want those things that are so skilfully promoted through advertisements and endorsements.

A child cannot be blamed for wanting things that appear to be so wonderful, and equally they cannot be blamed for throwing the desired object to one side when they finally get it and find it to be disappointing.

In fact, as a parent, one should be deeply concerned that one is robbing one's child of their innocence by allowing them to be so cynically exploited by an industry that is willing to pursue a profit at almost any price.

Pressure to own these toys also comes from schools, nurseries, playgroups and friends. If a parent puts their child in a social situation with a lot of unhappy children who are themselves being manipulated by television and who judge their own and everyone else's worth by the toys that they possess, then they cannot blame their child for wanting those toys as well.

Good Toys

Good toys can still be found if you are prepared to look for them.

Traditional toys, that have been enjoyed by children for countless generations, are just as capable of providing pleasure now, as they ever were.

Toys, hand-made from natural materials, such as wood, cotton or wool, are the best. They are more expensive than mass-produced, plastic toys but they last longer and offer a child's imagination more scope to invent games for themselves.

A few high-quality toys will be treasured and give far more pleasure than a mass of cheap toys that end up being discarded.

Babies

Very small babies are quite self-sufficient. People love to buy them toys but these often remain unused: babies usually prefer to look at your face or hold your finger or feel your clothes.

When they are a little older they sometimes like rattles and bells - anything that makes an unusual noise. They also like small things that they can pick up and throw out of the pram or cot.

Babies usually like to put things in their mouths and that is why plastic is such a popular material for babies' toys. When buying wooden toys for babies you have to be one hundred per cent convinced that any paint or wood stain used in their manufacture is completely non-toxic.

Toys are definitely of secondary importance for babies. Babies love, above everything else, to have hours and hours of their parents' time.

Toddlers

Once a child can start to move around, toys become much more significant. The best toys are those that mimic some aspect of the wider world and present it to a child in a way that they can manipulate for themselves.

Everyday objects can themselves make the best toys. Things like saucepans and wooden spoons, hosepipes and buckets can be a source of almost unlimited amusement for a small child.

Bath Toys

This is an area where plastic, modern toys might be best.

Ducks, fishes, divers, submarines, balls and boats of all shapes and sizes provide hours of enjoyment in the bath.

These toys are educational as well as being fun. There is no better way of learning about the property of matter than by exposing it to a few bath-time sessions with a toddler.

A child soon discovers which things float and which things sink, which things absorb water and which things are impermeable, which things are destructible and which things are indestructible.

Building Bricks

Building bricks provide a good example of a traditional toy. They allow a child to build constructions that represent the shapes and forms that they see around them.

A good set of building bricks should contain pieces of wood of all different shapes, sizes and colours. It is then a completely flexible toy which can be incorporated into almost any game. The bricks can be used to make houses and towers, fences for farm animals, roads for toy cars, patterns and all sorts of odd constructions. The more irregular the shapes, the better, because then the shape of the bricks does not force a particular style of building on the child.

You can make your own collection with offcuts. Each brick should be carefully sanded so that it does not have any rough edges that may cause splinters and can then be left bare, or stained with environmentally-friendly, non-toxic, coloured wood stain.

Farm Animals

Most children love toy animals, even if they live in a city and have few opportunities of seeing the real thing.

If you feel ambitious you can make some wooden farm animals yourself. Make a plasticine model of the animal first, so that you get a feel for the three-dimensional shape of the animal concerned. (A plasticine model also allows you to decide what size animal you want to make.) You can then carve the animal with a sharp knife from a piece of wood. It is not as difficult as you might think.

Wooden animals can also be bought in the shops. There are some very good plastic animals available, but somehow wooden ones seem better.

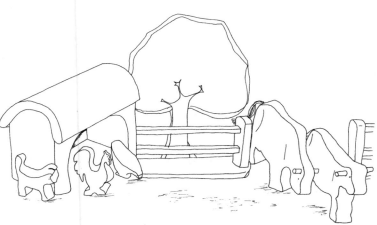

Four and Over

Once a child gets over the phase where they want to put everything in their mouth or hit everything with a hammer or hide everything in a place where it will never be found, their taste in toys starts to settle down and they can be trusted with a wider range of objects.

Marbles

Traditional toys, such as marbles, hold as much appeal for children now, as they have ever done.

Marbles come in different sizes and with innumerable different patterns. A good collection of marbles can keep most children amused for hours *(see page 115 for marble games).*

Wooden Toys

Good-quality wooden toys, such as the train sets made by Brio, can combine some of the benefits of traditional toys with the techniques of modern toy making.

Alternatively, it is not too difficult to make wooden toys oneself (albeit less sophisticated than a Brio train set!) and these can give children at least as much pleasure as a factory-made toy.

Dressing up Clothes

It is difficult to say at what age a child develops a taste for dressing up, but even very small children seem to enjoy walking around in silly hats and other people's shoes.

You can encourage your child to indulge in this pleasure by giving them a hamper of dressing up clothes.

Dressing up clothes that one buys for children (nurse's uniform, policeman's uniform etc.) can provide the basis of your collection but your children may get more pleasure from clothes that you make yourself. Dressing up clothes do not have to be of the highest quality – they just have to be a bit bizarre!

Alternatively, you can give your children your own old clothes – just adapt them for dressing up. Old disco dancing tops can make nice dresses for a very small person; old hats fit most heads and jackets make good coats if the sleeves are rolled up.

Dolls

For many children, their doll remains their most treasured possession throughout their childhood. A doll is a small human figure that a child can care for in the same way that they are cared for by their own parents. (The word 'parent' in this sense is used to denote an adult who takes responsibility for providing a child with a safe and loving home in which to grow up – not necessarily a 'biological' parent.)

This means that care should be taken in selecting a doll in order to ensure that it is capable of enduring several years of being played with and that it is aesthetically pleasing.

Porcelain dolls are a traditional toy and some of them have very nice faces and beautiful clothes, but they are, perhaps, too delicate for everyday play.

Plastic dolls are often neither well-made nor pleasing to look at. Gimmicks such as dolls that laugh or cry do not meet a child's real needs. A child has to be allowed to develop the personality of their doll for themselves.

This does not mean that children should not have modern plastic dolls. Barbie dolls can be fun. However, they are not suitable for young children and it is upsetting when one sees piles of old Barbie dolls in a child's toy cupboard with their heads and arms pulled off. One cannot help but think that the child has not been able to benefit from the pleasure that can be gained from having a really nice doll.

The best dolls are made of cloth but good ones are difficult to find in the shops because they cannot be mass-produced *(see recommended books on page 313)*.

Cloth dolls are soft, they feel warm to the touch and can take the rough and tumble of life with a young person. They can also be washed. They are a toy that gives lasting pleasure to a child.

Stilts

Stilts are a toy for an older child (at least seven or eight years old) because they require quite a high level of coordination in order to make them work.

This, however, is an advantage because toys that present a challenge are always more interesting than ones that work on their own.

Stilts are particularly fun because they make a child feel tall and one of the most annoying things about being a child is that everyone else is bigger than you are.

You can, of course, buy stilts but, on the other hand, they are not difficult to make. You just need two upright pieces of wood, approx 5 cm x 5 cm x 120 cm (2″ x 2″ x 4 ft) to which you attach footrests. These do not need to be more than 15 to 20 cm (6″-8″) above the ground. The higher the footrests, the more difficult the stilts are to use, and one has to bear in mind that the real fun with stilts comes from being able to walk with them at all – there is not a great deal of extra pleasure to be gained from having them really high.

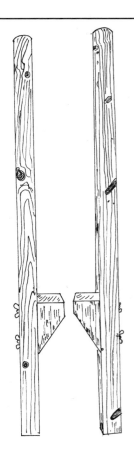

Kites

In some ways, kites cannot be called toys: kite flying is a traditional pastime for adults in many parts of the world.

However, if you can buy, or make, a simple kite that is capable of flying in a moderate wind (without crashing to the ground all the time) then your child will definitely enjoy flying it.

There is something almost magical in holding on to one end of a kite string and to see the kite flying above one's head – attached to the other end of the same string. It somehow makes one feel that part of oneself is flying free with the kite high up in the air.

Pre-School Education

The pressures on parents increase as their children get older. In addition to financial constraints that inevitably come with a young family, there are social pressures as friends, neighbours and relations expect parents to bring up their children in a certain way.

These can combine to make pre-school educational facilities (nursery schools) appear a very attractive option – parents are free to go to work and everyone approves of what they are doing.

However, neither of these factors should really count. The primary concern should be whether or not children are happy in their nursery schools (a secondary consideration may be how educationally effective nursery school is, but even this is dangerous ground because once a parent starts to think that something is good for their child even when their child is not happy, it is hard to see to whom that child can turn for help and support).

The problems associated with nursery schools are social, and are symptomatic of the way in which children are not properly valued in our society.

There are many enterprises and businesses that are fundamentally immoral and from which many parents try to protect their children, but which are nevertheless allowed to pursue their activities without any sort of restrictions.

This could be considered to include parts of the toy industry, the sweet industry, certain aspects of the broadcasting industry, the music industry and the computer industry. These businesses often seek to exploit young children in order to enhance their own profits and status.

Regrettably, this is all perfectly legal and the only way that parents can prevent their children from being overwhelmed by the intensity of the barrage maintained by these industries is to keep them at home for as much of the time as possible. Nursery schools, as well as having their own inherent problems, expose children to the watching-television, eating-sweets, computer-games, consumer culture.

Bunnies go to Nursery School continued from page 6

Institutionalisation

Nursery schools cannot offer children one-to-one attention and this inevitably leads to children having to conform to the requirements of the nursery school, as opposed to the nursery school meeting the needs of the individual child.

Each child ceases to be someone special and, instead, becomes one of a group. They are only tolerated in so far as they conform to what is required of the group as a whole.

This is institutionalisation, and the fact that many people do not see it to be a bad thing shows how far we have strayed from seeing children as they really are. We do not see that they are capable of making their own decisions about what they want to do, when they want to play, when they want to sleep, when they want to eat etc. and that these decisions are good decisions that lead to them getting the most out of each day.

Peer Pressure

It is to be doubted whether peer pressure can ever be a good thing: it must be better for someone to follow the dictates of their own conscience rather than the promptings of their friends, and there can be no doubt that it is wholly negative in the case of children too young to have formed their own judgements of the things that they see around them.

Unfortunately, children who attend nursery schools suffer intense peer pressure. However well-balanced some children in a class might be, there will always be others who are not at all happy and who will be drawn to experiences that, in better circumstances, they would have the sense to avoid.

Children who try to hold themselves aloof from these activities soon find themselves isolated from the group: they basically have to watch children's television, listen to pop music, play computer games, wear designer clothes and eat junk food in order to survive in their class.

Needless to say, when children start to demand all these things from their parents, the idea that nursery school makes family life easier and less stressful quickly evaporates.

Television

There are various reasons why television falls into the category of being something that is not good for young children.

A good toy engages a child on a physical level – they develop manual dexterity as they play with the toy – but it leaves their imagination free to develop a game in whichever way they want.

Television does the opposite of this. It fixes the attention so that there is no room for the imagination and it does not involve any physical activity at all: watching television leaves children feeling over-stimulated mentally and under-stimulated physically.

In order to compensate for this inherent deficiency in the medium, programme makers sometimes make their programmes for children as loud and as garish as possible in an effort to hold a child's attention. In the long run this is probably not a good thing.

Here are some things that you can do to protect your child from the worst aspects of television:

- Do not put your child into a situation, such as nursery school, in which they need to have watched all the previous day's television programmes in order to be accepted by their peers.

- When there is a programme that your child wants to watch, watch it with them.

- Talk to each other about what you have been watching. (This may not make for a very interesting conversation, but it is very good for your child.)

- Do not have the television switched on when your child is playing in the room.

- If possible, do not have the television in the room of the house in which you spend most of your time.

- Do not make a big issue of watching television. If your child wants to watch it, let them. Give them space to discover the good and the bad things about television for themselves so that they can make up their own mind about whether that is how they want to spend their days.

Computer Games

It is often asserted that computer games have an advantage over television in that they allow a certain amount of 'interactivity' between the child and the television screen. They are promoted as being educational, and parents are encouraged to believe that giving pre-school age children simple computers will somehow prepare them for working in a technological world when they get older.

It seems probable, however, that this argument does not represent the true picture: there is no reason to suppose that children need to be exposed to the latest technology in order to be able to cope with technical things in later life (it is quite possible that the reverse is true) and, in addition, however innocuous games for young children may appear to be, it is quite clear that computer games themselves encourage a culture of violent imagery and an enormous amount of time-wasting.

Children need to be given time to come to terms with the fundamental aspects of human life such as learning to talk, learning how to relate to other people and developing an understanding of the world around them.

There is an appropriate time for them to learn about technology, but it is probably when they are a little older and, even then, computer games are unlikely to be the ideal medium.

Sweets

Sweets seem innocent enough, but cheap sweets are a cocktail of sugar and artificial chemicals that can transform a peaceful, happy state of mind into a raging tantrum over the space of a few minutes.

They have the same effect upon children as addictive drugs have upon adults, and most responsible parents restrict, or totally deny, their children access to sweets. Once a child starts to attend nursery school this is no longer possible because there is always at least one child in every class who has access to sweets and who will use them to gain status or extract favours from other members of their class.

Generally speaking, once a parent loses control over what their child is eating, they more or less lose control of their child.

A Better Approach

There is a simple alternative to sending your child to nursery school: you can choose to carry on looking after them at home.

This has certain advantages:

Educational

Nursery schools cannot resist making some attempts to introduce children to the fundamentals of reading and writing. For most children, this is inappropriate. They are much happier if they are left alone and allowed to learn to read and write when they are older.

Artistic

Art and drawing is very important to young children. The next section of this book shows how a home environment is much more conducive to a child developing their artistic skills than a school environment.

Family Harmony

Children who are being cared for in a loving home environment will inevitably be more secure and well-balanced than those who are having to deal with all the pressures to which they are exposed at nursery school.

Many parents send their children to nursery school because they do not think that they can cope with having them at home all the time. When their children start to behave in a way that is more and more difficult to deal with, they are confirmed in this belief and the idea of looking after their children becomes even more alarming.

Much of this bad behaviour, however, is the result of going to nursery school and, given a little time, will disappear once the child starts being cared for at home again.

Family life becomes easier, not more difficult, for everyone concerned.

Common Sense

Parents of young children often spend the greater part of their time trying to work out ways of getting other people to look after their children for them. Eventually the children grow up and leave home. The parents spend all their time reminiscing about when their children were young and wishing that they had spent more time with them when they had had the chance.

It is common sense for parents to realise that they will not always have young children in their care, and it makes sense for them to reorganise their lives so that they can spend as much time as possible with their children when they *are* young.

The fact that there are other people out there who have set up whole industries based on looking after other peoples' children is really irrelevant.

To a Butterfly

I've watched you now a full half-hour,
Self-poised upon that yellow flower;
And, little Butterfly! indeed
I know not if you sleep or feed.
How motionless! - not frozen seas
More motionless! And then
What joy awaits you, when the breeze
Hath found you out among the trees,
And calls you forth again!

This plot of orchard-ground is ours;
My trees they are, my Sister's flowers.
Here rest your wings when they are weary;
Here lodge as in a sanctuary!
Come often to us, fear no wrong;
Sit near us on the bough!
We'll talk of sunshine and of song,
And summer days, when we were young;
Sweet childish days, that were as long
As twenty days are now.

William Wordsworth

Full-Time School

When a child reaches four or five years of age, education becomes compulsory. Many people are unaware that it is up to the parent to decide where and in what form their children will receive this education. It does not necessarily have to be in a school.

Parents do, in fact, have three basic options. One is to enrol their children in the state-run education system, another is to enrol them in a private school and the third is to keep them at home and take personal responsibility for their education.

Few people give active consideration to the option of not sending their young children to school. This is a pity, because going to school too early can cause a lot of problems. Children who do not respond to doing schoolwork when they are five or six years old are all too often branded as troublemakers, or as having learning difficulties. Conflict can develop between the child and the teaching staff and, when a parent steps in to help, they themselves are perceived as being the problem.

Once this happens it becomes very difficult for parents to do anything – the education authorities even resist the parents withdrawing their child from school. (These problems tend not to arise with private schools, which are generally only too pleased to see the back of a child who is causing problems.)

Parents can avoid this potential hazard by deciding for themselves whether or not they consider that their individual children are ready to start school at the age of five, six, seven etc. Generally speaking, parents who do not register their young children with a school, but who do take a responsible attitude to caring for them at home, are treated with a reasonable amount of respect by the various authorities.

For most people this is not a question of whether or not their children should ever attend school, it is simply a matter of getting the timing right.

There are a lot of disadvantages to school and it causes many children much anguish. Rather than assuming that their own children will be immune from problems, it makes sense for parents to put great care into deciding when their child should first go to school.

The History of Primary Schools

Given the lack of discussion about whether or not it is in the best interests of children to go to primary school, one could be forgiven for imagining that all children have always gone to primary school and that there is no other way in which young children can be educated.

This is far from being the case. Whereas secondary schools have been around since Roman times, primary schools only started to appear in the sixteenth and seventeenth centuries.

They were started by minority religious groups such as the Quakers and the Presbyterians who did not like the way in which they had to rely on clergymen to tell them what was in the Bible, and at that time they represented a revolutionary way of breaking the stranglehold that the upper classes had on learning.

Initially, the Church of England and the government were opposed to primary schools because they were seen as a threat to the established power structures in society but, as time passed, members of the dissident religious groups became more and more successful when compared to the population as a whole. Their ability to read and write gave them an advantage in trade and commerce and in exploiting the opportunities of the Industrial Revolution.

By the end of the nineteenth century it had become apparent to everyone that maintaining a large proportion of the population in a state of illiteracy did not benefit anyone and it was at this point that the government stepped in and started to fund primary school education for all children.

The twentieth century saw primary schools achieve the objective of reducing illiteracy to very low levels but it also saw the emergence of school-related problems that had not been envisaged and which have not yet been faced up to.

One of these problems is that primary schools no longer have a clear educational role. They have proved to be very good at teaching the children of illiterate parents to read and write, but children of parents who *can* read and write do not need to go to school to acquire these skills.

In an attempt to invent a new role for primary schools a whole range of subjects has been added to their curriculum. Rather than improving the situation, this seems to be reducing their effectiveness in assisting those children who do need help with the basic skills.

The Current Role of Primary Schools

Childcare

Many parents use primary schools as a means of keeping their children occupied whilst they go out to work. This is not a new phenomenon. Mill owners in the eighteenth and nineteenth centuries built schools for their workers' children with this very purpose in mind. The results have always been pretty disastrous. Children do not like to be abandoned in this way and it causes a very bad atmosphere to build up in schools.

Social

Parents worry that if they do not send their child to primary school then that child will be deprived of having a good social life. This view reflects a lack of clear thinking.

In school, children are put in a group with other children of their own age. This is a highly abnormal situation which can cause many difficulties. Children need to be able to develop meaningful relationships with people of all sorts of different ages.

For example, they should be assuming a caring role towards younger children, and they should be spending time with elderly people, with working people, with children slightly older than themselves etc.

The intense nature of school tends to restrict a child's social life to obsessive friendships with a few members of their own class, to the exclusion of everyone else.

Educational

Now that most children are capable of learning to read without going to school, it is unclear what educational role primary schools can play in the lives of the majority of children.

Children for whom English is not the first language

The most positive role that primary schools now perform is in helping children who come from homes where English is the second language to become fluent in the English language.

'Good' Schools

Most parents believe that there are 'good' schools and 'bad' schools. They believe that, if possible, their children should not be sent to a 'bad' school but that most children sent to a reasonably 'good' school should be reasonably happy. They believe that if a child does not prosper at a 'good' school, then the fault lies with the child and not with the school.

The most significant factor in determining whether or not a school is 'good' is the social status of the parents who send their children to it. Fee-paying schools are the 'best' and state schools situated in the heart of wealthy suburbs are the next best.

Everyone is aware that this is unfair and there have been many attempts to change the way in which the system works, but without success.

If you can afford to send your child to the 'best' schools then they will eventually leave with the 'best' qualifications and will be able to get the 'best' jobs, which means that they will be able to send their children to the 'best' schools and so on and so on.

Few parents who have enough money to ensure that their children can go to the 'best' schools can resist this logic, but it is still worth asking whether the system serves even those children who are able to go to 'good' schools.

The purpose of education should be to bring out the best in someone and help them to develop to their full potential, but the aim of these schools is principally to make their pupils do well in examinations, irrespective of the real interests of the children concerned.

Children who are subjected to this sort of treatment become very confused. They think that they should be grateful for being given such a privileged start in life but cannot understand why it does not make them happy.

Sometimes it is the children who have been sent to the 'good' schools who find it the most difficult to throw off the legacy of their schooling. It can take years before they are able to develop enough self-confidence to start following their own path in life and perhaps no one really benefits from a system that is so blatantly unfair.

'Bad' Schools

'Bad' schools reverse the picture painted by 'good' schools.

No one wants to send their children to a 'bad' school. 'Bad' schools are dangerous, violent and a breeding ground for crime and drug-taking. Their pupils get appalling exam results and rarely go on to University.

'Bad' schools are not nice places to visit or spend time in. The children play truant and the staff have nervous breakdowns.

Notwithstanding all of this, it is 'bad' schools that do most of the good work that is done by the education system. Children who go to 'good' schools do not really need to go to school at all: they come from comfortable homes that offer ample opportunities for home study. Children who go to 'bad' schools, on the other hand, may live in overcrowded and impoverished conditions and they may be experiencing severe family difficulties.

For some of these children, school is the only stable point in a turbulent life and their teachers are the only people who care enough about them to give them even the rudiments of learning.

Children who go to 'bad' schools seldom leave with useful academic qualifications but they do learn something about having to survive in an unforgiving environment and they do not expect things to be handed to them on a plate.

However, there is no getting away from the fact that 'bad' schools are bad. If you live in a deprived area and all of your local schools fall into the category of being 'bad', then you should definitely consider teaching your children yourself. However much you might sympathise with the plight of the local children and the teachers in the local schools, you must recognise that sending your child to one of these schools will not help anyone and will involve your child in a great deal of unnecessary distress.

Learning at Home

There are many different types of school but they all share the problems that arise from gathering children together in a classroom-based environment, and the only alternative to school itself is for a child to learn at home.

This solution may seem slightly out of step with the way that most people now live their lives but it is an approach to education that has been tried and tested over hundreds, perhaps thousands, of years, right around the world.

The object of primary education is to teach a child to read, to write and to be able to do simple arithmetic. This can be achieved by any parents in a few hours per day (for a few months at a time) at some point before a child is ten or eleven years old. It does not require five or six years of full-time school work.

The problem that really worries most parents is not so much how they can teach their child to read and write, but what they are going to do with them for the rest of the time if they do not go to school.

The fact that even the idea of having our children at home causes such alarm should make us realise that we need to do something to make our lifestyle more child-friendly. Common sense must tell us that there is nothing more natural than parents and children living and working together at home.

There are some basic points that you can follow when teaching a young child at home. *(See also Working With Your Child page 272.)*

- Avoid creating a school-like atmosphere in the home.
- Do not try to work the same hours as the local school.
- Restrict any reading and writing to the morning when you and your child are more wide awake.
- Establish a rhythm to your days.
- Try to spend some time out of doors every day.
- Involve your child in the things that you have to do.
- Always have some ongoing projects in hand.
- If your child wants to watch television, watch it with them. Do not use it as a babysitter while you get on with something else.

Continued on page 152

Art - Introduction

Art provides the ideal introduction to the world of learning. It gives a child a chance to become familiar with paper and pencils without making them conform to an educational curriculum.

The desire to express oneself through drawing and painting is common to everyone and young children do not need to be encouraged or persuaded to start drawing - they take to it perfectly naturally.

Allowing a young child to fully develop their artistic potential has many advantages: it boosts their self-confidence, it provides a painless introduction to writing (which in turn provides an introduction to reading) because writing is a form of art, and it opens the door to all sorts of artistic and creative activities in later life.

Generally speaking, schools do not provide an ambiance that allows children to fully develop artistically. Art, being a creative process, requires freedom and a sense of self-determination - being given specific periods of time in which to draw, and particular things to draw, combined with a chaotic or repressive atmosphere does not help children to develop their innate abilities in this subject.

The home, on the other hand, does offer the perfect environment for drawing and painting: children can have their own materials, can use them whenever they wish and can draw whatever they want.

Sometimes children develop the idea that they are no good at art, but in reality this means that they have not had sufficient opportunities to develop their talents and that insensitive people have criticised their work. Art should not be seen as a competitive activity at which some people are good and others bad: it is a means of self-expression and everyone's efforts have equal validity and worth.

Helping children to overcome any lack of self-confidence that they may have in this area is one of the simplest and most useful things that parents can do for their child in the field of education: they just have to provide the materials, the space and a little encouragement and their children will soon start painting and drawing at home. The more they practise, the more pleased they will be with their results.

The value of this sort of help cannot be overestimated: it addresses the ills at the heart of the education system in which children are taught to read and write at too young an age. This stifles their natural inclination for creative activities and the consequences of this are that many children lose their enthusiasm for academic subjects just when their interest should be beginning.

Unfortunately, many children never manage to rediscover the creative side of their nature once they have entered the school system.

Art at the Heart of the Curriculum

One of the biggest obstacles to any reform of the education system is the erroneous belief that children need to be taught to read and write when they are only five years old. Whilst this early tuition may help a minority of children to succeed in the school system, it does not help any of them to develop to their full potential, which should be the aim of education.

Concentrating on reading and writing when they are very young curtails a child's ability to focus on other activities more in keeping with a young child's mental and emotional development, but the reverse is not the case. Children who are encouraged simply to play and to enjoy themselves when they are young soon catch up with children who have been reading and writing for years, once they do start to take an interest in these subjects.

Painting and drawing is the link between these two worlds. It does belong in the world of play but it introduces a child to working with paper and pencils; it allows a child to express their own creativity but, in doing so, they also learn how to make the shapes and forms that they will one day use for writing.

This means that it is art and not reading, writing and arithmetic that should be at the heart of the educational curriculum for young children.

Once a child has developed an affinity for the subject, there is nothing more natural than for them to want to continue to improve and develop their technique as they grow older.

Materials

This is an important issue. It is easy to become dogmatic about which artistic materials are best and not to let a child use things like felt-tip pens or biros. Even a young child enjoys trying out different types of crayons and pens: it is part of the learning process and it is therefore a good idea to have as many different artistic materials available as possible.

All the same, you do have to be sensitive to the fact that young children are not comfortable with some of the drawing materials that older children can use with ease: they find some pens, brushes and crayons difficult to hold; are likely to break delicate materials and may spill inks and paints all over themselves, and their pictures. You have to give them appropriate materials with which to work.

In fact, it is the availability of the right sort of materials that largely determines the degree of enthusiasm that a child has for art.

Young children need a plentiful supply of simple materials with which they cannot do any harm to themselves or their surroundings, while older children need a wide range of good quality materials if they are to be able to develop their interest in the subject.

Age One to Three

You can start drawing with children when they are very young but you do have to provide the right sort of crayons. The best ones are, obviously, those that are easy to use and enable your child to produce beautiful pictures.

Stockmar crayons (marked on the tin 'Wachsfarben' - literally, wax colours) are exceptionally good: they are made from beeswax and use natural pigments; they start off in a pleasing cuboid shape, but constant use rounds off the edges and allows them to nestle comfortably into a small hand.

The overwhelming advantage of these crayons is that, because they are big and thick, they encourage a child to cover every square inch of a piece of paper with colour.

When this is achieved it represents a huge step forward from lines and scribbles in the middle of a white expanse. Drawings made up of lines can be very good, but when a child realises that a picture can be made up of colour covering the whole page, the world of art opens up to them.

If you cannot get hold of these chunky wax crayons, have a look around an art shop. Wax crayons in general are the best for young children if only because they cannot easily harm themselves when using them.

The earlier you start drawing with your children, the better. Admittedly the exercise may not be very rewarding for a parent in the early stages. Typically, a very young child will grab a piece of paper, scribble on it, grab another piece of paper, scribble on it etc.

This does not mean that you are wasting your time. You can do a lot at this stage to establish good habits and develop appreciation of good materials. Here are some tips:

1. Always use plain paper. A3 photocopy paper is good as it allows a child scope to express themselves. Lined paper detracts from the child's work.

2. Have a good supply of paper. Don't pressurise a child to do more work on a particular picture than their own inclination dictates.

3. Let them start a new piece of paper whenever they want.

4. Work alongside your child, using the same materials. Take some time over your picture, trying to cover the whole sheet in colour. Don't worry if your child does several pictures to your one: in time they will slow down and start to take as much care over their work as you do over yours.

5. Keep your child's pictures safe. Don't let them scrumple or tear them up.

6. Keep the 'best' ones in a folder.

7. Always praise your child's efforts. Remember that a very young child is not capable of doing sloppy or second-rate work. Everything that they do is an expression of themselves. To you it may be a scribble and perhaps you think that you can make helpful suggestions, but you have to try to remember that the time for critical analysis comes later. For young children, if you criticise their pictures, you criticise them - there is no distinction between them and their work.

8. Let your child decide when to finish the drawing 'session' – don't make them carry on when they are bored.

9. Keep the crayons in a safe place.

10. Don't devalue the exercise by allowing your child to scribble all over the table and the walls. A child derives far more enjoyment from drawing when they see that their efforts are treated with respect by their parents as opposed to them just being allowed to run amok and nobody really caring.

Ages 4 to 7

The situation changes when a child gets a little older: painting becomes a feasible activity; they can experiment with different sorts of crayons and they are more able to draw or paint specific things.

Having developed good habits when they are young, children soon start to work on their own, creating masterpieces without your assistance. Obviously, a child who has been producing copious pictures since the age of 18 months is going to have more confidence than a child who has not, but you can adapt your technique as a 'teacher' to cope with this.

It is never too late to start doing artwork with your child. Use the methods discussed for very young children i.e. have plenty of paper; do not make negative criticism, in fact don't make criticism; work alongside your child and be prepared to spend plenty of time painting and drawing. No one just picks up a brush and is instantly a brilliant artist. Like anything else, it is something that takes practice and commitment. Whilst the object need not be to make a child into a 'good artist', it is worthwhile for them to develop their self-confidence and to be able to feel pleased and proud of what they produce on paper. This is achieved through practice and is within the capabilities of everyone. No one is inherently bad at art. If as an adult you feel artistically inadequate, reflection will probably let you acknowledge that this was an idea about yourself that you picked up at school.

Working with a child will not only help them, but will also help you - it will help you to discover your own undeveloped artistic talents.

Drawing

Drawing remains the most accessible artistic activity: it does not require much preparation and children can do drawing more or less whenever they want when they are at home.

Paper

You can carry on using A3 photocopy paper but, if your budget allows it, try buying different grades of good quality drawing paper from an art shop, to be used for special pictures.

Crayons

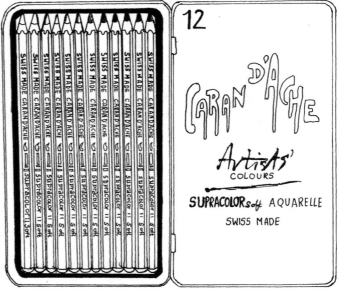

At some point, coloured pencil crayons will probably become your child's preferred medium.

Buy the best quality crayons available. It is better to have a tin of 12 really good crayons than a set of 50 cheap crayons. Caran d'Ache is the make that we have always favoured, but other people prefer Derwent.

Keep your best crayons safe. Don't let them be taken to school and be careful about leaving them lying around when friends come to play. Individual crayons can be replaced when they are lost or damaged, but children soon come to view their crayons in the same way that a craftsman regards his tools. Each crayon assumes its own personality and has to be looked after carefully.

Cheap crayons are not an acceptable alternative: the leads break and the colours are flat. Children need good crayons if they are to produce beautiful pictures.

Felt-Tip Pens

Felt-tip pens are cheap and for this reason are often given to children as presents. However, they are not easy to use. Producing a beautiful picture with a felt-tip pen requires skill and it is not being fair to a child if felt-tip pens are their only drawing implements, because they then have little chance of producing really pleasing pictures.

Painting

Painting requires much more preparation than drawing. It also creates more mess, so you have to build up a sort of painting kit, which may include:

- **a plastic tablecloth** to cover whatever surface you are working on.

- **painting aprons** for yourself and your child. This could be an old apron but it may be better to use one of your old shirts (the bigger, the better), as this covers everything up more efficiently.

- **paint** – use water soluble paints. Oil-based paints can make a terrible, irreparable mess. You can use blocks of paints, squeezy bottles of concentrated liquid paint (which you dilute) or powdered paint that you mix with water. As a minimum you need the primary colours: red, blue and yellow. You will, however, find life easier if you have a white, a green, a purple etc. A black is also useful, although some children use it too much and produce completely black pictures. If this starts to happen you can remove the black for a while.

- **brushes** – large brushes are the best for young children. They should have long handles and the brush itself should be about half an inch across.

- **paper** – you need a fairly absorbent paper, for example you can use a roll of lining paper from a wallpaper shop. Buy the most expensive because it is the thickest and will not tear so easily.

Painting is not as easy as you might imagine. Do not just give your child some blocks of paint and expect them to enjoy themselves: they are much more likely to have a good time if you work with them.

You do not have to be good at painting yourself, the fact that you are working together gives your child all the encouragement that they require.

Here are some suggestions you can make:

- it is best to cover the whole page with colour

- keep washing your brush

- change your water from time to time

- have some little plastic pots handy in which you can mix up new colours

- do not get too much water on your paper. Mop up excess liquid with a tissue

It is not easy to get a satisfactory painting with a big brush and water colour blocks, so do not be discouraged if your pictures are not as good as you would like them to be: children do enjoy painting and this makes it worthwhile.

Painting on wet paper
If you are not happy with the paintings that you are producing, you can try painting on wet paper: the colours run into each other and the overall effect is much softer.
Immerse the paper in a bowl of water for a few seconds, lay it on a board and remove excess water with a sponge. You will find that the paper will stick to the board.
You will have about half an hour to paint your picture while the paper dries out.
This is a good technique for painting flowers, trees, sunsets, water and fires.

Modelling

Modelling is another form of artistic activity that all children enjoy and take to naturally. Drawing and painting are two-dimensional art forms and do not allow an accurate representation of three-dimensional objects. Young children will make models out of anything that comes their way - especially out of mud and soil. Most parents try to direct them towards materials that do not make quite such a mess - such as sand.

You cannot trust young children not to put modelling materials into their mouths, so they need to be non-toxic and, preferably, edible. Bread dough is ideal *(see page 208)*.

Age Seven to Eleven

As a child gets older, all sorts of opportunities for them to further develop their artistic abilities present themselves.

Drawing

Coloured crayons

Coloured crayons remain the favourite artistic medium for most children, so a big tin of 40 – 80 top-quality crayons is a worthwhile investment.

Pencils

Once someone has acquired the basic skills of drawing they may prefer to use graphite pencils instead of colours.

In some ways pencil drawing is more difficult than colour drawing as you have to pay more attention to shading.

You can make a collection of different pencils. HB pencils are the most commonly used but not all HB pencils are the same. You have to experiment with the pencils that you have, to find which ones suit you best.

If a drawing is sketched out with an HB pencil then the shading can be done with a 2B or even a softer-leaded pencil – anything up to 9B.

Hard pencils (H, 2H etc.) are not often used for drawing – they are reserved for technical work and designs.

Charcoal

Charcoal sticks and pencils are traditional artists' materials but they are more difficult to use than pencils and the pictures may smudge unless you spray them with a fixative when they are finished.

Pastels

Sets of pastel sticks are available at quite reasonable prices. Oil pastels come in vivid colours which appeal to all ages, but to achieve the gentle, slightly blurred effect associated with pastels, the traditional sort should be purchased. They give an effect somewhere in-between crayon and painting, but they are not terribly easy to use.

They offer the opportunity for experimentation - just using them like crayons does not work very well: it produces a striking effect but the pastel tends to be too thick and falls off the paper. Using a large amount of white in pastel drawings gives a sense of light to the picture and rubbing with a finger or piece of tissue makes the colours merge together.

Pastel drawings can be 'fixed' with a fixative to prevent them from being rubbed off. Liquid fixatives that you paint on with a brush can smudge the picture unless you are very careful. Spray-on fixatives may, therefore, be a better idea but both liquid and spray fixatives can alter the appearance of the colours.

Painting

Watercolours

If your child enjoys painting, then at some point they will have to graduate to proper watercolours.

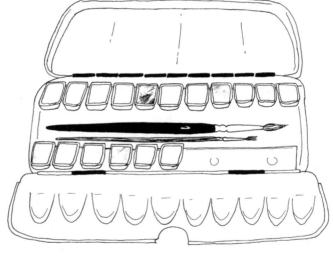

Good artists' materials are always expensive, but they are worth buying because they last a long time and it is impossible to create beautiful pictures without them.

The simplest course of action is to buy a watercolour set from an art shop.

You do not need many colours to start with and most watercolour tins have space to add more colours as you need them.

The same applies to brushes. One good brush is enough to begin with and you can buy more as you go along.

You will need one watercolour set for yourself and another for your child. They are not something that can easily be shared.

It is also very important that you buy proper watercolour paper. The paper contributes almost as much to the picture as the paint. You can either buy a sheet of watercolour paper and cut pieces off it as you need them or else buy a pad of watercolour paper.

When you produce a picture that you are pleased with, you can frame it and hang it on the wall. Watercolour pictures need a glass frame. It is surprising how much they improve a picture and it will greatly encourage your child to see their favourite pictures hanging on the wall in a proper frame. Second-hand frames can be bought from car boot sales, jumble sales, etc.

Oil Painting

Oil painting is quite a different technique from watercolour painting.

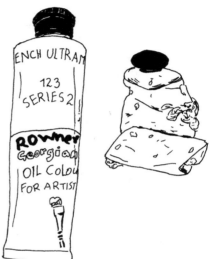

Painting-by-number sets can provide an introduction to oil painting. They give an opportunity to experience working with oil paints, but anyone who is used to painting their own pictures will find them a little restrictive.

A more comprehensive introduction to oil painting requires a slightly greater investment. You have to buy a few tubes of paint, one or two oil-painting brushes, some oil-painting boards, turpentine, linseed oil and a palette. A book that describes different oil-painting techniques will also be useful.

Oil paints dry very slowly so you generally have to take quite a long time over each picture – repeatedly working on one section of the picture and then leaving it for a few days to dry.

There is no reason why children of this age group should not use oil paints. It is not a medium suitable for children taking their first steps in art, but any child who has spent time developing their technique by drawing with coloured crayons will enjoy the detail and the colours that can be achieved by using oil paints.

Initially, it is probably best to paint on oil-painting boards rather than on canvas or oil-painting paper. Boards are available in a variety of sizes from art shops.

The picture can be sketched out beforehand with a pencil.

Mistakes can be corrected by removing paint with a cloth soaked in turpentine or by allowing the paint to dry and painting over it at a future session.

Improving Your Technique

There are many resources available to help parents and children further their interest in art:

Books

Art shops and libraries usually have a wide range of books that give advice on how to develop one's artistic abilities. They vary in difficulty and it is possible to find books suitable for everyone, whether they be a complete beginner or an advanced student.

To be 'good' at art one has to learn how to combine one's own unique abilities with techniques that have been developed by other artists over hundreds of years.

It is not realistic to read a book on painting or drawing and hope thereby to become a good artist. Books can help, however, by giving tips and ideas which make it possible to recreate on paper the pictures that one has in one's head.

In addition to self-instruction books, there are also countless books containing reproductions of famous pictures (often available at reduced prices in discount bookshops). Books of this sort are an invaluable resource which give a child a chance to study the work of great artists from the comfort of their own home - a privilege that has not been available to previous generations.

Lessons

There is no substitute for a sympathetic teacher. If you can find an artist who is willing to give you and/or your child lessons, then you should take the opportunity. Nevertheless, art is a means of self-expression and if a teacher tries to impose a particular style or way of working, then lessons should be discontinued.

Adult education centres, art shops and community centres often run art classes. These can prove to be a very good way of picking up tips on how to improve one's art work. Students learn from each other as well as from the teacher.

If your child does not want to go, you can attend the classes on your own and pass on everything that you learn.

Copying

Copying the work of great artists has always been one of the best ways of learning to draw and paint and should not be regarded as an inferior activity.

The ready availability of good quality, printed reproductions of great works of art means that everyone now has the chance to copy the work of the very best artists.

Art books, postcards sold in art galleries and greetings cards in general are all good sources of material from which to copy.

Art Galleries

Art galleries become a lot more interesting when you have tried to copy some famous works of art yourself: they give you the opportunity to look at pictures close to and to really understand how the artist has managed to create the effects that have made some pictures so famous.

When you see the original of a picture you can distinguish the individual brush strokes and the things that are not apparent in reproductions – however good they may be.

Cartoons

Certain art forms are looked down upon as being second-rate and this attitude is sometimes applied to cartoons, which is a mistake, because cartoons provide an excellent outlet for creative abilities.

It is an area in which a child can quickly develop their own distinctive style. Children enjoy making up their own cartoon characters, drawing cartoon strips and making their own comics.

They can start out by copying cartoon characters from commercial comics and from the television – which you might not consider to be a very good use of their time – but, if you refrain from criticism, they will soon move on and use cartoons as a means of expressing their own perspective on life.

Landscapes, Portraits etc.

The more interested your child becomes in art, the more different styles and techniques you can try.

Landscapes are, perhaps, best done from a photograph. If you decide to go out into the country to do a day's painting in the open air it will almost definitely rain and will probably be windy. You can try making a quick sketch of any good views that you find and take a photograph of them. This will allow you to take your time over the picture itself, at home.

If you are interested in portraits you might like to get some tips from a book about portrait painting and drawing. You can also experiment by trying to draw portraits of famous people from pictures that you cut out of newspapers and magazines.

Much the same applies to drawing animals. Each animal has distinctive features and a few tips from a good book can be a great help in getting them right.

Still life

Still life is the simplest exercise for improving technique. Make an arrangement of objects – you can use pieces of fruit, vegetables, crockery, jugs etc.

Flowers are another traditional element of still life drawings but you have to be sure that you can finish your drawing before the flowers wilt and the petals fall off. It is fine if you work on consecutive days but it is not feasible if, for instance, you are only available at weekends.

You can use crayons, pencils, charcoal, watercolours, pastels or oil paints.

As an alternative to working on white paper you can try using brown paper or black paper. White chalk on black paper gives an interesting effect and charcoal on brown wrapping paper is also worth trying.

What Children Draw

It has long been recognised that the pictures children draw can tell us a lot more about their state of mind than what they say or what they write.

Children who have had traumatic experiences produce disturbing pictures.

If your child produces dark, gloomy pictures or pictures full of violent images, then you should take this as a sign that action must be taken to change their lifestyle.

In some cases, just encouraging them to watch less television may be sufficient. In other cases you may find that a particular 'friend' or group of 'friends' is causing your child distress.

Often it is school that is the root of the problem.

Whatever it is, you must do something about it. You will know that you have resolved the problem when your child's pictures become lighter, more colourful and depict happy scenes.

Modelling

When children are older, their ability to make three-dimensional models increases. This is an important aspect of art and of education in general. Modelling an object helps one to discover something about its nature that cannot be learnt from reading books or even by drawing pictures of it.

Plasticine

Plasticine is a traditional modelling material that is very versatile and can be used by everyone - from beginners to skilled modellers. It is probably the best all-round modelling material available for use in the home.

Although it is a clay-based material, it does not dry out, and this means that you can keep working on a model over a period of days or even weeks.

The only problem is that it can ruin carpets and soft furnishings if it is trampled in or sat on, and this makes it an inappropriate material for very young children.

You cannot make permanent models with plasticine but you can keep models that you particularly like for quite a long time and then simply recycle them to make new ones.

It is available in big single-colour blocks from art shops - you do not need to buy a variety of different colours.

FIMO

There are various brands of modelling material available that come in a variety of colours and which can be hardened in the oven. FIMO is one of these.

These products are good for making small items – pieces of jewellery, fridge magnets, ornaments, etc. - but are not suitable for large models. Their overwhelming advantage is that they allow a child to make relatively permanent models without the need for a kiln.

Clay

Clay is the ultimate modelling material: it costs next to nothing (it is just dug out of the ground) and it is used to make pottery, which has always been counted amongst the greatest achievements of human creativity - but it only comes into its own if you have access to a kiln. If you are not able to fire your work, the things that you make just dry out, become dusty and fall apart.

There are clays available that do harden to a certain extent in an ordinary oven but they are not really satisfactory. The firing of clay involves a chemical reaction that changes the chemical composition of the clay itself. This requires a high temperature and if, you want to make clay models that will last, you either need to have a kiln of your own or an arrangement with a potter who will fire your work for you.

Art—Summary

More than any other subject, art is an activity that parents and children can pursue together at home. There is no conflict between work done at home and work done at school (as there sometimes is with other subjects such as writing or arithmetic) and children who become proficient at drawing and painting at home will find that it makes their time at school more enjoyable because they will always receive praise for presenting their work attractively.

Parents need not be too formal in their approach: art needs to be pursued in a free and unrestricted atmosphere and children have to feel free from external constraints in order to fully develop their talents.

It is a therapeutic activity and is one of the few things that can be done in the evenings after a hard day at school. If you can develop a habit early on in your child's school career of sitting down with them when they come home and doing some drawing together, you will find that it gives them a perfect opportunity to unwind and to tell you about their day. This simple activity can help to avoid a gulf opening up between you and your child once they start to attend school - a circumstance which causes so much distress to so many parents.

Home-taught children can have art as the foundation of their education. They should be able to do as much art as they want, and up until the age of seven or eight all their work can be done in the form of pictures. It is commonly said that a picture can speak a thousand words but this self-evident truth is rarely made use of in education. A young child who draws a picture of something is bound to understand more about that thing than a child who writes about it.

Many parents who teach their children at home make the mistake of trying to emulate the work that takes place in school. This approach invariably runs into problems: children who go to school do not want more of the same at home; and children who do not go to school do not want school work at second hand - they are perceptive enough to realise that if they are going to do that sort of work, they may as well do it in school.

Art provides the alternative. It is something that is never covered properly at school and yet it opens up the whole world of learning to a child.

Writing

Learning to Write

The ability to write is related to a child's physical development.

If children are made to write at too young an age, they experience an actual physical discomfort in forcing their hands to form the letters on the page. These physical difficulties can give writing (and by association, reading too) painful connotations that can lead to a permanent aversion.

Thus writing is an area of education where an adult can do immeasurable damage by seeking to impose a rigid programme of instruction upon a child. Different children develop the motor skills required for writing, at different ages, and it is far better to be guided by the inclination of the child than by fixed ideas that children should be able to do certain things at specific ages.

When is the Best Age to Learn?

Preparation for learning to write comes from art and drawing. Children who have plenty of opportunity to express themselves by drawing will, over a period of years, build up the skills necessary for writing.

This principally involves acquiring a familiarity and dexterity with a range of writing implements and being able to create forms on a page that are pleasing to the eye. A child who has developed the habit of producing pictures that are beautiful and of which they are proud would never dream of lowering these standards by producing messy and untidy handwriting.

This basic fact about handwriting is better understood in the East than in the West. Writing has been a well-established skill for millennia in China and Japan and is still regarded as an art form in its own right. In our culture we have come to see writing as a purely utilitarian exercise where the content is everything and the appearance is nothing.

This is not the way in which to introduce writing to a child. Children have a natural affinity for beauty and enjoy creating elegant and symmetrical shapes on the page, and a child who has spent a lot of time drawing and painting will enjoy learning to write.

Initially, the fact that the shapes that they draw make letters which convey a particular meaning is of only secondary importance, but once a child has learnt to write letters, and can join them together to make words, they will naturally start to associate meaning with what they have written.

In this way children develop an interest in reading that arises out of the writing that they do themselves. It is, in fact, much better to learn to write before learning to read rather than the other way round.

School vs. Home

Schools tend to make children learn to write before they are ready and this means that they have to start by teaching them to write in printed letters – they are not able to form joined up letters because they are too young.

This makes the whole process of learning to write unnecessarily difficult and leads many children to see writing as an arduous and unpleasant chore.

Children who are allowed to wait until they are a little older before learning to write – age seven or eight – can start off with joined up writing.

This has many advantages but it does, of course, present a problem for parents who send their young children to school. It is not possible to prevent a school from teaching children to write – the whole school curriculum is based on writing.

If your child is learning to write at school then it is best not to interfere. Anything that you say or do will only make matters worse. The following pages apply to parents who have decided not to send their children to school until they have first learnt to write at home.

Writing Materials

Children have to be allowed to select their own writing implements. A child who is made to use a pen or pencil with which they are not comfortable will never be happy with the work that they produce.

As a child grows older their preferences are bound to change, so it is a good idea to have a wide range of writing materials available. Very young children often learn to write their names with thick, wax crayons while slightly older children usually prefer a soft pencil.

Biros are not free-flowing and are not ideal for learning to write, but there are now a variety of similar pens – roller points etc. – that do write very well.

Good quality fountain pens still make the best writing implements but they can be difficult for young children to use (it is easy to press too hard, which bends the nib and everything gets covered in ink).

This is another good reason why children should wait until they are seven or eight before they learn to write – they are then old enough to use a fountain pen with relative ease.

The best solution is to have as wide a range of writing materials available as possible. Your child can then keep experimenting with them and use the ones that they prefer.

This is where children who have always spent a lot of time drawing will come into their own. They will already be familiar with the properties of all their pens, pencils and crayons and will have no problem in selecting the one which they will find most comfortable for writing.

CAPITAL LETTERS

Capital letters provide a good starting point for learning to write because most of them are formed from straight lines and have quite distinctive shapes. This makes them easy for children to identify and reproduce.

They are quite adequate for the requirements of young children who generally only want to know how to write their names and a few messages to members of their family.

Initially, capital letters do not have to be introduced in sequence. Different children want to learn different things. For example, one child may want to know how to write their name when they are as young as two or three years old and, once they have mastered it, not show any more interest in learning to write for four or five years, while another child may want to write messages to all their friends and relatives from the age of four or five.

The simplest way to deal with this is to write out anything that your child wishes to write, in capital letters, and let them copy it. They will eventually start to learn the shapes of the capital letters for themselves.

Later on (when they are six or seven years old), you may like to go over how each of the capital letters is written to make sure that they know them all.

Practical Points

- Learning to write the letters can be taken as slowly, or as quickly, as a child wishes.

- The direction of the strokes for writing each of these letters is shown opposite.

- You do not have to restrict yourself to writing the letters on pieces of paper. You can walk the letters out on the ground, following the pattern outlined by the direction arrows. You can also draw the letters in the air. You can make a game out of this, with you and your child guessing which letter each of you is drawing.

- You can also try to draw the letters in the air with your eyes closed. This is surprisingly difficult for a young child, but they generally enjoy it.

- Finally you can draw the letters on a piece of paper using chunky wax crayons. You do not have to write the letter over and over again. It is fun to write big letters, with one letter filling a sheet of photocopy paper.

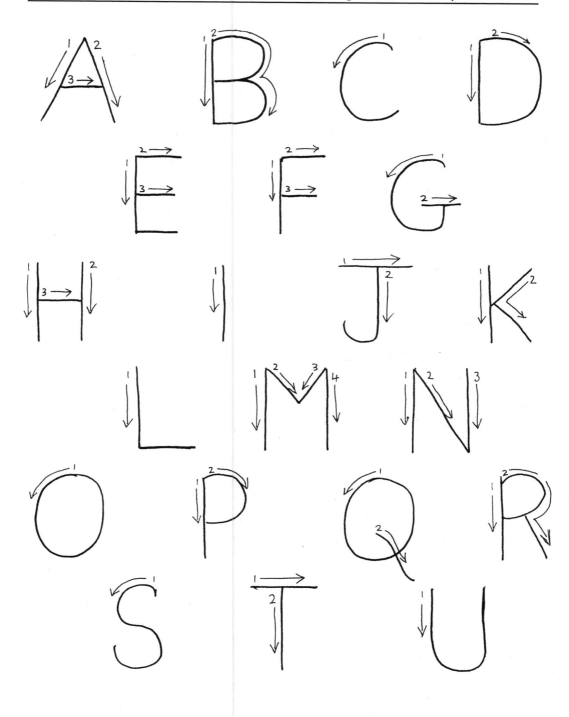

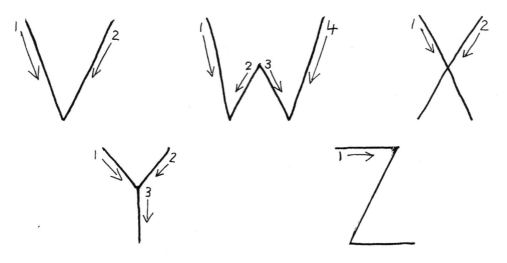

If you have decided to take responsibility for teaching your child to write, it is at this point that you will encounter the biggest obstacle to success in teaching – possibly for the first time.

This obstacle is your own attitude.

Most of us believe that in order to teach a child properly we have to behave like a school teacher, with us explaining things and our children listening obediently. This does not work in practice.

Instead, one has to make learning a continuation of play and you can only do this if you already have a good rapport with your child through other activities that you do together.

For example, if you think that it is a good idea to do some writing, you can suggest that your child add a few words to a birthday card that you are making for someone, or you can show them how to write a title for a picture that they have drawn.

You can make learning to write the letters into an interesting activity by telling a story that introduces one letter at a time. When a new letter is introduced, you stop and learn how to write it. You can draw a picture of the character or item represented by the letter.

There is no need to teach the letters in sequence. Each letter can play a part in the story and it can be fun to guess which one is coming next. Alternatively, your child can suggest which letter should be introduced – this gives you more of a challenge.

You can use this story to introduce the idea of working in an exercise book. Try to find an A4-size (U.S. letter size) exercise book with *plain* pages for drawing (exercise books with lines should be avoided as much as possible because the lines detract from illustrations and even restrict writing). Write the capital letter on one page and draw an accompanying illustration on the facing page. It is best if you and your child have a book each.

Here is an example of how a story involving capital letters might start :-

__A__my is a little girl. She lives with her mummy and daddy on a high __M__ountain Her favourite toy is a __B__all which she accidentally drops down the mountainside...

or

__A__drian is a little boy, he lives in a __H__ouse with his mummy and daddy. Every day a __B__ird comes to his __W__indow....

You can introduce one or more new letters each day, depending on how it goes.

This exercise teaches a lot about the art of storytelling. A story that develops at the rate of only a few sentences per day has the potential to captivate the imagination of a young child – the simpler the story the greater the appeal.

Practice

The next step is to practise writing the letters. Rule lines 5 cm (2 inches) apart on a piece of A3 paper and, using a 3B or 4B pencil, carefully repeat the same letter along one row yourself. Your child can then copy these on the lines that you have drawn below.

This gives them a chance to improve their technique and gets them into the habit of writing on a straight line and doing a series of letters all the same size.

This process can be repeated until all the letters have been drawn and you are both happy with the result.

Capital letters are quite adequate for most children's needs until they are old enough to learn to use joined up writing.

Printed letters – lower case

As has already been mentioned, there is no need for a child to learn to write small printed letters. It is tedious, unattractive and of little use in future life. They can always learn them when they are older should they be keen to do so.

Children learn printed letters in school because they are too young to be able to write in joined up writing. They expend a lot of time and heartache trying to master this skill only to discover a few years later that it is of no use - they have to start all over again learning to write joined up letters.

Most children cannot just forget their printed letters and consequently their writing is often a combination of the two styles. It looks a mess and makes the child feel discouraged.

Joined up Writing or Running Script

A child who has not been burdened by having to learn to write printed letters but who has, instead, been allowed to enjoy themselves through lots of drawing, will probably be happy to learn to write in joined up letters when they are about seven or eight. (It is a big mistake to be too rigid about this. Every child is different and it does not help to either hold a child back or to try to push them forward. You have to be sensitive to their real needs.)

Children who have been allowed to develop their artistic skills will automatically want to produce a good standard of handwriting. Children who have never learnt to write in printed letters will not have been able to acquire any bad writing habits.

This results in their seeing writing as something of which they are proud and which they enjoy.

Lower Case letters (i.e. small letters)

The following describes a tried and tested approach to learning to write. The entire process need only take a couple of weeks if a child wants to learn.

- Buy a ream of A3 (U. S. 11″ x 17″) photocopy paper.

- Rule out lines about 2 cm (¾″) apart (using a pencil and ruler) on one of the sheets.

- Fill in rows of letters on alternate lines.

- Let your child copy each row of writing, on the line below.

- Work slowly, taking care to make each letter as perfect as possible.

- Go through the alphabet writing out a line of each letter.

- If necessary, practise writing the letters yourself to ensure that you can consistently make them the same size and shape.

The following pages show the suggested strokes for each letter. Although the strokes are numbered, each letter in this script (with the exception of 't', 'i' and 'j') should be done without lifting the pencil from the paper. This gives a feeling of flowing and continuity, which will make it easier later on when you actually join up the letters to make words.

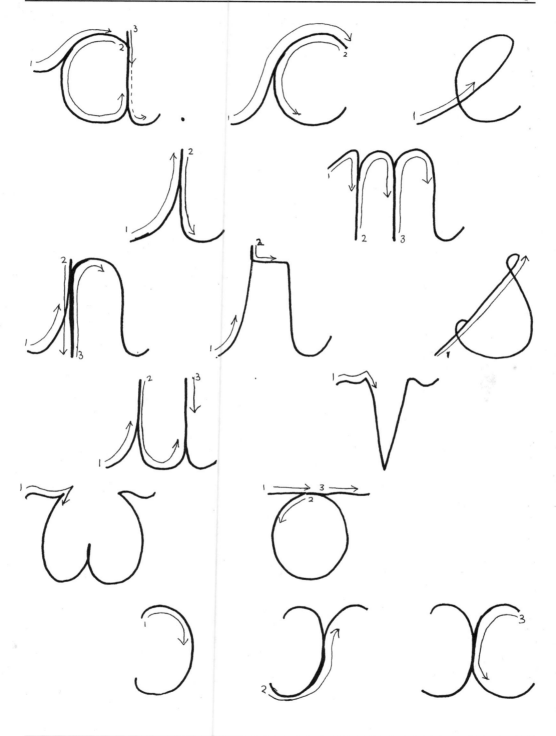

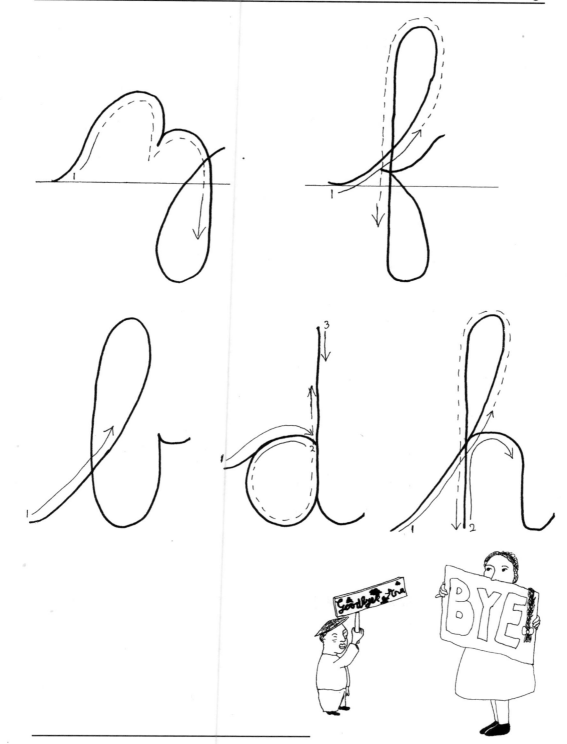

ttttttt... uuuuu...

vvvvvv... wwwww..

xxxxxx... yyyy...

yyyy...

- Repeat letters that you (or your child) find difficult.

- Repeat letters that you find particularly fun.

- Overleaf are some suggestions on how you can experiment with combinations of different letters.

- Spend as much time on this as you want. If a child is really ready to learn to write, they will probably want to spend an hour or two per day doing this sort of work. At the end of a few weeks they will be able to produce perfect handwriting.

- At first concentrate on having fun. Don't try to write words. The object of the exercise is to learn to enjoy making the shapes of the different letters.

- You can experiment with combinations that the child may recognise from their reading books, building up short words from the combinations of letters that you have learnt to draw.
  For instance, the exercise over the page shows how the combination of *cacaca* can be used to form words such as *cat, ace* and *act*. It is better if *i, j* and *t* are dotted or crossed after the word is written, so the child does not have to lift the pen off the paper.
  This exercise also introduces the idea of leaving a space between words.

- Keep all this work in a big folder. Don't just leave all the pieces of paper lying around as scrap – this would show a want of respect for the work that has gone into them.

cacacaca....

lililililili....

dededede....

hmhmhmhm....

jkjkjkjkjk....

oeoeoeoeoe....

dqdqdqdqdq....

gdgdgdgdg....

wscwscwsc....

pupupupupu....

yzyzyzyzyz.....

caca → cat ace act

lili → little tilt

dede → deed lad

hmhm → him hum

jkjk → jack lack

oeoe → joe jack

qdqd → quid queen

gdgd → god good

wxwx → wax

pupu → puppy

nmnmnm → name

grgrgr → grin ring

The advantages of working together

All this may seem like a lot of work for you – which indeed it is – but it does have some advantages.

Firstly, it may make you feel much better about your own handwriting – especially if you had a bad time at primary school and have felt somewhat inadequate with regards to your handwriting ever since (not as rare as you might think).

Secondly – and this is very important – it will mean that you are able to write in a style almost exactly the same as that of your child. Young children experience great difficulty in reading different styles of handwriting. In primary schools most children can read their own teacher's handwriting but if a supply teacher comes in to teach the class, chaos can erupt because half the class cannot understand what is being written on the blackboard.

If you teach your child to write using the method just described then you will be able to write things down in the form that your child finds most easy to read i.e. the same as their own handwriting.

Upper Case Letters
(i.e. capital letters)

Once you are happy with the lower case joined up letters, you can learn some capital letters that will match them for elegance.

The following pages show the direction of the strokes for each of these.

Once again, rule some lines approximately 2 cm (¾ inch) apart on plain paper. Complete one line yourself and let your child copy it on the next line.

Go through the alphabet in this way, taking care to draw each letter as beautifully as possible.

Extra Exercises

Once upper and lower case letters have been mastered you can combine them by writing the names of people that you know. This is a very useful exercise because it teaches you which capital letters are best joined up to the rest of the word and which look better when not *(see page 61).*

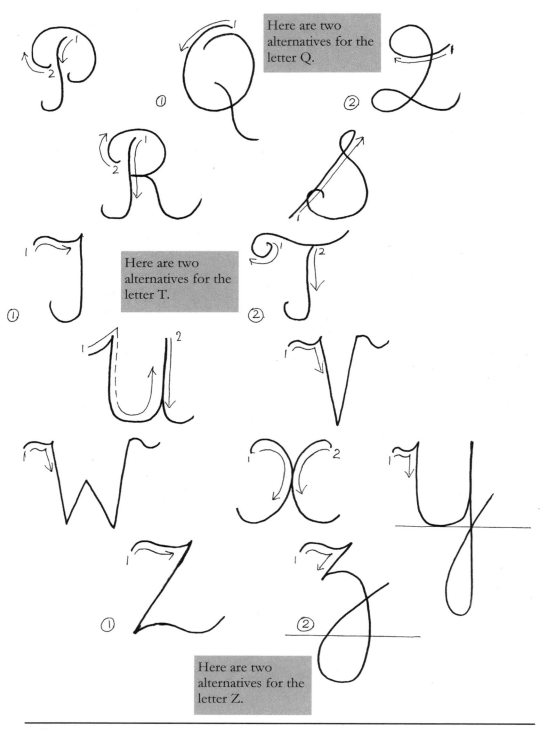

Here are two alternatives for the letter Q.

Here are two alternatives for the letter T.

Here are two alternatives for the letter Z.

Anna   Boris

Chris   Daddy

Ellie   Fred

George   Helen   Idris

Joel   Kirsty Lily

Mark   Naomi

Oliver   Pop   Queenie

Rudi   Simone

Terry   Ursula

Venus   Walter

Xavier   Yolande

Zak

School

Of course, if your child is going to school this method of teaching is not really open to you. They will be subjected to the National Curriculum and will have to acquire some means of putting words on paper long before the time is really appropriate.

Teaching them a style of writing that is different from that which they learn at school will only confuse them and make matters worse. You can help a little, however, if you try to keep abreast of their progress by learning to write in the same way that they learn at school.

Their joined up writing probably won't be very different from that outlined on the previous pages – but take care to pay attention to details.

For instance if your child has learnt to write an *h* with a loop they may not recognise it when it hasn't got one!

h (*with loop*)   *h* (*without one*)

This may seem like a small point but it can make a great deal of difference. For example, if your child can read shopping lists that you write, then they can help you with the shopping; it means that you can write notes to each other and it opens up the possibility of your being able to help them with their schoolwork. It is demoralising for a child to work hard at school learning how to write and then not even be able to understand their own parents' handwriting.

Another way in which you can help is not to insist on your child doing a lot of writing at home. If they are being made to write at school before they are ready then you cannot expect them to have any enthusiasm for writing in their spare time. They need to have home as a haven, into which the pressures of school life cannot penetrate.

Sensitivity on your part to issues like this can help them to survive early schooling relatively unscathed.

The final thing that you can do to ameliorate the effects of enforced writing practice at school is to keep up with your drawing and painting sessions. Drawing is an antidote to the restriction and narrowness of writing. It allows a child to express themselves freely.

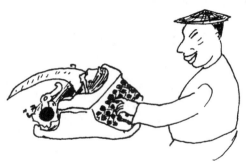

If you continue to spend time doing a lot of drawing with your child – after school and at weekends – then they will continue to have a positive attitude to paper and pens and will probably enjoy writing when they are a little older, and will forget any early problems that they may have encountered.

Reading - Introduction

Being able to read and write has always been the definition of an educated person and literacy is still the foundation upon which education is built. It does not matter how many other skills someone may acquire, if they cannot read they will experience great difficulty in coping with modern life.

This means that a child's whole life will be affected by how they are taught to read. Children who are introduced to reading in an inappropriate way can be put off to such an extent that they never manage to catch up.

It is particularly difficult for children who are trapped within the school system to alter either their own perception of themselves or other people's perception of them once they are classed as being poor readers. They become caught up in a vicious circle of low expectation, low achievement and low enjoyment and, even if they do manage to learn to read, it is often not to the standard that is required to achieve success in today's world.

Despite all the efforts that have been made to improve standards of literacy, evidence suggests that reading levels in Western countries are now actually in decline and that schools are unable to do anything to reverse this trend: in fact they may be the cause of the problem.

Schools and Reading

Broadly speaking, the situation is now that children who come from families where everyone does a lot of reading, do well at school, and children that do not, tend to do badly. Schools continue to help about twenty per cent of the intake to achieve high academic standards but have been less successful in addressing the needs of the majority.

The problem is that schools are seen historically as the means by which mass literacy was made possible and people now find it hard to recognise that the whole idea of sending children to school is working against the best interests of some children.

As a result, instead of looking for alternatives to school, more and more resources are being put into schemes aimed at improving schools. It is easy for parents to be beguiled into believing that these schemes will be effective and that their own children will be spared the traumas that they experienced themselves when at school.

Unfortunately, this is not realistic. The constant stream of new initiatives is a sign that something is going badly wrong but it does not offer any hope that the real cause of the problem is being addressed. No amount of tinkering with the way that schools are organised is likely to have much effect and it is parents themselves who will continue to have to take primary responsibility for helping their children – especially when it comes to learning to read.

The Role of Parents

It is parents, not schools, that have the biggest effect upon a child's development and this means that current problems are not caused so much by badly-run schools but, rather, by the presence in those schools of large numbers of children who are not being cared for properly by their parents. This disrupts everything that schools try to do and makes it difficult for them to provide any of the children who attend with a really satisfactory education. Consequently the onus is put back on those parents who *do* care, to help their children at home.

This creates a slightly peculiar situation, which will be dealt with in more detail later, in which many parents find themselves teaching their children to read in order that they can do well at school – even though the only reason that school was ever created for young children was to teach them to read!

Parents do, in fact, make the natural and ideal teachers of reading for their children. They can nurture an interest in books from a very young age, which will make reading a natural extension of daily life for their child and they are the ones who can do the most to bolster their child's self-confidence. Self-doubt is a major obstacle for many children when it comes to learning to read, but when a child feels that their parent believes in them (but is not putting any pressure on them to learn to read to a particular timetable), they can relax and learn in their own time and in their own way.

A Short History of Reading

In order to come to terms with the paradoxical situation in which five-year-old children are being taught to read by their parents so that they will do well at school, one has to understand a little of the history of the subject.

Until recently schools existed solely to improve standards of literacy and, to a lesser extent, numeracy. Other skills (relating to trades and crafts for example) were acquired in the workplace itself. Literacy holds a very special place in a civilised society and the spread of literacy, and the way in which it has been achieved, is closely related to the social and economic reforms that have taken place in European countries over the past five hundred years.

The Middle Ages

The Middle Ages saw people turning back to the old Roman model of education in an attempt to re-establish law and order after the years of anarchy that followed after the collapse of Roman civilisation.

This involved the Christian church setting up grammar schools that taught boys, who were destined to work in the Church and in the government, to read and write in Latin. More or less everyone else in the country was illiterate, but having a small core of clerics made it possible for the rule of law to be re-established.

The Reformation

In the 1500s some people started to take exception to the power wielded over their lives by the Church. One way in which they exercised their independence was by learning to read – this process was accelerated when the Bible became available in English.

For the first time, people could study 'God's Word' for themselves without having it interpreted for them by a priest. Puritans, Quakers, Presbyterians and

Nonconformists led the way by learning to read themselves and by setting up primary schools for their children.

It is difficult for us to imagine how radical a step this must have been. There had never previously been a time when ordinary people had been able to read for themselves.

The established Church did not respond in the same way to the greater availability of written material. The Church of England was happy to keep the great mass of its followers in as much ignorance as possible, possibly because this helped to maintain the power and status enjoyed by its vicars, bishops and other clerics.

The Seventeenth Century

Many factors led to fundamental changes in European life in the sixteenth and seventeenth centuries. The discovery of the New World and other voyages of discovery had fired people's imaginations and stimulated trade; the feudal system had more or less collapsed and methods of agriculture had improved.

Many of these changes favoured those people who could read and write. Soon a new, wealthy class of merchants and tradespeople arose – drawn mainly from the Puritan, literate minority. The English Civil War saw a transfer of power from the old institutions of King and Church to this new middle class.

The Eighteenth Century

Change continued to take place and machines were invented to improve efficiency in fields and factories. This led to the Industrial Revolution which affected every aspect of life. Once again it was the literate minority who prospered.

It became obvious to everyone that reading should no longer be seen as the preserve of religious zealots and fanatical Puritans – it was the passport to material success.

Primary schools started to appear all over the country – but on an ad hoc basis - and many children only gained the very rudiments of learning.

The Nineteenth Century

By the middle of the nineteenth century, panic was starting to set in amongst the ruling classes. There was a danger that Britain might fall behind in the race against its Continental rivals due to the illiteracy of a huge proportion of its population. Some other countries, notably Protestant countries such as Germany, had a better organised system of education than Britain and mass literacy was becoming a possibility in many areas of Europe.

In an effort to catch up, various Acts of Parliament were passed that made sure that every parish had a primary school and that primary school education was available, without charge, to every child. This marked the beginning of the system that we have today.

The Twentieth Century

During the first part of the twentieth century, the school system proved to be a great success. Literacy levels improved dramatically and by the middle of the century Britain was considered to have achieved one hundred per cent literacy for the first time.

However, problems began to emerge as responsibility for education was perceived to have shifted from parents to the government. The latter half of the century saw children having to spend more time at school but achieving less, and this problem is yet to be addressed.

The Situation Today

The situation that we have inherited is complex. The population enjoys a high level of literacy but there is a great deal of dissatisfaction with the education system. This has led to it fragmenting along social and economic lines: the better-educated sectors of society are still able to provide an education for their children (at least partly with the help of the school system, private and public), but standards of literacy are declining in other sectors of society.

The response from the educational system to the lack of success in improving reading standards is to continue with the same approach that it has always had, but with greater intensity. Thus children now spend longer at school than they have ever done and learn to read at an earlier age than ever before. It does not seem to have occurred to anyone that this might be making things worse rather than better.

The pressure being applied to very young children at school may actually be the cause of the reading difficulties that many children experience. It is now quite common for children, even from homes where everyone can read well, to experience difficulty at school.

This is a new phenomenon and the most likely explanation for it is that schools simply apply too much pressure on children and thereby alienate them from reading – sometimes permanently.

Summary

Education has not been a fixed process; it has changed from generation to generation. Over the course of five hundred years Britain has transformed itself from being a largely illiterate country to having one of the best educated populations in the world. The impetus for this revolution came from ordinary people, largely through their desire to learn to read.

This revolution seems to have lost its momentum and most people now expect someone else (schools, teachers and the government) to take responsibility for their children's education. This has inevitably led to standards starting to slip.

If we are to be successful in teaching our children, we have to have the same flexibility and determination as was demonstrated by our forebears.

The problem now is not that we don't have the resources to provide our children with a good education, it is that we are using the resources wrongly. Schools are applying inappropriate methods, especially in the teaching of reading, and are in danger of now doing more harm than good to the education of young children.

WHY ARE SCHOOLS FAILING?

At first glance it may seem strange that an institution, school, that did so much to improve literacy in the seventeenth, eighteenth and nineteenth centuries should be cast in the role of villain in the twenty-first century.

The problem is that success in school is now seen as an end in itself. The ability to read is seen as a good way of getting ahead in school.

In some affluent areas we have the bizarre situation in which a child has to be able to read before being accepted by a school – at the age of five! It has been found that the earlier a child learns to read, the better they will do at school. The process becomes self-perpetuating.

Children who learn to read early get off to a better start (in school). Once they get ahead of their classmates they receive more praise and more encouragement, they are treated with more respect and have their self-confidence boosted. This helps them to move further ahead from their non-reading classmates and the gap widens. The early readers do better and better and their erstwhile friends fall by the wayside.

Naturally enough, this message has not been lost on parents who put more and more effort into teaching their children to read at younger and younger ages.

Teachers and administrators have similarly lost sight of the fact that it is only success at school that is being gained by learning to read early, not overall educational excellence.

The current approach to schooling fails to take into account that each child is an individual who has their own desire to learn. It assumes that children need to be directed and does not recognise that in reality they just need to be helped.

Neither those children who are able to conform with what is expected of them, and get ahead at school, nor those who are left behind, are really served well by this system. All are subject to unnatural pressure and none are allowed to fulfil their individual potential.

British schools teach reading to five-year-olds, which is patently too young, and reading problems would undoubtedly be reduced if the Continental practice of teaching reading at the age of six or seven were followed.

However, the problem is more deep-seated than that. It is not a good idea to set any age as being the time by which all children must learn to read.

Learning to read is a big step and not all children are ready to take it at the same time. Ideally the education system should be sensitive enough to allow each child to take this step when they are ready.

It is hard to see how this could be achieved in a school setting, where a small number of teachers look after a large number of children and no individual child can receive the personal attention that they require.

Problems Arising from Learning To Read Too Early

In this country, most research into the teaching of reading has tended to focus on the fact that the younger a child is when they learn to read, the better they do at school. This has encouraged people to try to teach children to learn to read at younger and younger ages without taking into account the harm and distress that is caused to children who fail to respond to the reading programme imposed upon them.

These children are often labelled as having reading difficulties – a label that can scar them for life.

This over-simplistic interpretation of what is happening also ignores the fact that those schools that do not teach children to read at the age of five are just as effective as those that do. For instance, Rudolf Steiner schools, of which there are hundreds around the world, are vehemently opposed to the early teaching of reading but their graduates do at least as well as any other schoolchildren and in Germany, where the movement originated, Steiner education is highly sought after by all sections of society.

This indicates that it is the way in which schools are organised, rather than something about the nature of children themselves, that makes it necessary for reading to be taught so early. Once we accept that it is not essential to teach children to read when they are very young, we can perhaps reflect upon the harm that we may be causing by forcing them to do so.

We do not understand everything about the process of child development. Great changes take place as a baby learns to walk and then to talk. Speech brings a revolution in understanding. At the same time, a child is constantly learning through play, through observing the world around them and through interaction with other people.

We have to be careful when we interfere with this process, especially when it involves something as fundamental as reading. Common sense would suggest that reading is an abstract activity that is best learnt when other important stages of development have been completed.

Just as not all children learn to walk at the same age, or to talk at the same age, they are not all ready to read at the same time. We do not actually know what damage we are doing when we arbitrarily force a child to acquire this skill against their wishes. Parents and teachers often pursue this goal in the face of tears, temper tantrums, depression and all manner of distress displayed by a child.

This lack of sensitivity encapsulates everything that is wrong with the way that we educate our children.

Instead of an arrogant assumption that we know what is best for children in general, we should approach each child with a degree of humility and try to understand what they really need.

Reading Difficulties

If a child is not ready to read, then reading will, obviously, be difficult for them, the squiggles on the page won't make any sense and they will always be wishing that they were somewhere else when they are being made to read.

At the very least, this will cause them to dislike reading and it will also probably lead to them being considered to have reading difficulties, a label that, once applied, is very difficult to remove.

Young boys, in particular, can find lessons based around books boring and they often develop a habit of messing around and not paying attention. This is something else that can stay with them throughout their time at school.

Dyslexia

Estimates for the number of dyslexic children in Britain vary, but some people think that up to twenty per cent of children in schools experience some form of dyslexia. It is difficult to make a more precise estimate because people cannot agree about what types of reading difficulties should be classified as being the result of dyslexia.

The steady rise in the reported number of children suffering from dyslexia must, however, be a cause for concern. Perhaps more cases are now reported because it has become a fashionable condition to have; perhaps more cases are uncovered as more effort is put into improving literacy; perhaps factors outside the control of the education system are responsible for at least some of the rise, but schools must take their share of the blame.

School teachers and other professionals try to help children who cannot read by giving them extra reading practice. In most cases, this makes matters worse.

Young children should be encouraged to do things that they enjoy. If children who already dislike reading are made to do extra reading practice, we should not be surprised when they develop more serious reading-related problems.

The opposite approach is much more likely to be successful. If a child has difficulty reading, then it is best to protect them as much as possible from being made to read and to encourage them to do other things that do not involve reading.

In the vast majority of cases, children treated in this way will eventually start to read on their own. They may be nine or ten years old before they do so, but they will never see themselves as having a 'problem' and, in the meantime, may have acquired skills that make other children envious.

Children who do have an innate problem with reading will also benefit from this approach. If they are never going to be able to read very well, it makes sense to protect them from books until they have had a chance to build up their self-confidence by concentrating on things that they do enjoy, and at which they can be successful.

Coping With School

Children who go to school are inevitably going to be taught to read, whether they want to learn or not. Parents can do a great deal to mitigate this lack of sensitivity on the part of the school system.

- It is up to the parent to choose the school that their child attends. You can select a school that you feel will take a sympathetic approach to your child.

- You must remember that a child is much more strongly influenced by their parents than by their school. If your child is not getting on very well with reading at school, you can let them know that this does not worry you. You can explain to them that your expectations for them are still high; that you have confidence in them and that being a 'late developer' often leads to greater eventual success. Basically, help them to maintain their self-confidence. This is the most important thing. If they retain a belief in themselves, they will have no difficulty in catching up with their classmates when they do finally get the urge to read.

- If reading is becoming a tedious activity for your child at school, make it fun for them at home. Keep up the habit of reading them a night-time story. Read comics and magazines to them. At home, take the strain of doing all the reading upon yourself.

- If your child does want to read to you, make sure that you have the time to listen. Do not be impatient. Do not make lots of corrections. Enjoy the story that is being read to you.

- Do not force your child to do homework and do help in whatever way you can to make schoolwork easier for them.

- Be prepared to go and see your child's teachers if you are not happy with the treatment your child is receiving at school.

- Be prepared to change your child's school if necessary.

- Most children do want to read by the age of seven or eight. A few children have more difficulty in coming to terms with the written word. These are the children that may become labelled as severely dyslexic. If you feel that your child may be starting to fall into this category be prepared to take drastic action (this may mean that you have to withdraw them from school altogether for a few years so that they are not put under any pressure to pursue 'academic' activities).

Learning to Read

Whether or not your child goes to school, you can adopt some elements of the following approach. Reading with you at home can only help to make your child feel more comfortable with books when they are at school.

The principal objective must be to give your child a sense of the pleasure that can be gained through reading, then sooner or later they will learn to read for themselves. You do this by reading to them: it is very simple and there is no real alternative.

It is never too early to start reading to your children, but do not despair if this is something that you have neglected during the early years of your child's life. It is surprisingly easy to wean a child off a diet of television and computer games and on to the more intimate activity of reading to each other.

These are some of the stages that one goes through when reading to a child:

- You can start 'reading' to your child when they are still a baby. Cardboard books can keep a baby amused for hours.

- Very soon, you can progress to nursery rhyme books. It does not matter if you are not very good at singing, young children are not critical in that way. Your child will soon recognise the pages on which their favourite nursery rhymes appear and this may help them to learn to read later on.

- Pop-up books are also a favourite with small children.

- Story books become appropriate once a child is old enough to understand and enjoy being told a story.

- In the early years, it is best not to let your children look at the books on their own. Young children can be quite destructive and don't take too long to rip pages out of a book, or scribble over all the pages. This doesn't improve their appreciation of literature but does reduce the appeal of the books concerned.

- Books, particularly books that a child knows well, are a very good way of calming children down when they are getting over-wrought. Books allow a high level of interaction between parent and child, and can help to defuse potentially explosive situations that can build up very rapidly when one is on one's own with a young child.

- Illustrations are at least as important as the text in children's books. It is best to avoid books that have frightening or weird illustrations – even though these seem to be very popular with publishers.

- As a child gets older, their desire to hear the same story over and over again starts to diminish, but this does not mean that you have to stop reading to them. It just means that you have to buy more books and/or find a good library. The more books you have in the house, the better. As your child gets older, keep all their books in a more accessible place, so that they can look at them on their own.

- Books are a source of useful information. Children always have lots of questions. If you have good reference books in your home to which you can refer for the answers, this also helps to cast reading in a favourable light.

- There are many other examples of written material around, including magazines, newspapers, comics and text on computer screens: all these can have an input into a child's life. The more advantages they see to being able to read, the more likely they are to learn. It is books, however, that remain the best way of introducing children to the written word.

One has to bear in mind that children do not look at the world in the same way as an adult.

Until they try to read for themselves, they assume that it is something that they will be able to do one day – like so many other things that they see adults do. They are generally quite happy to be surrounded by books without being able to read them for themselves. Reading aloud to children does not make them lazy, it lays the foundation for a lifelong interest in the written word.

Unfortunately, in our society people do not have the patience to let nature take its course. Pressure comes from all sides to try to make a young child read – from grandparents, from other children and above all – at school.

Nonetheless, it must be re-emphasised that it is parents who have by far the biggest influence over a child's state of mind. Parents can do an enormous amount to redress the balance and reassure their children that there is no rush.

In reality, children do not need to be taught to read: given the right conditions they learn by themselves.

The First Steps

- If you have filled your child's life with interesting and stimulating books you will not have to teach them to read. They will teach themselves in the same way that they learnt to talk.

- In many ways, contrary to current wisdom, it is better if a child learns to write before they start reading. Once a child starts to write words, they have a much stronger connection with them and this obviously helps them to read.

- Once your child decides to start reading you have to be prepared for the tables to be turned. Whereas you were in the habit of reading to your child, you have to let them read to you. There is no substitute for this. Children can read on their own but will derive infinitely more satisfaction from reading aloud to someone else.

- Listening to a child read is not as easy as you might think. One instinctively remembers the behaviour of one's own teachers and it is all too easy to slip into unpleasant habits.

- It is a mistake to jump in all the time with officious corrections. It is also a bad idea to try to hurry a child up: they have to be allowed to read at their own pace.

- On the other hand, you have to help them with words that they find difficult. If your child is stuck on a particular word, tell them what it is, so that they can get on with the story. Encouraging a child to work out what the word is by building up the letters is a waste of time.

- 'Learning to read' books can be excruciatingly boring and pointless. They are written for children who are four or five years old who shouldn't really be reading anyway. Let your child pick a book from their own collection that they want to read. It doesn't matter if they virtually know it off by heart – this may even be an advantage.

- Be prepared for a few false dawns. Children do feel the pressure placed on them by others and may announce at any time that they want to learn to read. Often they will learn to read one book and are then satisfied. As far as they are concerned, they have learnt to read and can now go back to playing. If this happens, don't keep on nagging them to read every day.

- When a child really does want to read they won't restrict themselves to just one book. They will read anything that comes in their path, from road signs to cereal packets. Reading becomes a revelation and they see the world in a new light.

Achieving High Levels of Literacy

As has been mentioned previously, the challenge facing today's parents is not so much to teach their children to read, but rather to teach them to read well.

The simplest way to achieve this is to continue reading to your child once they start to read for themselves. In this way you can continue to inspire them to read good literature. It enables you to introduce books that are a little more advanced than the ones that your child is reading for themselves. This helps them to keep up their momentum in developing their own reading skills.

If a book is a hit as a bedtime story your child will probably want to read it again on their own and, in this way, will soon be reading all the classics of English literature.

Even though there may appear to be no connection between a novel and much of the printed material that one has to deal with today – such as official forms, scientific documents and technical manuals – reading 'classical' literature remains the best way of becoming a really adept reader.

Suggested Reading Material

Everyone has their own taste in books and, when reading to your children, it is better to be guided by your own preferences than by reading lists drawn up by someone else.

The following pages provide a list of some tried and tested children's books, and has been included in case you are daunted by the vast array of books available: it is not meant to be a definitive list of suitable books.

In particular, modern books are probably under-represented. There are so many new books being produced all the time and people's tastes vary so greatly that it is perhaps better for everyone to make their own selection in this area!

Political Correctness

Some of the books that have been included could by no means be considered 'politically correct'.

Unfortunately, traditional classics of English literature do not reflect the social and cultural realities of the modern world. Women's issues, race issues and class issues are often treated in a way that may offend a modern reader.

Many characters in classic children's books go to boarding schools or have governesses, there are rarely any non Anglo-Saxon characters (unless they are included to be ridiculed or pitied) and boys and girls tend to have stereotyped roles.

Some books spend a lot of time dealing with social issues that are largely irrelevant today, such as the divisions between the upper and lower classes.

These perfectly valid criticisms have led to many books being removed from reading lists and library shelves in spite of the fact that they have always been popular with children. Unfortunately, comparatively second-rate books have been included in their place.

Such books are often specially written to have heroes and heroines drawn from a representative cross-section of ethnic groups and to reflect current social issues ranging from divorce to inner city deprivation and drug abuse.

Although this effort is well-intentioned, it is misguided. It arises from the mistaken belief that children derive their sense of belonging from what they read. In reality, children get this from the environment in which they grow up.

Their sense of right and wrong, their attitudes to the roles of men and women, family life and racial equality come from their families, their school and people that they meet.

If you read old-fashioned books with your child it gives you a chance to discuss changes that have taken place in people's lives over the years. It does not indoctrinate them or make them feel alienated.

The real value of books is that they can teach children about good writing and about the good use of language.

In fact, I cannot personally remember ever reading many books that I could relate to in terms of my own life. Passages that do touch one are usually to do with events that transcend race, creed, gender or colour such as births and deaths, loves and marriages, joyful reunions and painful separations.

Reading about these things happening to a character from whom one is separated by every conceivable social distinction can help one to realise that all human beings share the same concerns, and that divisions between people are far less significant than we are led to believe.

Parents can therefore feel justified in selecting reading material for their children on the quality of the writing and the interest of the story. They need not pay too much attention to whether or not it is 'politically correct'.

Obviously you have to retain your sense of discrimination and you do not have to read books that you find offensive or that your child finds frightening. You can miss bits out or change things that you don't like when you are reading a book aloud.

A further consideration is that if a book has managed to stay in print for many years and has appealed to successive generations of children, then it must have something to recommend it. Sometimes modern books are launched in a blaze of publicity but ten years later have been completely forgotten. It is a shame to waste your time reading books that are basically not very good.

Books for Babies and Toddlers

To a certain extent one is at the mercy of publishers and their marketing departments when looking for books suitable for very young children. Publishers arbitrarily promote different titles at different times and it is often impossible to find books that were popular just a few years previously.

This leaves no alternative but to search the shelves of your local bookshop for books that you like. The illustrations are the most important aspect of a book designed for young children, but its size, its texture and what it is made from can also affect its appeal.

Some board books are very good, as are some hard-backed paper books. In either case, you have to keep hold of the book all the time or the baby will find a way to do something unspeakable to it. (Books made from plastic or cloth are a complete waste of money.)

Part of the reason why the following books have been recommended is that they have managed to remain in print for a number of years and should therefore be readily available.

Mother Goose – Nursery Rhymes

This is a classic collection and probably contains all the nursery rhymes that you have ever heard.

It is a little too big for comfort (A4 size) but is definitely worth buying if you see it for sale at a reasonable price.

Ladybird Book of Nursery Rhymes

Ladybird Books produce hundreds of titles, many of them excellent. Unfortunately, they have a policy of only keeping a proportion of their titles in print at any one time. This can result in a particular book, that one really wants, not being available.

The Nursery Rhyme books are, however, perennial favourites.

Some of the modern, updated editions have new illustrations that are supposed to appeal to modern children. The older editions are better and can often be found in second-hand bookshops at very reasonable prices.

The Ladybird series includes many other books which contain simple rhymes – such as 'Tootles the Taxi' – that have become classics in their own right.

Fairy Stories

Fairy stories such as Cinderella, Sleeping Beauty, Snow White, Rapunzel, Puss-in Boots, The Frog Prince, The Princess and the Pea, The Six Swans, etc. remain the very best stories for young children.

They have evolved over hundreds of years and have an appeal that transcends time and cultural differences.

The Ladybird books of fairy stories are very good but there are many other versions.

You may have to peruse them carefully, as the illustrators sometimes get carried away and produce pictures that are frightening or grotesque. The Disney fairy story-books are based on their films and are rather bland.

Young children may not have the patience to listen to you reading text and you may have to tell the story yourself as you look at the pictures in the books.

This Little Puffin... Finger Plays and Nursery Games

This book contains a wonderful collection of rhymes and songs that children find irresistible. It is essential reading.

Pop-up Books

Most small children like pop-up books but you have to be careful – you only have to leave a toddler alone with a pop-up book for a few seconds and it is not a pop-up book any more!

Specific titles do not stay in print for very long and you have to look through those that are available at any particular time. Pop-up alphabet books, counting books and fairy stories are among the most popular.

Three to Five Year Olds

Some of the books already mentioned will remain favourites for years, but at some point a child's interest starts to shift from the pictures in a book to the story being told. Illustrations remain important but you can also start to read proper stories to children once they are about three years old.

Enid Blyton

Enid Blyton remains the doyenne of writing for children of this age group. She had the ability to tell a story in such a way as to capture, and hold, the interest of children of a specific age.

Her stories have suffered a great deal of ridicule over the years and are taken off library shelves from time to time when their political incorrectness is discovered by a new generation. The stories are sometimes racist, often sexist and habitually recommend violence as a method of correcting naughty children.

These are good reasons to shun her work, but in mitigation one must remember that she produced books with such rapidity that they were bound to reflect her inherent prejudices and faults. Many of them were never edited, because she kept total control over her own work.

Most modern editions have removed anything that is liable to offend, sometimes making them rather insipid. Originals can still be found in second-hand bookshops.

The Enchanted Wood, The Magic Faraway Tree, Adventures of the Wishing-Chair

These are very simple books that can be read and re-read to children from age 3 – 4 upwards.

They are stories of magical adventures and are ideally suited to the imagination of this age group.

Enid Blyton also wrote hundreds of short stories which make good material for bedtime reading.

It is difficult to recommend a particular collection because they keep appearing in new editions.

Thomas the Tank Engine by Rev. W. Awdry

This is a perennial favourite that has found a place on most children's bookshelves for many years. The illustrations are excellent but I have always found the stories slightly tedious. They do not hold a young child's attention.

Mister Men books/Little Miss books by Roger Hargreaves

These are another sort of classic. They are simple and appeal to children from a very young age upwards.

Another advantage is that they are not expensive.

Popular favourites include:

> **Mr Mean**
> **Little Miss Chatterbox**
> **Mr Muddle**
> **Mr Bump**
> **Mr Strong**
> **Mr Small**
> **Mr Tickle**
> **Mr Clever**...but they are all good.

Grimm's Fairy Tales

Children of this age should still enjoy fairy tale books with plenty of illustrations but it is well worth buying a copy of Grimm's Fairy Tales as well. It is not always illustrated, but the stories are told in a way that makes modern books seem dull in comparison.

The brothers Grimm collected traditional stories that were being told to children in Germany in the nineteenth century. Similar stories existed, with only slight variations, in different countries right across Europe, so these stories really do represent a significant part of our cultural heritage.

Other Fairy Stories

There are many other, less famous, collections of fairy stories from other countries, which are also worth reading – Russian stories, Scandinavian stories etc.

Stories from other parts of the world, such as Africa, Asia and North America, are more difficult to find, although The Arabian Nights is normally available, and is as much a classic as Grimm's fairy tales.

Hans Christian Anderson's stories are regarded as fairy tales but are often frightening in a way that traditional stories never are. This is probably because he made them up himself.

When We Were Very Young by A.A. Milne

Poems and rhymes are always more appealing to young children than prose. A.A. Milne's poems are some of the best written for young children, in the English language.

This book includes the poems 'Lines and Squares', The King's Breakfast, Halfway Down, Market Place and Hoppity.

Beatrix Potter – **The Tale of Peter Rabbit, The Tale of Jemima Puddleduck, The Tale of The Flopsy Bunnies, The Tale of Benjamin Bunny, The Tale of Mrs Tiggywinkle, The Story of Miss Moppet, The Tale of Mrs Tittlemouse**

Beatrix Potter's books are children's classics. Her illustrations are beautiful, the text simple and the books themselves beautifully produced.

It is much better to get the original versions, published by Frederick Warne, than the updated editions.

The titles listed above are some of the best.

Postman Pat by John Cunliffe

Postman Pat has established himself as a favourite with successive generations of children.

Milly Molly Mandy by Joyce Lancaster Brisley

The Milly Molly Mandy books describe the everyday adventures of a little girl growing up in an English village in the 1920s. The style of writing is very simple and yet manages to speak directly to modern children.

A Child's Garden of Verse by Robert Louis Stevenson

Robert Louis Stevenson is best remembered for his adventure stories but he also wrote beautiful poetry for children. This book contains poems such as:

ESCAPE AT BEDTIME

The lights from the parlour and kitchen shone out
Through the blinds and the windows and bars;
And high overhead and all moving about,
There were thousands of millions of stars.
There ne'er were such thousands of leaves on a tree,
Nor of people in church or the Park,
As the crowds of the stars that looked down upon me,
And that glittered and winked in the dark.

The Dog, and the Plough, and the Hunter, and all,
And the star of the sailor, and Mars,
These shone in the sky, and the pail by the wall
Would be half full of water and stars.
They saw me at last, and they chased me with cries,
And they soon had me packed into bed;
But the glory kept shining and bright in my eyes,
And the stars going round in my head.

Aesop's Fables

Aesop was a Greek slave, who lived about two thousand six hundred years ago.

He became renowned for his wisdom and, after being freed by his master, went to live in the court of King Croesus.

His stories have been told and retold to generations of children, and include such classics as 'The Hare and the Tortoise', 'The Fox and the Grapes' and 'The Wolf in Sheep's Clothing'.

Six and Over

Children aged six or seven years old still enjoy illustrated books that they look at on their own, and with which they learn to read, but they may also appreciate quite complex books and stories that you read aloud to them. You do not have to limit yourself to children's literature. By the time they are eleven years old your child should enjoy being read classics by authors such as Charles Dickens or Jane Austen.

Billy Goats Gruff – Ladybird Books

Ladybird Books produce a 'Read it Yourself' series, which contains many traditional fables and stories.

Billy Goats Gruff is particularly good.

Rupert Bear

Rupert Bear annuals are just right for young children. They are bigger than a lot of books, they are usually inexpensive and children like the characters.

The stories are magical and can be read quickly (they are summarised in little verses beneath the pictures), or slowly by reading the full version at the bottom of each page.

Teddy Bear Robinson by Joan C. Robinson

These stories ought to be included amongst the classics of children's literature. They describe the adventures of a little girl and her teddy bear.

They are well written, perceptive and humorous.

Prince Siddhartha by Jonathan Landaw and Janet Brooke

This book describes the life of the Buddha. It is written for children but is not patronising, and it is well illustrated.

When it is not in print in the UK it can be ordered from America (any bookshop should be happy to do this for you).

Toad and Frog, Grasshopper on the Road, Little Bear by Arnold Lobel

These are high quality books, with beautiful illustrations and simple text. Children can teach themselves to read with these books.

Now We Are Six, The House at Pooh Corner, Winnie the Pooh by A.A. Milne

Now we are Six is another book of poems by A.A. Milne and is every bit as good as 'When We Were Very Young'.

The Winnie the Pooh books make good material for reading aloud. Sometimes the humour is a little too subtle for young children to appreciate, but they generally love the characters. Most adults really enjoy reading these books to their children.

Stories for Eight-Year-Olds edited by Sara and Stephen Corrin

This is an excellent collection of short stories that helps to introduce young readers to authors such as Charles Dickens, Rudyard Kipling and E. Nesbit.

It also contains traditional stories retold by modern authors.

Alice in Wonderland, Alice Through The Looking Glass by Lewis Carroll

Time has not lessoned the appeal of Alice and she remains as popular with today's children as she has ever been.

The brilliant rhymes, many of which are parodies of the sanctimonious poems of the time, are classics in their own right, and the fact that Lewis Carroll was a mathematics wizard lends another dimension to the stories.

They are so unconventional that children cannot fail to be fascinated by them.

Swallows and Amazons by Arthur Ransome

Arthur Ransome wrote a series of books for children, most of which are set in the Lake District in the 1930s. Swallows and Amazons is the first of the series, and the most famous.

The stories are now slightly dated: all the children involved go to boarding school and are immersed in the values of the Empire – keeping a stiff upper lip in the face of all problems etc.

However, the books are very well written and one cannot help but identify with the characters in spite of these disadvantages.

We Didn't Mean To Go To Sea is a gripping adventure story involving the same children as Swallows and Amazons, and is probably the best of all Arthur Ransomes's books.

Ramayana

This is a traditional Indian story describing the life of one of the Masters in the Hindu religion – Lord Ram.

It is one of the best stories ever told, being not only inspiring but also exciting and moving. Unfortunately I cannot recommend a particular translation. The story has still not gained the recognition it deserves in the West and versions appear and disappear in the shops. We have a translation imported directly from India, which has a certain authenticity, but it is not the easiest book to read. You may have to search through your local bookshop or library for a copy that suits you.

The Hobbit by J.R.R. Tolkien

This forerunner to The Lord of the Rings was written as a children's story and most children enjoy it – although some may find the battles at the end unnecessarily cataclysmic.

Five Children and It, The Amulet, The Phoenix and The Carpet, The Railway Children, The Treasure Seekers, The Wouldbegoods, The New Treasure Seekers by E. Nesbit

E. Nesbit's stories are amongst the best ever written in the English language for children. They convey a clear sense of life in Edwardian England but do not come across as dated or propagandist as other books of the period sometimes do.

Lorna Doone by R.D. Blackmore

A historical novel that is fun to read aloud and perfectly suitable for children. It combines romance with some good adventures and is slightly ironic and humorous in its style.

Little Women by Louisa M. Alcott

This American classic is often mocked for its schmaltzy story line, but it is a jolly good read and is simple enough to appeal to children.

It does not involve its young heroes and heroines in unlikely adventures (which is the usual style of children's literature) but manages to make an interesting and moving story out of essentially everyday events.

The Cat in the Hat, Fox in Sox, etc. by Dr Seuss

Dr Seuss started writing books to help young children to learn to read, but his books do not have the stultifying effects that afflict most 'learning to read' books.

They manage to convey a real sense of fun that appeals to children over a wide age range. Their imaginative use of language in poems and rhymes stimulates an interest in words and reading.

Dr. Seuss represents a different side of the American culture from Disney. His books are witty, intelligent and respectful of their young readers.

Wind in the Willows by Kenneth Grahame

Everyone knows the story of Ratty, Moley and Mr Toad, but if you haven't read the book since you were a child you may not be aware that it is an exquisitely written story. In fact you will probably only be able to read a few pages at a time, because the prose is quite complex and old-fashioned and it requires concentration to follow it – but it is well worth the effort.

The Lion, The Witch and the Wardrobe, the Narnia books by C.S. Lewis

The Narnia books have remained popular with children ever since they were written. C.S. Lewis was a committed Christian and some children may find the imagery in some of the stories verging on Christian propaganda (especially in 'The Last Battle') – but few books are perfect!

'The Horse and His Boy' is considered by many to be the best.

Norse Myths

Stories of Odin, Thor, Freya and Loki (the Norse gods) come in many different versions. **Myths of the Norsemen** by Roger Lancelyn Green is one of the best. Libraries can be a good source of books of Norse Myths.

The stories are ideal for children aged about nine or ten. They deal with the issues that affect everyone's lives in a way that is still vibrant and refreshing thousands of years after they were first told.

If you enjoyed telling fairy stories to your children when they were younger, then these stories will let you continue the tradition with new material.

The William Stories by Richmal Crompton

Richmal Crompton wrote over thirty books of short stories describing the adventures of William Brown and his friends. They were originally written for an adult audience but quickly became popular with children.

They are surprisingly anarchical and make ideal bedtime reading.

Secret Seven by Enid Blyton

The Secret Seven books appeal to young readers and have provided an introduction to reading to successive generations of children.

Island of Adventure, Ship of Adventure, Circus of Adventure
by Enid Blyton

These are classic Enid Blyton adventure stories. They are more complicated than the Secret Seven books and are very exciting if you read them at the right age.

Enid Blyton had the knack of being able to finish each chapter in such a way that one wants to read the next one. This makes the books ideal for reading aloud.

There are other books in this series but these are probably the best.

Famous Five by Enid Blyton

This series is amongst Enid Blyton's best-known work and is very exciting. The books are dated however and some of the plots will stretch even a young child's credulity.

Peter Pan by J. M. Barrie

The original story of Peter Pan by J. M. Barrie is not the version with which most people are familiar. It agonises over the nature of growing up and getting old in a way that seems to reflect the author's personal problems rather too much.

An abridged version, **The Story of Peter Pan** retold by Daniel O'Connor, has been in print since 1914. It is beautifully illustrated and tells the story in a much simpler form.

Bible Stories

At one time children were subjected to almost unrelenting propaganda that sought to brainwash them into becoming paid-up members of the Christian church.

In such circumstances parents were right to try to protect their children from excessive exposure to the Christian message.

Now the pendulum has swung too far in the opposite direction and many young people do not know the classic stories from the Bible: they do not know the story of Adam and Eve, Noah's ark, Joseph and the coat of many colours or the details of the life of Jesus.

This is an obvious lack in their education because these stories are full of wisdom as well as being fundamental to an understanding of our culture and history.

They are also good stories in their own right.

Little House on the Prairie by Laura Ingalls Wilder

The Little House on the Prairie series of books are autobiographical and describe the continuing adventures of Laura and her family in America at the turn of the century. They make interesting reading and children can easily identify with the characters. **Little Town on the Prairie, On the Banks of Plum Creek** and **Farmer Boy** are probably the best, but you have to read the whole series if you want to be able to follow the story.

The Adventures of Mardie, The Bullerby Children by Astrid Lindgren

It is difficult to recommend books that were originally written in another language (in this case Swedish) because one never feels that a translation can do them full justice, but these stories are so good that they should not be missed.

Greek Mythology

Stories of the Greek gods are similar to the stories from the Old Testament in that they have had an enormous effect upon the development of Western culture.

One cannot really appreciate the novels and literature of previous centuries without a good understanding of Greek mythology because they are invariably full of classical references.

Libraries are a good source of books on Greek mythology. There are so many different versions available that it is difficult to recommend any one in particular.

Kidnapped, Treasure Island by Robert Louis Stevenson

'Treasure Island' is often voted the best adventure story ever written for children. In some ways, it is a little too convincing, and although the plot is improbable some of the situations in which the hero finds himself are genuinely frightening.

'Kidnapped' is at least as good and not so scary.

Peanuts by Schulz

It is easy to dismiss cartoons as a second-class form of literature but good cartoons such as 'Peanuts' are an art form that manages to express complex ideas with the minimum of words.

Anthologies of 'Peanuts' cartoons are widely available. Some editions contain a lot of jokes relating to American subjects, such as baseball, but are very funny, nonetheless.

Finn Family Moomintroll (and many other titles) by Tove Jansson

These books are modern classics from Finland and can be appreciated by children from around six years upwards.

They are simple, magical stories and yet are slightly weird. Once you start to read them you'll be hooked!

Harry Potter by J.K. Rowling

The publishing sensation of the 1990s, the Harry Potter books have won the hearts of millions of children. They demonstrate that books have lost none of their traditional hold on children's imagination.

Tintin by Hergé

The Tintin books have the advantage that they can be enjoyed by people with a wide range of reading abilities.

This makes them particularly suitable for people who learn to read when they are eight, nine, or ten years old.

Most learning-to-read books seem banal and boring to four-year-olds and are just unbearable to older children.

The Tintin books are not easy to read but the interesting stories and quality of the pictures encourage children to make the necessary effort.

Hans Brinker or the Silver Skates by Mary Mapes Dodge

This book, written by an American about a brother and sister in Holland, is an evocative and moving story that takes the reader back to a bygone era.

Although young children may find the parts dealing with Dutch art and architecture slightly hard going, no one can fail to be stirred by the thrilling final chapters.

The Oz Books by L. Frank Baum

The first title in the series – **The Wizard of Oz** – is the most well known, but this is largely due to the success of the Hollywood film and has nothing to do with the relative merits of the books themselves.

L. Frank Baum wrote fourteen books about the fairytale land of Oz (not all of which are readily obtainable these days) and anyone who has read them will agree that the subsequent stories are an improvement on his first effort.

They are, of course, best read in the correct order, but our personal favourites are **Ozma of Oz, The Emerald City of Oz** and **Tik-Tok of Oz**.

Facsimiles of the original editions are to be found, and the illustrations lend much to the charm of the stories themselves.

Poetry

This reading selection has concentrated on prose, but poems should in no way be neglected.

There is, of course, good poetry and bad poetry and one has to be guided by one's own tastes in the selection of poems, as with everything else. However, poets such as Wordsworth, Blake, Keats, Shakespeare, Tennyson, the Brontë sisters, Burns, and Shelley all deserve the acclaim they have received over the centuries and it is a good idea to keep a lookout for collections of their work when browsing through second-hand book shops; anthologies are also useful, not least because they can introduce you to poems that you would not otherwise come across.

A child who has the opportunity to read and enjoy good poetry will write poetry themselves, and everyone involved in the world of education agrees that that is a highly desirable outcome.

The Tyger

Tyger! Tyger! Burning bright
In the forests of the night,
What immortal hand or eye
Could frame thy fearful symmetry?

In what distant deeps or skies
Burnt the fire of thine eyes?
On what wings dare he aspire?
What the hand dare seize the fire?

And what shoulder, and what art,
Could twist the sinews of thy heart?
And when thy heart began to beat,
What dread hand? and what dread feet?

What the hammer? what the chain?
In what furnace was thy brain?
What the anvil? what dread grasp
Dare its deadly terrors clasp?

When the stars threw down their spears,
And water'd heaven with their tears,
Did he smile his work to see?
Did he who made the Lamb make thee?

Tyger! Tyger! Burning bright
In the forests of the night,
What immortal hand or eye
Dare frame thy fearful symmetry?

William Blake

The Sleeping Beauty

Year after year unto her feet,
She lying on her couch alone,
Across the purple coverlet,
The maiden's jet-black hair has grown,
On either side her tranced form
Forth streaming from a braid of pearl:
The slumbrous light is rich and warm,
And moves not on the rounded curl.

The silk star-broider'd coverlid
Unto her limbs itself doth mould
Languidly ever; and, amid
Her full black ringlets downward roll'd,
Glows forth each softly-shadow'd arm
With bracelets of the diamond bright:
Her constant beauty doth inform
Stillness with love, and day with light.

She sleeps: her breathings are not heard
In palace chambers far apart.
The fragrant tresses are not stirr'd
That lie upon her charmed heart.
She sleeps: on either hand upswells
The gold-fringed pillow lightly prest:
She sleeps, nor dreams, but ever dwells
A perfect form in perfect rest.

Alfred, Lord Tennyson

Introduction

Mathematics (or arithmetic – the two are essentially the same), reading and writing, are the foundations of learning. Once someone can read for themselves and understands the principles of arithmetic they are capable of pursuing any other branch of learning, whether it be in the arts or in the sciences, on their own. This was always well understood in the past and that is the reason why the three 'Rs' (reading, writing and arithmetic) made up more or less the whole of the primary school curriculum until relatively recently.

The thing that marks mathematics out from reading is that whilst levels of literacy steadily rose after the introduction of primary school education, levels of numeracy did not.

Even today, schools are remarkably ineffectual in their efforts to teach this subject. A few children enjoy maths, understand it and do well in it; the majority struggle with the subject, do not understand it properly and forget most of what they have learnt as soon as they leave school; a significant minority hardly understand it at all and come to dread maths lessons from a very early age.

As a society we have become conditioned to failure in this area. We no longer find it remarkable that children should have maths lessons every school day from the age of five to sixteen years old (eleven years!) but at the end of it be unable to pass the fairly undemanding GCSE examination. Rather than blaming ourselves for having wasted countless hours of our children's time, we consider that the fault lies with them and that they should have tried harder.

In order to understand how this situation has come about, it may be useful to look at the history of mathematics and the attempts that have been made to make it more widely understood.

History

Most of us know that scholars in ancient Greece possessed a knowledge of mathematics equal to that of University mathematics professors today, but we may be surprised to learn that the same is also true of ancient Babylon, India, Egypt and

China. Ancient Chinese astronomers could track the movement of the planets so accurately that they were able to make precise predictions of the solar eclipses; mathematicians in Egypt were masters of trigonometry and geometry and clay tablets survive from ancient Babylon giving values for square roots, sines, cosines and tangents to incredible levels of accuracy.

Thus, contrary to popular belief, there has not been progress in this area over the millennia. The overall mathematical abilities of a modern society do not vary greatly from that which existed in the ancient civilisations. Like them, we have a small elite of very skilled mathematicians, a slightly larger section of society (shopkeepers, bankers etc.) who have a certain degree of competence and a mass of people who only know enough maths to enable them to go about their daily lives.

People have always been able to do the arithmetic necessary to manage their household finances and pursue their trade or craft, and this remains the level of mathematical ability that exists today. Most people do not understand the more complex mathematics learnt at school, such as algebra and trigonometry, and consequently cannot make any use of it in later life.

Maths teaching in schools has failed to raise the level of numeracy in society as a whole. Maths remains as useful a skill, and in as short supply, as it ever was and people who are good at maths rarely find themselves out of employment. It does, therefore, seem remarkable that more effort has not been made to find an alternative to school that would enable this subject to be taught more successfully.

What has gone wrong?

In order to understand the cause of the failure of maths teaching one has to understand something of the way in which people relate to numbers. Anyone who has spent time with very young children, including babies, will know that they have an inherent fascination for numbers. Children count things without any prompting from adults. In many ways numbers seem to be more natural to them than words and speech.

They are also happy to add things up and to take away – in fact simple *mental* arithmetic does not upset any child. Difficulties arise when the step is taken from mental arithmetic to written work. Different children are prepared to take this step at different ages. Unfortunately, the school curriculum encourages children to make this step too early and this gives rise to the first big schism in maths.

Some children literally stop relating to their maths education at this point – at the age of five or six! Others only just manage to struggle on. It is only for a few that everything remains fine.

The problem is often nothing to do with maths itself – it is to do with unfamiliarity with things written down on the page. (For example, some young children cannot tell from which end a number should be read when they see it written down.) This sort of problem generally diminishes with age and, consequently, waiting a few years before starting formal maths teaching could prevent hours of tears, distress and trauma.

Furthermore, when a child starts to become confused in maths, it is difficult for them to catch up: it is more likely that they will lose their self-confidence and fall further and further behind.

In this sense, the mechanics of school itself works against successful maths teaching. Teachers do not have time to stop and help those pupils who are struggling, because the rest of the class then becomes unmanageable. They cannot give the subject a rest for a few weeks, to give everyone a chance to recover, because the timetable demands constant maths study. Sometimes maths teachers are little more than helpless witnesses watching one after another of a class (who all start off so keen and enthusiastic at the age of four or five) become confused and discouraged by their experiences in the maths lessons.

It may well be that the successful teaching of numbers can never take place in school and that this is a subject that always requires the sensitivity of approach that can only come with one-to-one tuition.

Abstract Concepts

Further problems arise when moving from straightforward ideas, such as adding up and taking away, to more abstract concepts of numbers, such as fractions and decimals.

Whether or not they can work out sums on paper, nearly all children have an intuitive understanding of the principles involved in adding, subtracting, multiplying and dividing whole numbers: this is not necessarily the case when it comes to fractions. Some fractions are readily understood and when teachers restrict themselves to questions such as 'What is a half plus a half?' or 'What is a half plus a quarter?', few problems are likely to arise. It is all too easy, however, to stray into areas for which a child is unlikely to have an intuitive feeling and, if they are asked a question such as 'What is a half plus a third?', most young children will not know how to begin to find the answer.

Of course, as adults, our reaction may be to solve the problem of $\frac{1}{2} + \frac{1}{3}$ by the theoretical method that *we* were taught at school:

This runs something like this:		$\frac{1}{2} + \frac{1}{3}$
What is the lowest common denominator of 2 and 3?	6	$\dfrac{}{6}$
How many times does 2 go into 6?	3	
What are three ones?	3	$\dfrac{3 +}{6}$
How many times does 3 go into 6?	2	
What are two ones?	2	$\dfrac{3 + 2}{6} = \dfrac{5}{6}$

Thus: $\quad \frac{1}{2} + \frac{1}{3} = \frac{5}{6}$

Perhaps some readers managed to follow this reasoning with equanimity but, no doubt, for others it will have reawakened feelings of panic that have lain buried since their schooldays. Whatever the case, it should be obvious to everyone that this method does little to help a small child, who knows that a half and a quarter make three quarters, to understand that a half and a third make five sixths.

This example illustrates that even basic maths can require complex, abstract thought that is not appropriate to the majority of primary school-age children.

It also shows that most of us are ourselves the victims of inappropriate maths teaching and that we therefore have little idea of how the subject should be approached properly. We remember having to struggle to understand mathematics when we were young. We remember being confronted by homework questions that made us cry. We remember being confused and intimidated by the subject and we assume that it will have to be the same for our own children when their time comes.

Nothing could be further from the truth. In fact, maths is a subject that must be enjoyed if progress is to be made. When a child wants to learn, they are able to gain an understanding of the principles involved and how to apply them.

Timing

The key to success in maths teaching lies in timing. One child will grasp a new mathematical idea and be keen to progress to the next one. They will be impatient, bored and frustrated if they have to keep going over the same ground because other members of the class are unable to understand something the first time that it is explained. Other members of the class (perhaps even children who came top of the class in other subjects) may be incapable of understanding this particular mathematical idea – and may not be able to do so for one, two or three more years. It does not mean that they are stupid, it just means that they are developing in a different way or at a different rate.

To make matters worse, the child who does not understand the work may be traumatised to such an extent by being made to look foolish in front of their class, that they never manage to progress beyond that particular point during the rest of their time at school.

Surprisingly perhaps, those children who are first introduced to mathematics when they are of secondary school age tend to do well in the subject, especially if they are reasonably competent at mental arithmetic before they begin.

Mathematics is not really as difficult as many people imagine. It only seems difficult because people first encounter it when they are seven, eight, nine or ten years old and forever afterwards cannot see a maths problem without recalling how they felt at that time.

A More Enlightened approach

Some systems of education do take account of the mental and emotional development of children in determining the curriculum. It is incredible that the bulk of mainstream educational thinking does not. An assumption is made that it is up to committees to write the curriculum and that it is the duty of children to comply with what the committees decide. When it all goes wrong, it is the children, their parents and the teachers who are blamed.

The secret of successful maths teaching is to totally reject this way of thinking. It is the child themselves who should be allowed to provide the impetus for progress in the subject. When they say that the sums that they are doing are too easy, they should be allowed to go on to the next stage; when they are having difficulty with something, they should be allowed to retrace their steps and pick up something that they have done before and enjoyed.

If they are finding maths to be tiring then it should be given a rest for a while.

We have to believe that children do want to discover things about the world around them – including maths – and that, given time, they will ask the right questions and will be keen to learn everything that we can teach them.

The Curriculum

The study of maths is like a journey. It starts with counting, progresses through simple sums into fractions, decimals and other number work. It leads from there to algebra, geometry and on to trigonometry, calculus and higher forms of logic.

You cannot reach the end if you do not start at the beginning and take it one step at a time from there. For a child to be taught an aspect of mathematics is not sufficient. The important thing is that they understand it.

The early stages of mathematics involve learning things, and acquiring skills, that are useful in everyday life – money, measuring, finances, percentages, timetables, betting odds, etc. It makes sense for everyone to master these skills.

Later on, more refined concepts, such as algebra, trigonometry, geometry and calculus, are encountered. Some people find these to be a joy in themselves and to others they provide an entry into a profession and a means of earning a living. Many people, however, are not greatly interested in these areas and it makes little sense to force them to study something that they never understand and will never use.

The length of time that an individual needs to explore the subject of mathematics to their own satisfaction bears no relationship to the time devoted to it at school.

In school, the mathematics curriculum is spread out over eleven or twelve years. Children are introduced to a formal study of maths before they are ready, but from then on cover the subject at much too slow a rate to maintain their interest.

Any maths teacher who has worked with a well-motivated student, with an aptitude for the subject, will know that it takes about three to four years to progress from simple arithmetic to 'A' level mathematics. There is only a certain amount of work to be covered and, as everything in maths is interrelated, it helps to keep everything fresh in one's mind by maintaining a momentum.

Child Prodigies

This is the reason why home-taught children often do 'exceptionally well' at maths and pass their 'A' level in their early teens. It is not that they are all maths geniuses, it is simply that, by studying on their own, they are able to progress through the subject at a sensible rate.

However, not everyone wants to study maths to 'A' level and for most people one or two years of regular work will take them to the level of mathematical knowledge that they require.

This has implications for all aspects of maths teaching. In particular, it means that we should give careful consideration to when is the best time to move forward from working with whole numbers to working with fractions.

Not only is this a confusing step for the majority of young children, but taking it too early also fails to serve the interests of children who are gifted in maths.

Once a child grasps the idea of fractions there is no reason why they should not then go on to see how these concepts can be applied to algebra and other areas of mathematics. If you try to delay further progress and tell the child that they have to spend two or three years just working out fractions and decimals, you run the risk of losing their interest forever.

If, on the other hand, you allow a child to progress at the rate at which they feel comfortable, they may be sitting their 'A' level by the time they are twelve or thirteen which puts them in a difficult situation: the only way for them to maintain the momentum of their studies is for them to then go to University, but they are not old enough to cope with the demands of an adult environment. If they do not go to University, all the work that they have done up until that point may be wasted.

It is far better to delay the study of maths rather than risk exposing a bright child to an unpleasant experience at the age of fourteen or fifteen. Most children are far better employed pursuing more down-to-earth activities when they are young and leaving mathematics until they are older.

As a general rule, it is a good idea to spend as long as possible doing mental arithmetic and working with simple things like whole numbers. This does not do anyone any harm. It allows children gifted in maths to become well-versed in the basics, and to develop other interests before plunging into the world of mathematics. It allows everyone else to acquire the number skills that they need without being made to feel inadequate.

Conclusions

Adults are frightened that if they do not force children through a programme of maths instruction, the child will end up uneducated and disadvantaged. This fails to take into account the fundamental importance of maths. The desire to understand it is innate. The job of the teacher is to be ready to answer questions and provide shorter routes of solving problems – one does not have to force maths down someone's throat.

It is unlikely that schools will ever be able to approach the subject in this way. They are now wedded to teaching children in classes and it is difficult to see how these could ever metamorphose into places where children receive one-to-one tuition in a sensitive and caring environment. Parents who want to help their children in this subject have little choice, therefore, but to take matters into their own hands and do some teaching themselves. This may be a daunting prospect for some people, particularly if their own experience of maths at school has left them feeling inadequate. However, all that is really required is an open mind and a willingness to approach the subject in a new way. Very good mathematicians often make the worst teachers – they sometimes forget how difficult maths can be for the uninitiated.

The following pages give an outline of the rough order in which the various subject areas of mathematics can be approached. It is more difficult to say what should be done when because this varies so much from child to child.

As a rough guide it is fair to say that you cannot start mental arithmetic too early, but that everything else can be delayed for a considerable amount of time without doing any harm. The older a child is when they do something new in maths, the more likely they are to understand it.

Even some of the work included in this book – long multiplication and division for example – can be safely left, in the majority of cases, until a child is of secondary school age.

Children who do well at maths at primary school do not necessarily understand the work that they are doing, and would not suffer at all if their study of the subject was deferred for a few years.

Practical Tips For Helping Children Who Are Having Difficulties With Maths at School

The typical reaction to children who are having problems with maths at school is to try to encourage them by 'helping' them with their homework, buying extra maths books and arranging private tuition. Well-intentioned though these efforts might be, they can often be counter-productive.

If a child is not ready for a new mathematical idea, then no amount of extra help is going to make them understand it. It would be far better to leave the subject alone altogether but, as this is not possible for children who go to school, here are some things that you can do to ameliorate the situation.

Give Your Child Praise

Parents have a much greater influence on their children's experience of school than they give themselves credit for. If you let your child know that you are not in the least bit concerned about their inability to do maths at school, then you will be going a long way to relieving any stress or anxiety that they might feel. You can reassure them by telling them that it is quite common for people who eventually become very good at maths not to understand it when they are young.

This will help to counter the idea they may pick up at school that, because they can't do maths when they are seven or eight, they have basically blighted their chances of success in life.

Do Their Homework for Them

Homework is at best a waste of time for young children and, when it involves something that they do not enjoy, it can be positively harmful. One solution is to do the work for them. This is not a perfect solution but you can combine it with explaining to the teacher that you do not agree with the principle of homework. You will not necessarily receive a frosty reception. Many teachers do not like homework and only set it because it is expected of them by parents and administrators.

Approach the Subject from Another Angle

'Helping' children with their sums just prolongs the agony associated with maths, but approaching the subject from a completely different angle can be a source of enjoyment for all concerned.

Practical work such as measuring or working with money is enjoyed by most children. Many games involve adding up or working things out or using logic. If you pursue these sorts of activities at weekends or during the holidays when your child is not tired, then maths can become fun again.

Three Basic Rules of Maths Teaching

1. You have to write your own textbook.

When I started teaching maths, I spent hours in bookshops and in libraries looking for the perfect textbook. I just assumed that, given the fact that children had been learning sums for hundreds, or perhaps thousands, of years, someone must have written the perfect textbook by now.

Eventually I came to understand that no such thing can ever exist. Each child approaches maths from their own perspective and you have to react accordingly.

For example, one child may love adding up. For them, a page of adding up sums every day is a source of almost endless pleasure and enjoyment. Taking away, on the other hand, may be incomprehensible and distressing.

Another child of the same age and perhaps even from the same family may master the idea of adding up in a few days and be keen to go on to taking away immediately.

It is not that one of these is better than the other or that we should encourage one child to conform to the standards of the other, but it leaves us with the challenge of having to produce a different set of sums for each child that we teach.

2. Don't give children sums they can't do.

At one time, I used to add a few more difficult sums to the end of an exercise, to challenge the more able students in the class, and keep everyone on their toes.

Eventually, I realised that this was not very helpful: giving children sums that they cannot answer does not help them to understand the subject better, it only serves to encourage a culture where failure is acceptable. In school seventy per cent is considered to be a good mark.

In real life you either have to get the right answer or say that you don't know. Imagine if a shopkeeper, an engineer or an aircraft designer only got 70% of his or her sums right – at best he or she would be out of a job, at worst they could have caused a disaster to take place.

One may as well get into good habits early on. Real mathematicians cannot afford to make wild guesses at the right answer. They have to know their limitations and be prepared to seek help when they need it.

These days, when I set sums, I expect the children to get them all right. If they don't, I consider the fault to be mine, not theirs. If they don't know how to do one of them, they ask me – and I show them.

If you are worried that a child hasn't understood how to do the work for themselves, then you can set some similar sums next day – and if they still can't do them, do them yourself again.

Sometimes (often) I have made the mistake of setting a sum that is, at the time, beyond the comprehension of the child who is trying to do it. When I realise that I have done this, I work out the answer myself and move on to something else — or back to something already done. Months, or years, later, when we look back through the book, we can laugh at the fact that a particular sum seemed so difficult.

3. Work with a child on a one-to-one basis.

Mathematics is not one of those subjects that lends itself to group work. It is difficult to learn maths when you are a member of a large class and have to compete for the teacher's attention every time you have a problem.

Put yourself in the child's position. You have a sum to do. You can't remember exactly how to do it.

$$\begin{array}{r} 2\,4 \\ +4\,8 \\ \hline \end{array}$$

Take the example on the left:

- You remember that you start off by adding the eight and the four.

- You get the answer 12.

- You can't remember whether you put down the 2 and carry the one or put down the one and carry the 2.

$$\begin{array}{r} 2\,4 \\ +_14\,8 \\ \hline 7\,2 \end{array}$$

- This is not easy and not many children under the age of about 16 are likely to be able to work out what to do by a process of logic. You simply want someone to remind you.

- If the teacher is sitting next to you, they can say 'put down the 2 and carry the 1'. No problem. The sum is done in one or two minutes and all the rest of the sums on the page are done correctly.

What happens, however, if the teacher is not there?

The child can make a guess. They will know that it is a guess and feel slightly unsure.

$$\begin{array}{r} 2\,4 \\ +_24\,8 \\ \hline 8\,1 \end{array}$$

They might make alternate guesses for the rest of the sums on the page, to cover themselves, and end up more confused than when they started.

Alternatively, they may not attempt the sum until they can get their question answered. If this takes a long time they may lose interest in the whole thing and just start drawing in their book or throwing things round the classroom.

The good news is that work that can take years in the cumbersome setting of a schoolroom can be covered in a few hours of interactive activity when both you and your child are prepared for the effort.

There is no substitute for one-to-one tuition in mathematics. The fact that schools cannot offer this to their pupils accounts for their failure to improve standards of numeracy.

When is the Best Time to do Maths?

Children who go to school cannot be expected to do maths in the evenings: they are too tired and need a break from schoolwork. For the same reason, it may not even be a good idea to do maths at weekends, during term time. This leaves the holidays.

Doing maths in the holidays is not as bad an idea as it might sound. Taken out of the school environment, maths is fun and puts everyone in a much better mood than many of the alternative holiday activities such as television or computer games.

Whether you do sums with your child, play games that involve calculation and logic, or involve your child in some practical mathematical activity, you will find that mathematics helps to create a harmonious atmosphere in which you and your child can communicate with each other.

Any maths that you do manage to do in the holidays will have a beneficial effect on their subsequent schoolwork. The main problem that children experience in maths is lack of self-confidence. A positive, relaxed experience of maths in the holidays can do much to restore a child's belief in their own ability.

If you have an older child who is experiencing problems with mathematics, they too may appreciate going over the basics again. You can be sure that their difficulties do not arise from a failure to understand algebra or trigonometry. The problem will lie in the maths that they never really understood at primary school. Once they understand fractions and decimals they will probably be able to cope with any maths that they encounter at secondary school.

If you do not send your child to school, then you can be far more flexible in your approach. Most children enjoy doing some sort of mathematical activity every day. Early morning is a good time to do mental arithmetic as it wakes everyone up.

From time to time you can concentrate specifically on maths and spend two or three hours per day, for two or three weeks, working on a new aspect of the subject – the multiplication tables, money, weights and measures, shapes etc.

The important point about these suggestions is that they are designed for a situation in which you are teaching your child one-to-one. This means that you can tailor each lesson to suit the needs of the child concerned.

The type of work and the order in which it is to be tackled can be very similar to the National Curriculum but the result will be very different from that achieved at school, because it is the child, not the teacher, who is providing the impetus for learning.

Mental Arithmetic

The first objective should be to stay in the realm of mental arithmetic for as long as possible. Being able to work sums out in their heads is the thing that gives children real confidence in maths, and mental arithmetic skills are more difficult to acquire once one has moved on to written sums.

It is a fascinating subject in its own right – there is no standard method by which it is done. You ask a child 'What is two plus two?' They answer 'four'. It is difficult to see how children arrive at the correct answer.

Demonstrating with marbles or conkers or counters doesn't really help. The numbers have a life of their own in a child's mind. Two and two simply fit together to make four without any outside assistance.

Failure in mental arithmetic doesn't hurt in the same way as failure in written work. There are no crosses on the page, no corrections to be made, no evidence of what has passed. One nearly always instinctively knows when one has got the right answer and every child that I have ever known has been prepared to keep trying until that answer comes – this does not apply to written sums!

Mental arithmetic is best done as a game. It should not involve writing answers down. Just ask the child questions and let them reply. Tell them if they are right or wrong. If they are wrong they will try again. You can keep a score if you want, but it is not necessary.

> The little matter of distinguishing one, two, and three – in a word, number and calculation:— do not all arts and sciences necessarily partake of them?
>
> *Socrates*

Adding Up

You can start this with very young children.
Ask questions to which the answer is less than 10.

$2 + 2 =$ $5 + 1 =$
$1 + 3 =$ $8 + 1 =$
$4 + 4 =$ $4 + 2 =$

If this is providing a lot of fun, you can experiment with sums to which the answer is 10.

$6 + 4 =$ $3 + 7 =$
$5 + 5 =$ $8 + 2 =$

You can keep repeating these or you can move on to the decidedly more difficult additions to which the answer is more than 10.

$6 + 5 =$ $8 + 5 =$
$7 + 4 =$ $9 + 6 =$

Answers

$2+2=4$	$5+5=10$
$1+3=4$	$3+7=10$
$4+4=8$	$8+2=10$
$5+1=6$	$6+5=11$
$8+1=9$	$7+4=11$
$4+2=6$	$8+5=13$
$6+4=10$	$9+6=15$

Once your child can answer these questions, they can basically add up. It is just a small step to sums such as

$$16 + 5 = \qquad\qquad 21 + 7 =$$
$$21 + 3 = \qquad\qquad 24 + 7 =$$

and even

$$116 + 5 = \qquad\qquad 121 + 7 =$$
$$121 + 3 = \qquad\qquad 124 + 7 =$$

There is an infinite number of adding-up sums and you will never exhaust all the possibilities. It does not do any harm to keep repeating the same ones over and over again. You can spend years just doing adding-up sums – they are the most important aspect of mathematics.

Adding up leads directly to multiplication (or 'timesing') and taking away (subtraction), which can be introduced whenever you want to have some variety.

Multiplication

Multiplication is a specialised form of adding up.

Three twos are $\qquad 2 + 2 + 2 = 6$

Three twos means three lots of 2 (we write this as 3 x 2, but this is just a shorthand way of referring to two plus two plus two).

Children who can add up in their heads can usually answer questions such as :

two twos	two threes
three twos	three threes
four twos	four threes
five twos	five threes etc.

If you have the patience to keep asking the questions, your child will develop a close relationship with these numbers and, hence, the multiplication tables.

They will recognise the multiples of two to be **2, 4, 6, 8, 10, 12, 14, 16, etc**. and will come to know which numbers exist in each multiplication table. (I am not suggesting that young children should learn the tables by rote and you need not introduce the idea that three times two is the same as three twos unless your child can take it on board with ease.)

Arithmetic has a very great and elevating effect, compelling the soul to reason.

Socrates

This lays down a solid foundation for future work and, if your child is enjoying the exercise, you can experiment with big numbers.

You can ask such questions as:

what are two hundreds?
what are two thousands?
what are two millions?

two twenty fives
three twenty fives
four twenty fives
five twenty fives
six twenty fives

Taking away (subtraction or minus)

Terminology can be confusing for a child.

The question 'Five take away three' is usually met with the answer 'two', but the question 'five minus three' can be met with blank non-comprehension. If a child cannot grasp that in this case 'minus' is another way of saying 'take away', don't bother pushing the point. Just keep saying 'take away'.

Take away sums like these do not usually present a problem:

$6 - 3 =$

$8 - 4 =$

$9 - 2 =$

$3 - 2 =$

$7 - 3 =$

$14 - 2 =$

$18 - 6 =$

$24 - 3 =$

$37 - 5 =$

$49 - 9 =$

Answers

$16+5 = 21$	$2 \times 2 = 4$	$2 \times 100 = 200$	$6 - 3 = 3$
$21+3 = 24$	$3 \times 2 = 6$	$2 \times 1000 = 2000$	$8 - 4 = 4$
$21+7 = 28$	$4 \times 2 = 8$	$2 \times 1\,000\,000 = 2\,000\,000$	$9 - 2 = 7$
$24+7 = 31$	$5 \times 2 = 10$		$3 - 2 = 1$
$116+5 = 121$	$2 \times 3 = 6$	$2 \times 25 = 50$	$7 - 3 = 4$
$121+3 = 124$	$3 \times 3 = 9$	$3 \times 25 = 75$	$14 - 2 = 12$
$121+7 = 128$	$4 \times 3 = 12$	$4 \times 25 = 100$	$18 - 6 = 12$
$124+7 = 131$	$5 \times 3 = 15$	$5 \times 25 = 125$	$24 - 3 = 21$
		$6 \times 25 = 150$	$37 - 5 = 32$
			$49 - 9 = 40$

And have you further observed that those who have a natural talent for calculation are generally quick at every kind of knowledge; and even the dull, if they have had an arithmetical training, although they may derive no other advantage from it, always become much quicker than they would otherwise have been?

Socrates

It becomes more difficult when they involve such questions as:

$$11 - 7 = \qquad 12 - 3 =$$
$$17 - 9 = \qquad 22 - 5 =$$
$$13 - 8 = \qquad 33 - 4 =$$

It is best not to go too fast with subtraction. Children will usually really enjoy it if they are allowed to approach it in their own time, but it can be quite confusing if they are not ready. They know that numbers that can be added, can also be taken away. This means that you can wait for them to ask about it.

Don't even think about sums such as 'four take away five is minus one'. Such concepts are 'counter-intuitive' and undermine a child's understanding of maths rather than increase it. It is much better to get a firm understanding of the fact that 'four take away five cannot be done' than to introduce the idea of minus numbers. After all, in reality it cannot be done and if a child doesn't understand this then they will not appreciate how clever minus numbers are, when you come to study them later.

Division

Division is a difficult concept to grasp and it is difficult to do in one's head. That is why it is left till last. It does fit in quite well with multiplication, but is best introduced using the words 'shared between'.

'What's six shared between three people?' makes more sense than 'What's six divided by three?'

Doing this type of division is further preparation for learning the multiplication tables: it provides another way of working with multiples of a number. You can ask questions such as:

Two shared between two people
Four shared between two people
Six shared between two people
Eight shared between two people
Ten shared between two people
Twelve shared between two people

You can see how this sort of work can easily lead to a good understanding of the tables.

You can also ask questions to which there is not an exact answer, so that **seven divided by** (or shared between) **2 is '3 with one left over'**. (In this example a child might quickly realise that 7 divided by 2 is three and a half, but one should be wary of fractions and not force them into the conversation.)

And, for these reasons, arithmetic is a kind of knowledge in which the best natures should be trained, and which must not be given up.

Socrates

Mental Arithmetic and Everyday life

Many other things can be drawn into mental arithmetic. Big numbers are always fun. Ideas such as a million add one making a million and one are enthralling to children.

Sums involving money make good sense. Working out how much the shopping costs or just adding up different amounts of money is both useful and interesting.

Most children are interested in questions involving age: how much older than you am I; how much younger than granny are you; how much younger than granny am I? etc.

If you do cooking with your child, then you will be using weights and may have to convert from grams to ounces.

If you are making things together then you will probably have to use measurements.

Basically, if you lead a normal life with your child, then mathematical ideas will crop up all the time and you will not have to go out of your way to convince your child of the usefulness of numbers.

Children Having Problems With Maths

There are very few children who do not enjoy mental arithmetic (contrary to what you might expect). Mental arithmetic involves some communication with another person – it is not such a lonely struggle as working out sums on paper – this makes it an ideal activity for children who are experiencing difficulties in maths.

Do not ask a child to work out sums in their head and write the answers down – it must be an oral exercise which allows them to make mistakes without seeing their work criticised on a piece of paper.

Much of what is written here represents knowledge gained through bitter experience. In some ways it is easier to teach maths badly than to teach it well. If a child is having difficulties, therefore, do not assume that they are no good at maths. It is far more likely that they are the victim of poor maths teaching. The easiest way to remedy this is to return to the basics and do some mental arithmetic.

Children often miss out on this formative phase of maths study and are thrown straight into trying to work out sums on paper at school or – even worse – having meaningless answers presented to them by an electronic calculator.

In such cases it is essential that they be allowed to start again and to discover the pleasure that can be gained from playing with numbers in one's head.

Answers

$11 - 7 = 4$	$12 - 3 = 9$	$2 \div 2 = 1$	$8 \div 2 = 4$
$17 - 9 = 8$	$22 - 5 = 17$	$4 \div 2 = 2$	$10 \div 2 = 5$
$13 - 8 = 5$	$33 - 4 = 29$	$6 \div 2 = 3$	$12 \div 2 = 6$

Multiplication Tables

Having discussed maths with a lot of children, I am convinced that the secret of being able to do it lies in the multiplication tables.

For a while, many people thought that the invention of calculators might mean that children would no longer have to learn their tables. In practice the opposite has proved to be the case. One cannot get the right answers on a calculator if one doesn't know how numbers work.

This understanding comprises such things as knowing that **six sevens are the same as seven sixes**; that **four twos are half of eight twos**; that **multiples of 5 always end in 5 or 0 etc**.

The multiplication tables give a child a key into the inner workings of mathematics, and a familiarity with them vastly increases their self-confidence in the subject.

There is nothing wrong with learning tables by rote, but it is not the only way of becoming familiar with them. An alternative is to treat them as a quiz:

> What are three fours?
> What are five sixes?
> What are two eights?   etc.

Each child may find a different way of remembering the answer but everyone becomes quicker the more often they are asked. (Of course, you can't do this in a school because if you go round a class asking questions in turn, each child only has the opportunity to answer a question once every five or ten minutes, and everyone rapidly gets bored and distracted.)

Most people get stuck on the same elements in the tables.

Once you have learnt the basics, you can concentrate on questions like:

> What are six sevens?   What are six eights?
> What are six nines?   What are seven eights?
> What are seven nines?   What are nine sixes?

I didn't know my tables very well when I started teaching maths, but I learnt them pretty quickly when I had to work out sums on the blackboard in front of a class of children, and have found them very useful ever since.

I am sure that any parent who takes the trouble to teach their child the multiplication tables will derive similar benefits.

Answers

$3 \times 4 = 12$	$6 \times 7 = 42$	$6 \times 8 = 48$
$5 \times 6 = 30$	$6 \times 9 = 54$	$7 \times 8 = 56$
$2 \times 8 = 16$	$7 \times 9 = 63$	$9 \times 6 = 54$

Games

There is much more to mathematics than working out the answers to sums. Games offer an excellent way of developing mathematical skills with a minimum of difficulty.

The main requirement for games is time. (This is why they are not an appropriate activity in school. The teacher has virtually no time to spend with each individual child in their class and therefore cannot spend time playing games.)

When I worked as a private tutor, helping children who had experienced problems at school, I used to spend up to an hour per day playing various dice and card games with each child that I taught. I always felt that it was time well spent even though it was not quantifiable in the same way as working out sums in an exercise book.

Games are an ideal activity for parents and children to do with each other. Even children who have had a hard day at school will normally welcome the chance to sit down and play some games when they get home. This is far preferable to them watching the television or playing computer games, not least because it gives you a chance to talk to each other and for your child to keep you informed about what is happening at school.

They also have a strong educational value. All dice games involve some number skills (sometimes quite sophisticated ones) and card games require logic and being able to calculate the chances of success related to the various options available at each stage of a game.

Statistics and probability, two very significant branches of mathematics, owe their origins to the desire of Renaissance mathematicians to improve their chances of winning at various forms of gambling – usually dice – so there should be no reason to feel guilty spending maths lessons playing games!

Cheating and Temper Tantrums

If you are not in the habit of playing games with your child, you may find that you have to get over a few teething problems before it becomes an enjoyable activity.

Children often pick up, perhaps from school, an obsessive desire to win no matter what the cost. They may cheat outrageously and throw a temper tantrum if they look like losing. This makes playing games very difficult.

Of course it is not easy for anyone to cope with losing all the time and some games (like chess) could stretch the patience of a saint. You therefore have to select games that, played over a reasonable period of time, give every player an equal chance of success.

Dice Games

You can start playing very simple dice games such as Snakes and Ladders with quite young children. Once they reach the age of seven or eight they may want to try something a little more challenging, such as the following:

Yahtzee

Yahtzee is a dice game that is widely available from toy shops and games shops.

It involves getting certain combinations with successive throws of the five dice and adding up one's score at the end of each game.

It has the appearance of being a very simple game but there are innumerable ways in which the dice can fall and each game that you play is different. Working out the final scores also provides good adding up practice.

Shut That Box

Shut That Box is a modern game but it does contain all the elements required to make a good dice game.

Each player takes it in turn to throw the two dice and put down the tabs that correspond to their total, for as long as possible.

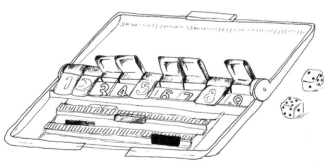

When the total of the dice cannot be matched by the tabs still standing, then the next player has their turn.

Each game of Shut That Box only takes a few minutes so no one gets too wound up about the result. (Games that take too long should be avoided.)

Another advantage is that if you can get all the tabs down in one go, then you win outright. This stops people becoming depressed when they think that they are losing.

Other Dice Games

Other dice games that may prove popular could include poker dice and 421.

Dominoes

Dominoes is another traditional game that has proved its value over many generations.

It teaches children to recognise numbers from one to six and it also introduces them to the fact that number games throw up almost endless permutations from seemingly simple origins.

Dominoes is a gentle game that seldom arouses great passions. It can offer a very pleasant way of passing half an hour or so with your child.

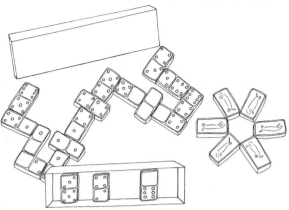

Marbles

There are many different games of marbles. Most of them contain some mathematical element, with different marbles having different values.

The game shown here involves making a target out of wood with a series of arches cut out of it.

The aim is to roll one's marbles through the arches. Each arch has a different value so one has to keep a record of each player's total.

The arches in the middle have the lowest value and should be slightly larger than the arches at the edges which have higher values.

You can allow younger players to roll their marbles from slightly nearer to the board as this considerably increases the chances of them going through the arches.

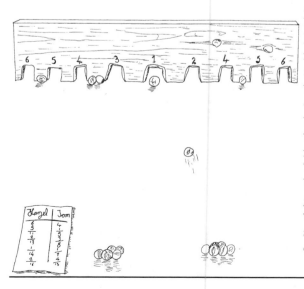

Another marble game involves balancing a dice on top of a marble. Players take it in turn to roll their marbles at this marble. If they succeed in knocking the dice off, they win the number of marbles corresponding to the number facing upwards on the dice when it comes to rest. If they miss, they lose their marble.

This game involves one person being the 'banker'. The banker gives each player their marbles at the start of the game, looks after the stock of marbles and replaces the dice when it is knocked off.

Battleships (2 players)

Battleships is a game that introduces a child to the use of co-ordinates to designate a particular place. This is a useful skill in map reading and, perhaps more relevant to the study of maths, in the use of graphs and charts in general.

There are many commercial versions of Battleships available but it is more enjoyable if you make your own game on a piece of paper. You have more flexibility to change the game to suit your needs.

The Aim: To destroy your opponent's fleet.

To make the game:
- Draw a grid consisting of ten squares by ten squares. It is best to draw this on squared paper because then you do not have to measure all the boxes with a ruler. One centimetre squares (½") are best, but you can play with smaller squares if you are careful.
- Label the columns from 1 to 10 and the rows from A to J (as shown below).
- Make another identical grid so that you have one for each player.
- Make sure that you have two sharp pencils (HB) and two erasers.

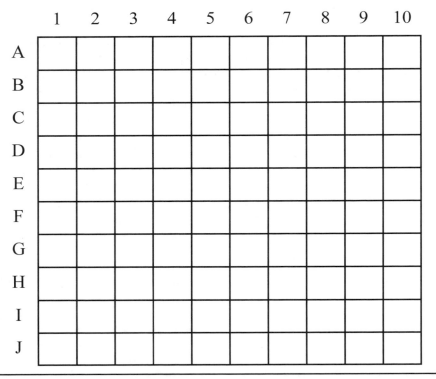

To play the game:

- Each player has a fleet consisting of:

1 Battleship	1 Cruiser	2 Destroyers	1 Submarine

- Each player marks all the items in their fleet on their grid. They can be either vertical or horizontal but not diagonal. They must not be in adjacent squares – not even diagonally adjacent squares.
- Do not let the other player see your grid.
- The first player 'fires' at one of the squares on the other player's grid.
  For example they could say 'A1'. If the other player has something on square A1 they must say '**Hit**'. If not they say '**Miss**'.
  If it is a hit, the first player marks an **H** in square A1 on their own grid and has another turn. They may say 'A2'. If this is a hit, they get another turn, and so on. When every square of an item has been hit, the other player must say '**Hit and Sunk**'.
  When the first player has been told that they have a '**Miss**', they put an '**X**' in that square and it is then the other player's turn to fire.
- Misses are more common than hits so turns normally alternate between the two players.
- The main problem with this game is that of becoming confused between which squares you have fired at and which squares your opponent has fired at. You have to know which squares your opponent has fired at in order to tell them that they have sunk one of your fleet. The easiest way to do this is to put a dot in the corner of each square that your opponent fires at. This will not get in the way of the '**H**' or '**X**' that you put there when you fire at that square.

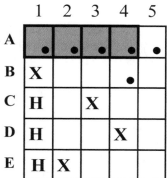

- If you draw out the grid with a biro, shade in the items of your fleet in crayon and mark on everything else in pencil. You will be able to rub out any mistakes that you make when playing the game.
- The winner is the first player to sink every single item in their opponent's fleet.

Advanced Game

You can devise a more advanced game by drawing a bigger grid and having a larger fleet. You can also have new craft in your fleet (both players must still have the same craft).

e.g.   aeroplane   aircraft carrier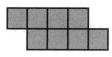

Card Games

Cards are the most versatile of all games. You can start playing games such as Snap with very young children. You will have to let them win, at first, because they will not be able to distinguish one card from another as quickly as you, but they will soon learn to recognise the different numbers and that opens the door to other games.

If you are not a committed card player yourself, you may find it a good idea to ask friends and relatives to teach you games that are suitable for young children.

There are also books, such as 'The Pan Book of Card Games' by Hubert Phillips, that describe a wide range of different games that vary in complexity from the simple to the very sophisticated.

(See pages 119-125 for a description of a few games that usually prove popular with children.)

Other Games

There are many other games that rely on mathematical ability.

Bagatelle is fun and involves adding up figures to keep track of the score.

Darts games such as 301 offer very good practice at addition and subtraction (but darts can be dangerous if not properly supervised).

Mastermind requires the use of logic and inspired guesswork which are essential skills in problem solving. Travel editions of Mastermind are not too expensive.

Draughts and chess are games that involve logical thought and being able to work out which of the available options is most likely to succeed, but they are games that accentuate the differences in ability that come with age and experience. They contain no element of chance and you would normally expect to beat a young child at these games every time you played them. This tends to make them less enjoyable.

There are of course word games such as Scrabble and Lexicon, that are also worth playing. Even these, however, have a mathematical element because they involve logic and strategy.

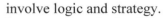

In a sense, maths itself is a game. It involves playing with numbers in accordance with certain pre-defined rules. This makes games a highly appropriate medium for acquiring numerical skills.

Playing Cards

'Packs' are made up of fifty-two playing cards, or fifty-four if the two 'jokers' are included. Each pack is divided into four sets of thirteen cards – 2, 3, 4, 5, 6, 7, 8, 9, 10, Jack (abbreviated to J), Queen (Q), King (K), and finally the ace (A) which can be the lowest or the highest card depending on the game.

To distinguish these ascending sequences, each has been given a symbol; two red and two black.

The names of these symbols are diamonds, hearts, spades and clubs. They look like this:

♦ Diamonds (which are red)   ♠ Spades (which are black)
♥ Hearts (which are red)   ♣ Clubs (which are black)

As with any game, there are specific words used to describe the different cards, and the manner in which they are played. Some of these are confined to certain games such as Bridge or Whist, but many are an essential part of whichever game you choose to play. These basic terms are listed below.

Suit – The name of a particular set of cards e.g. the suit of clubs, the suit of diamonds etc.

Trumps – The cards belonging to the suit chosen at the beginning of the game or 'round' are the most important. In Knock out Whist for example, if hearts were 'called' trumps then they would take precedence over the other suits, and a two of hearts (2♥) would actually be higher in value than an ace of spades, clubs or diamonds (A♠, A♣ or A♦).

Shuffle – To mix the cards together in one of a variety of different ways, the aim being to prevent the formation of sequences and the same assortment of cards being dealt out twice.

Deal – The process of distributing the cards to each player. The dealer begins with the person seated to his/her left, and deals the cards out one at a time going around and around the circle until the specified number of cards has been distributed.

Cut – Cutting is done either at the end of the shuffle, when the pack is divided into two and the lower half is placed above the upper half, or to determine which player will deal or call trumps. In the second instance the players take it in turn to lift several cards off the pack, upturning the 'bottom' of their pile when requested, in order to see which of the exposed cards is the highest.

A Hand – Literally the cards held in your hand during the game.

A Trick – When each player has put out one card upon the table in turn, the person who put out the highest card, or 'trump', gathers them together and places them face down in front of him/herself. The name of these assembled cards is a 'trick' and in many games the player who acquires the most tricks is the winner.

Over-trump – To play a trump higher in value than the one that preceded it.

Knock Out Whist (2 – 7 People)

The Aim: To win the final trick

This is an ideal game for beginners, and is one of the most popular card games. There are many slightly different variations of the rules, but those described below will guarantee you a balanced game in which few of the players will be 'knocked out' – always a major deterrent for young players.

The Rules

- The players cut the pack and the person who selects the highest card deals out seven cards face down to each player, starting with the person on their left. Once the deal is completed the player on the dealer's right cuts again – this time the card selected will dictate which is the suit of trumps during that round.

- Play begins with the player on the dealer's left. They lead a card from their hand, then the player on their left plays their card, and so on, until the dealer has had his turn and the person who played the highest card of that suit or of the suit of trumps, gathers up the trick and lays it face down before them.

Note: It should here be made clear that if the first player leads a club, then the other players have no choice but to follow suit – that is, also to play clubs. Only if they have no clubs in their hand may they play a trump or a card from another suit.

- Play continues in this way, with the winner of the preceding trick taking the lead, until all the cards have been played.

- The person with the most tricks chooses which suit will be trumps at the beginning of the following round. If two or more players have an equal number of tricks they cut the pack and the player who turns up the highest card picks trumps in the next round.

- The player on the dealer's left deals the cards for the second round. This time six cards are dealt to each player; in the next round only five and so on until the seventh round, when players receive one card apiece.

- In this final round, there is only one trick to be won and the player who gains this is the overall winner, irrespective of how many tricks they acquired during the preceding rounds.

Dogs' Chances

Obviously there will be some players who, at the end of the round, have won no tricks. In the first round this does not matter, as even if they come away with nothing the dealer has to give them six cards at the beginning of the next round. However, if a player fails to win a trick in the second round, they are allotted a 'dog's chance'.

This means that when the dealer is giving out the cards for the third round (five cards each), they only receive one – although they are allowed to choose it. They can also play it whenever they want, provided it is their turn.

If someone with a dog's chance wins a trick, then they are automatically reinstated in the game and will once more receive the same amount of cards as everyone else at the beginning of the next round.

However, those who have not met with success will be given a 'blind dog's chance' in the next round. This is basically the same as a dog's chance, except for the fact that they are not allowed to look at their card once they have chosen it from the dealer. They have to rely upon their intuition as to when to play it.

If bad luck still 'dogs' their footsteps, never fear: after a blind dog's chance comes a 'dead dog's chance' which is only different in so far as they have to play it on their first turn.

This is followed by a 'buried dog's chance'. By now they cannot look at their card, have no choice about when to play it and – because this is a buried dog's chance – cannot even choose it anymore.

If even this card fails to win a trick (an event which is admittedly rather unlikely) then they are knocked out of the game – hence the name 'Knock out Whist'.

Hints on How to Make the Most of Your Hand

- If it is your turn to call trumps pick the suit in which you have most cards.
- Avoid leading your high cards unless you are confident that they will win. It is annoying when your Queen is beaten by a King or an Ace and it may be better to wait until a round of her suit has been played before letting her venture forth.
- If an opponent leads a suit which you do not have in your hand, and it is trumped by another player, do not play one of your own trumps unless it is higher in value than the trump just played. It is far wiser to 'throw away' a low card in another suit and save your trump for a later round.

Black Jack (2 – 5 People)

The Aim: To be the first to play all one's cards

This game is simpler than Knock Out Whist and would, perhaps, be the better game to play with young children who have never played cards before.

It belongs to quite a different family of card games but the rules, once mastered, are very easy and will provide hours of amusement.

The Rules

- All players cut and the person who turns over the highest card deals out seven cards to each player, starting with the person on their left. Once this has been done, the dealer places one more card face up on the table and places the pack face down at its side.

- Play begins with the player on the dealer's left who has to look at their hand and either: play a card of the same suit as the one face up on the table; play a card of a different suit but of the same value (thus a K♦ may be placed on a K♣, a 9♣ may be placed on a 9♥ etc.); or, if they hold none of the appropriate cards in their hand, pick up a card from the pack which is face down on the table.

- Whichever option they choose, play then passes straight on to the person on their left and the same procedure is repeated.

- This system of play continues with the turns passing in a clockwise direction around the circle until someone puts out their final card and wins the game.

Note: If the cards in the pack on the table run out, take the top card from the pile, lay it face up on the table and then place the pile face down at its side. Do not shuffle this pile.

Aces, Twos, Eights, Queens and 'Black Jacks'

To make this otherwise rather uninteresting game more exciting, eighteen cards have been given special properties:

Aces

All four aces are very useful to the discerning player. They can be played irrespective of which card is upturned upon the pile, and enable the player to change the suit to one of their choice.

Example: A player has 3 clubs and an A♠ in their hand; the upturned card is a four of diamonds (4♦). Instead of having to pick up a card from the pile, they can put out the A♠ and inform the other players that the suit which they now have to play is clubs.

A player may put out an ace as their final card.

Twos

The twos, although not particularly useful to their owner, allow them to increase the number of cards in their opponents' hands and consequently improve their own chances of winning.

The player who puts out a two forces the next player to pick up two cards from the pack. (A two can only be played if it is of the same suit as the card on the top of the pile; if it is of the suit nominated by someone who has just played an ace, or if it is following another two.)

However, if this player happens to have a two in their hand, they can play it, making the following person pick up four cards. If four players play twos consecutively then the fifth player must pick up eight cards (if there are four people playing the game then this 'fifth' player will be the person who played the first two!).

Eights

The eights are the same in principle as the twos, except that the person who puts one out forces the next player to miss a turn.

If this player has an eight in their own hand, they may play it instead of missing a go. This makes the next player miss a turn, and so on.

Queens

Queens change the direction of play. If only two people are playing they enable their possessor to have several consecutive turns.

Black Jacks

The 'Black Jacks' are the J♠ and the J♣. The person who plays one of these cards forces their neighbour to pick up five cards.

As with twos, the value of Black Jacks can be doubled and, if two consecutive players place them on the pile, one hapless soul will find themselves left with no choice but to pick up ten cards!

Tips

This is primarily a game of chance but the following hints could be kept in mind:

- If possible, keep your aces to the end, as they can be played no matter what card is upturned on the pile.

- You are allowed to play an ace whenever you wish, but it is preferable to keep it in your hand until you would otherwise have to pick up a card from the pack.

Racing Demon (3 or more people)

Racing Demon is a game that can be enjoyed by the whole family and it is unusual in that it does not allow the adults to maintain their accustomed superiority for very long.

- Each player starts with their own pack of cards (it is advisable to use old packs because cards sometimes get bent in the frenzy of the game).
- The game is best played with everyone sitting round a large table which has plenty of space in the middle.
- Each player deals 13 cards into a 'stack' that they then place face upwards in front of them.
- Each player then deals a further 4 cards that they place in a row, face upwards in front of them, beside the stack.
- This leaves each player with 35 cards which they hold in their hand.

The Aim : The winner is the first player to get rid of the 13 cards in their stack

- One player gives the word to begin.

At any time there are six cards that can be played:

- The four upturned cards or, if cards have been placed on top of these cards (see below), the top card of the piles built up on these cards.
- The top card in the stack.
- Players are allowed to make a further pile of cards by turning over the cards that remain in their hand, three at a time. The top card of the pile formed in this way can also be played. Once all the cards have been turned over from the hand, this pile can be picked up and the process repeated, as often and as quickly as one likes.

Ways in Which These Six Cards Can Be Played

- Aces can be placed in the middle of the table.
- Once an ace has been placed in the middle of the table, any player can build up on it. For example, any player can place the 2♣ on the A♣ and then any player can place a 3♣ on the 2♣ and so on up to the K♣. (Speed is of the essence and when two players want to play the same card, it is the one who is first to place it upon the ace, who wins.)
- Players can build up on the four upturned cards. This is done in the same way as in some Patience games, using alternate colours and in descending sequence. For example, if one of the upturned cards is the 10♣, then a player can place the 9♦ or the 9♥ on top of it and on top of that they can place the 8♣ or the 8 ♠ etc. Players can only build up on their own upturned cards, not on anyone else's!

- When a space is created by placing one of the four upturned cards onto one of the piles being built up on the aces, or onto one of the piles being built up on the other upturned cards, then any of the remaining five cards that are available to be played can be placed in the space. (Normally, it makes sense to move the card on top of the stack into any spaces that occur.)
- Only one card can be moved at a time.

Speed is the key to success in this game and it is usually the player who can build up fastest on the aces in the middle of the table, who wins.

This is the stack of 13 cards. The top card, 3♠, can be played onto the 4♥. However, it is a good idea to first place the 4♥ onto the 5♣ as this will create a space. Remember that you cannot move two cards together.

This is the pile that is created by turning over three cards at a time from those cards held in the hand.

There is nothing that can be done with the 9♥ so, once all the other moves have been made, turn over another three cards.

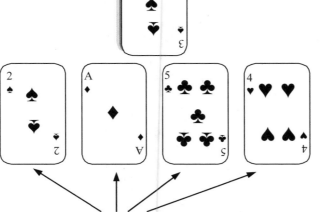

These are the four upturned cards:
- The A♦ can be placed in the middle of the table.
- The 2♠ can be placed on an A♠ as soon as someone puts one out on the table.
- The 4♥ can be placed on the 5♣

WRITTEN SUMS

At some point you will want to progress from mental arithmetic to sums done on paper.

A good time to do this is when a child is learning to write. Hopefully, by this time, numbers will be old friends and they will enjoy meeting them in the new setting that they are learning to work with – the written word.

There are a few basic points to be considered:

Writing Materials

You must bear in mind that if a child is not happy with their writing implement then they cannot be happy with what they write. This is difficult to appreciate for an adult who can happily pick up any pen or pencil that is lying around and start writing with it, but any primary school teacher can testify to how important an issue this is to some children, who can spend half an hour at the beginning of a lesson sorting through their pencil case for something to write with.

Other children are simply unable to work if they lose their favourite pen or pencil. In extreme cases, there are children who have never found anything that they are happy to write with.

The problem may be more acute for left-handed children, but many right-handed children also experience severe difficulties in finding a suitable pen or pencil.

If you are trying to do written sums with young children, then problems may be exacerbated by their hands not being sufficiently developed to hold a pen or pencil properly.

As with writing, things are much easier if you have done a lot of drawing with your child. They will not then have any difficulty in selecting something to write with – be it a crayon, a felt tip pen, a wax crayon or whatever. Sometimes adults can be dogmatic and may try to make children use a particular writing implement. For example, many people do not like to see children using biros or felt-tip pens, especially for doing sums, and constantly try to make them use pencils or fountain pens.

It is important for a child's work to be clear and legible, but the overriding consideration must always be that the child feels comfortable with their writing implement – it should not distract them from the work that they are trying to do.

Paper

The question of paper can also be surprisingly contentious. In Britain, children are usually given lined paper on which to work out sums, in some other countries, such as France and Germany, they are given squared paper.

The idea behind this is to give a child a structure within which to work so that they can keep their work neat. In practice, these lines and squares are too restrictive for young children: the lines are generally too close together and the child has difficulty keeping within them.

Most young children do not feel comfortable writing very small characters – they prefer big writing. This leads them to spread out from the limits defined by the lines, and the page is more of a mess than it would have been if there had been no lines at all.

If you use plain paper and set out the sums yourself, then you can adjust their size to suit the needs of the child you are teaching. This will allow them to concentrate upon the sums themselves and not upon the actual process of trying to fit the answer into a particular space. It does not mean that you ignore the basic principle of keeping maths work neat and making sure that all the numbers are in the correct columns, it just means that the child can work in a medium in which they are happy.

A ream of A3 plain white photocopy paper will keep you going for ages. There are advantages to working on individual sheets of paper: they are easier for a young child to manage than an exercise book – they are flatter – and working on plain paper allows you to write out the sums in the size with which your child is most comfortable.

Later on, when your child has become adjusted to the process of writing and working on paper, you can use any normal exercise book for your maths work. Children find it useful to be able to look back through their work to see how they have done certain sums before.

Calculators

Calculators provide an excellent means of getting the right answers to sums, but they do not help a child to understand them. This means that they have limited relevance to most children.

If a child is confronted by a practical problem, to which they need to find the correct answer, then a calculator may be useful. (Simple exercises that help them to understand how to use a calculator may also be appropriate.) However, using a calculator to find the answers to pages of sums is a waste of their time. Working out a series of different sums for themselves will increase their understanding and skill in the use of numbers, and is therefore a valuable, and often enjoyable, exercise, but using a calculator to work them out is repetitive and tedious and teaches no new skills – once they know how to push the buttons and copy down the answer, it does not matter how many sums they do, they will learn nothing new.

It is fine for a child to have a calculator, but it is not of much real use to them at this age.

Practical Points

Mathematics is a subject that has become notorious for how badly it is taught. Here are a few more tips to help you to avoid some of the worst pitfalls.

- Lengthy explanations do little to shed light on a mathematical problem. It is much better to teach by example. If you have a page of sums that are all similar, work the first few out yourself and let your child take over when they seem to grasp what you are doing.

- If you have set some work that is too difficult, leave it and return to it at some point in the future when you have prepared the ground better.

- Approach the subject in a logical manner so that each new idea follows on from what has gone before.

- Try to remember that maths is inherently enjoyable. If it is becoming a painful experience then you are not approaching it properly. Be prepared to stop what you are doing and to try something completely different.

- Do not feel that you have to do sums every day. You are not trying to make your child into a maths genius. A few sums, every now and then, is all that most children require to satisfy their interest in the subject.

- A more normal routine is to do sums every day for a few weeks and to then to leave them for a few weeks (or even months). This allows children to pursue other interests. Each time they return to doing sums, they will make more sense. This approach allows children to become good at maths, but not in an unbalanced way.

Adding Up

Begin with some old favourites that you have been doing in mental arithmetic:

5	3	5	7
+ 4	+ 2	+ 6	+ 5

Once you have completed a few sheets of these and you are sure that your child knows where, and how, to write the answer, you can move on to more difficult adding up sums:

2 3	1 7	4 3	3 1
+ 4 2	+ 3 2	+ 2 5	+ 5 4

The next big problem involves 'carrying' to the next column. When you add numbers in a column that come to more than ten, you have to put down the units and carry the tens.

Don't expect a child to understand an explanation of this – if they are good at mental arithmetic it will make sense to them because they will see that it leads to the right answer.

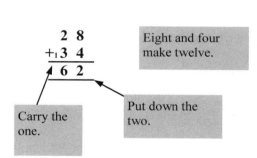

2 8
+₁3 4
6 2

Eight and four make twelve.

Carry the one.

Put down the two.

This idea of carrying a number over to the next column represents a huge step in a child's mathematical progress. They are being introduced to the fact that they can use techniques with a pencil and paper that will allow them to work out sums that are too difficult for them to do in their heads.

If you have managed to wait until your child is ready for this sort of work before introducing it, you will now find that they have an insatiable desire to explore the potential of this new skill. You may be surprised to discover how rapidly children can progress in mathematics when they are enjoying themselves.

Answers

5 + 4 = 9	5 + 6 = 11	23 + 42 = 65	43 + 25 = 68
3 + 2 = 5	7 + 5 = 12	17 + 32 = 49	31 + 54 = 85

It is well worth spending quite a long time doing adding-up sums. Adding up is the most fundamental and the most useful of all mathematical functions. Keep the work interesting by making up sums that have unusual answers, such as the following:

```
   1 7        1 8        3 7        5 6
 + 1 6      + 2 6      + 1 8      + 5 5
 _____     _____     _____     _____
```

```
   3 2        4 2 6      1 5 8 1      4 3 6 6 5
 + 2 3      + 1 2 9    + 3 9 7 4    + 1 1 8 9 0
 _____     _____   _____   _____
```

```
   3 5        7 0 8        2 1 9
 + 7 6      + 4 0 3      + 8 9 2
 _____     _____     _____
```

```
                2 1          1 2 4
                1 3          1 7 3
                2 4          1 1 5
                1 6          1 2 7
              + 2 5          2 1 1
              _____      + 2 4 9
                          _____
```

One of the remarkable things about maths is the speed with which people can progress when they are self-motivated. You may find that your child moves rapidly from simply adding two digits together to wanting sums that involve long columns of numbers.

```
1
5
6
9
2
9
4
4
9
5
7
9
8
3
9
1
+ 9
```

Try devising some sums that have interesting shapes.

```
      9
    1 8
  1 7 3
2 4 6 7
1 6 3 3 3
+ 1 8 1 0 0 0
```

Of course, it is also a good idea to include some sums that do not have predictable answers.

```
1 2 3 4 5 6 7
  1 2 3 4 5 6
    1 2 3 4 5
      1 2 3 4
        1 2 3
          1 2
+           1
```

Constant practice is the best way of becoming good at sums.

Sums that have a practical relevance to a child's life are the best and games, such as Yahtzee, that involve adding up columns of numbers, probably offer the simplest way of becoming good at adding up.

Taking Away (Subtraction)

Many children find it easier to understand the term 'take away' than 'subtract' or 'minus' and it therefore makes sense to carry on using this expression.

Start off with easy sums such as the following:

$$
\begin{array}{r} 2\ 7 \\ -\ 1\ 6 \\ \hline \end{array}
\qquad
\begin{array}{r} 4\ 8 \\ -\ 2\ 6 \\ \hline \end{array}
\qquad
\begin{array}{r} 4\ 7 \\ -\ 1\ 4 \\ \hline \end{array}
\qquad
\begin{array}{r} 6\ 6 \\ -\ 2\ 2 \\ \hline \end{array}
$$

$$
\begin{array}{r} 3\ 4\ 7\ 1 \\ -\ 2\ 3\ 6\ 0 \\ \hline \end{array}
\qquad
\begin{array}{r} 5\ 8\ 9\ 3\ 6 \\ -\ 3\ 6\ 7\ 1\ 4 \\ \hline \end{array}
\qquad
\begin{array}{r} 3\ 4\ 6\ 5 \\ -\ 1\ 3\ 2 \\ \hline \end{array}
$$

You will find that you soon have to introduce the difficult concepts involved in a sum such as **12 − 8**. Hopefully, your child will know that the answer is **4**, but to get this result on paper you have to work through the following steps:

- 2 take away 8 cannot be done

- Get 1 from the next column (which leaves 0 in that column)

- Put the 1 beside the 2 to make it into 12

- 12 take away eight is 4

- 0 take away nothing is 0

- The answer is 04 which is 4

$$
\begin{array}{r} 1\ 2 \\ -\ \ \ 8 \\ \hline \end{array}
$$

$$
\begin{array}{r} {}^0\!\!\!\not{1}\ {}^1 2 \\ -\ \ \ 8 \\ \hline \end{array}
$$

$$
\begin{array}{r} {}^0\!\!\!\not{1}\ {}^1 2 \\ -\ \ \ 8 \\ \hline 0\ 4 \end{array}
$$

Perhaps, as an adult, you can see that this process is perfectly logical – that one taken from the tens column is worth ten in the units column and that when this is added to the two that are already there, it makes twelve.

Most children, however, cannot understand the sum in these terms (these are in fact quite sophisticated mathematical concepts) but are happy to apply the method – especially as they can see that it gives the right answer.

There are different ways of doing take-away sums but the method described here is the one that is now taught more or less universally in schools.

Set some sums that develop this skill.

$$6\ 1\ 3\ 1$$
$$-\ \ 1\ 8\ 1\ 0$$

$$9\ 5\ 3\ 9$$
$$-\ \ 3\ 7\ 8\ 2$$

Once your child can do sums like this, there only remains one more thing for them to learn to completely master 'taking away':

A sum like **103 – 15** involves 'taking one' from a column that has a **0** in it, which clearly presents problems.

$$1\ 0\ 3$$
$$-\ \ \ 1\ 5$$

- 3 take away 5 cannot be done
- Take 1 from the next column – but there is nothing in the next column!
- Take 1 from the 'next column but one' (hundreds column) and put it in the 'next column' (tens column)
- This leaves 0 in the 'next column but one' and you now have 10 in the 'next column'
- Take 1 from the 'next column' (leaving 9) and put it next to the 3 (making 13)
- 13 take away 5 is 8
- 9 take away 1 is 8
- 0 take away 0 is nothing. (If there is nothing in a column then that counts as 0)
- The answer is 088 which is **88**

$$^0\cancel{1}\ ^1 0\ 3$$
$$-\ \ \ 1\ 5$$

$$^0\cancel{1}\ ^9\cancel{0}\ ^1 3$$
$$-\ 0\ 1\ 5$$

$$^0\cancel{1}\ ^9\cancel{0}\ 3$$
$$-\ 0\ 1\ 5$$
$$0\ 8\ 8$$

Here is a more difficult example that requires the use of this technique.

$$8\ 0\ 0\ 0\ 0$$
$$-\ \ \ \ \ 7\ 5\ 2\ 8$$

$$^7\cancel{8}\ ^9\cancel{0}\ ^9\cancel{0}\ ^9\cancel{0}\ ^1 0$$
$$-\ \ \ \ \ 7\ 5\ 2\ 8$$
$$7\ 2\ 4\ 7\ 2$$

Multiplication (Timesing)

This is another area where you have to be careful with the terminology. Most children will know that two fours are eight but they may not be able to answer the questions: 'What is 2 times 4?' or 'What is 2 multiplied by 4?'

In order to keep things simple it is best to explain that the sum '$2 \times 4 = $ ' is asking 'What are two fours?'

Multiplication basically involves using the multiplication tables.

It is a good idea to start off by setting very simple sums that give practice in using the multiplication tables on paper.

$$
\begin{array}{r} 2\ 3 \\ \times\ \ 2 \\ \hline \end{array}
\qquad
\begin{array}{r} 4\ 1 \\ \times\ \ 2 \\ \hline \end{array}
\qquad
\begin{array}{r} 2\ 4 \\ \times\ \ 2 \\ \hline \end{array}
\qquad
\begin{array}{r} 3\ 3 \\ \times\ \ 2 \\ \hline \end{array}
$$

Your child should be familiar (from adding up) with the idea of 'carrying' to the next column:

$$
\begin{array}{r} 2\ 6 \\ \times\ \ 2 \\ \hline \end{array}
$$

- Two sixes are twelve

- Put down two and carry one to the next column

- Two twos are four, add one – that makes 5.

- The answer is **52**.

If you put the numbers that you 'carry' below the sum, as shown here, it helps to avoid making the mistake of getting them mixed up in the sum itself.

$$
\begin{array}{r} 2\ 6 \\ \times\ \ 2 \\ \hline 5\ 2 \\ {\scriptstyle 1} \end{array}
$$

×	1	2	3	4	5	6	7	8	9	10
1	1	2	3	4	5	6	7	8	9	10
2	2	4	6	8	10	12	14	16	18	20
3	3	6	9	12	15	18	21	24	27	30
4	4	8	12	16	20	24	28	32	36	40
5	5	10	15	20	25	30	35	40	45	50
6	6	12	18	24	30	36	42	48	54	60
7	7	14	21	28	35	42	49	56	63	70
8	8	16	24	32	40	48	56	64	72	80
9	9	18	27	36	45	54	63	72	81	90
10	10	20	30	40	50	60	70	80	90	100

Drawing out and filling in a 'multiplication square' gives more practice and can be used as a reference. (There is no harm in looking up the answers in this way – if you look something up often enough you will eventually remember it.) There is no need to learn the tables beyond ten times ten.

Draw out a grid for a multiplication square; fill in some of the boxes yourself and let your child try to work out the rest of the answers.

Patterns start to emerge that make the exercise interesting in its own right.

✗	1	2	3	4	5	6	7	8	9	10
1	1								9	
2				8			14			
3					18					
4										
5								40		
6							42			
7		21								
8				40						80
9									81	
10		20								

Continual practice is the best way of learning the tables – so keep setting sums....

3 4 × 5 ———	5 6 × 5 ———	8 7 × 5 ———	1 2 3 × 5 ———

5 2 8 × 4 ———	2 0 2 × 5 ———	1 4 1 4 × 3 ———

135

Long Multiplication

Few people now work out long multiplication sums on paper – it is so much easier with a calculator. Nevertheless it still remains an essential part of the process of learning maths. Children need to understand the mechanics of long multiplication in order to have confidence in the work that they do with their calculators.

example: **216 × 34 =**

- Multiply by the units first i.e. the 4 (start on the right)
- Four sixes are 24
- 'Put down' the 4 and carry the 2
- It may be a good idea to put the numbers that you 'carry' at the right of the sum. This stops them getting mixed up with the sum

```
  2 1 6   2
× 3 4
      4
```

- Four ones are 4. Add 2, that makes 6 (cross out the 2 so that you do not use it again)
- Put down the 6
- Four twos are 8
- Put down the 8

```
  2 1 6
× 3 4
  8 6 4
```

- Next, you have to multiply by the tens. Put 0 in the units column
- Three sixes are 18. Put down the 8 (make sure that it is under the 6). Carry the 1

```
  2 1 6
× 3 4    1
  8 6 4
    8 0
```

- Three ones are 3. Add 1, that makes 4
- Put down the 4
- Three twos are 6
- Put down the 6

```
  2 1 6
× 3 4
  8 6 4
6 4 8 0
```

- Add up the two rows that you have worked out
- 4 add 0 is 4
- 6 add 8 is 14. Put down 4 and carry 1
- 8 add 4 is 12. 12 add 1 is 13. Put down 3 and carry 1
- 6 add 1 is 7
- The answer is **7,344!**

The secret of success with long multiplication is to keep all the numbers in the correct columns.

Always work from right to left.

```
  2 1 6
× 3 4
  8 6 4
6 4 8 0
7 3 4 4
  1 1
```

You can see that it takes time and concentration to do a long multiplication sum, so you do not need to set many at the same time. Once again, the work is more enjoyable if the answers have an interesting twist.

3 7	3 7	3 7	3 7	3 7
× 3 0	× 3 3	× 3 6	× 3 9	× 4 2

4 9 4 9	7 0 7	2 0 2	1 0 1
× 2	× 1 4	× 4 9	× 9 8

2 5 2 9 5	4 5 9 0 3	1 5 3 0 1	1 8 1 8 2
× 2 4	× 1 4	× 4 2	× 3 3

7 3 5 0 4 3	1 1 9 9 9 9 9
× 1 3	× 5

Mathematical problems can also be interesting – providing they have a practical relevance to your child's life.

You can work out how many months you have lived; how many weeks you have lived; how many days you have lived; how many hours there are in a year; how many seconds there are in a day etc.

Problems like this are good practice and also serve to show that sums have practical relevance as well as being fun.

Answers

		$25295 \times 24 = 607080$
		$45903 \times 14 = 642642$
$37 \times 30 = 1110$	$4949 \times 2 = 9898$	$15301 \times 42 = 642642$
$37 \times 33 = 1221$	$707 \times 14 = 9898$	$18182 \times 33 = 600006$
$37 \times 36 = 1332$	$202 \times 49 = 9898$	
$37 \times 39 = 1443$	$101 \times 98 = 9898$	$735043 \times 13 = 9555559$
$37 \times 42 = 1554$		$1199999 \times 5 = 5999995$

Division

Division completes the work involving whole numbers. It is the most difficult of the four functions (addition, subtraction, multiplication and division) but it does not present any real problems to a child who has acquired a sound knowledge of their tables through continued practice of multiplication sums.

example: $78 \div 3 =$

$$3\overline{\smash{)}7\ 8}$$

- How many times does 3 go into 7?
- Twice with 1 left over
- Put 2 above the 7 and put the 1 beside the 8

$$\begin{array}{r} 2 \\ 3\overline{\smash{)}7\ {}^18} \end{array}$$

- How many times does 3 go into 18?
- 6 times
- Put 6 above the 18

$$\begin{array}{r} 2\ \ 6 \\ 3\overline{\smash{)}7\ {}^18} \end{array}$$

- The answer is **26**. Three goes into seventy eight twenty six times.

Sums that involve remainders are not very satisfying and can be avoided until a child asks what happens when one number does not go exactly into another.
Division does take a little time to get used to and it is best to start off with very easy sums – even when a child is really good at multiplication.

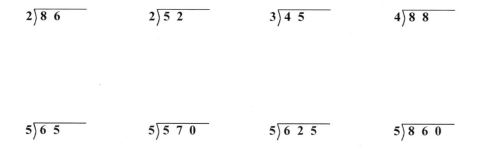

$$2\overline{\smash{)}8\ 6} \qquad 2\overline{\smash{)}5\ 2} \qquad 3\overline{\smash{)}4\ 5} \qquad 4\overline{\smash{)}8\ 8}$$

$$5\overline{\smash{)}6\ 5} \qquad 5\overline{\smash{)}5\ 7\ 0} \qquad 5\overline{\smash{)}6\ 2\ 5} \qquad 5\overline{\smash{)}8\ 6\ 0}$$

As with multiplication, the secret of success in division is to keep all the numbers in the correct columns. Do not forget to put in a 0 when a number will not go into another number.

example: **14 210 ÷ 7 =**

- How many times does 7 go into 1?
- No times. Put 0 above the 1
- Put the 1 beside the 4 in the next column

$$\begin{array}{r} 0 \\ 7\overline{)1\,{}^14\ 2\ 1\ 0} \end{array}$$

- How many times does 7 go into 14?
- Twice
- Put 2 above the 4

$$\begin{array}{r} 0\ 2 \\ 7\overline{)1\,{}^14\ 2\ 1\ 0} \end{array}$$

- How many times does 7 go into 2?
- No times. Put 0 above the 2
- Put the 2 beside the 1 in the next column

$$\begin{array}{r} 0\ 2\ 0 \\ 7\overline{)1\,{}^14\ 2\,{}^21\ 0} \end{array}$$

- How many times does 7 go into 21?
- 3 times
- Put 3 above the 1

$$\begin{array}{r} 0\ 2\ 0\ 3 \\ 7\overline{)1\,{}^14\ 2\,{}^21\ 0} \end{array}$$

- How many times does 7 go into 0?
- No times. Put 0 above the 0
- The answer is 02030 which is **2,030!**

$$\begin{array}{r} 0\ 2\ 0\ 3\ 0 \\ 7\overline{)1\,{}^14\ 2\,{}^21\ 0} \end{array}$$

$$8\overline{)4\ 8\ 0\ 0} \qquad 9\overline{)2\ 2\ 5\ 0} \qquad 7\overline{)7\ 1\ 4\ 0} \qquad 6\overline{)5\ 4\ 0\ 0\ 6}$$

Answers (page 138)		(page 139)
86 ÷ 2 = 43	65 ÷ 5 = 13	4800 ÷ 8 = 600
52 ÷ 2 = 26	570 ÷ 5 = 114	2250 ÷ 9 = 250
45 ÷ 3 = 15	625 ÷ 5 = 125	7140 ÷ 7 = 1020
88 ÷ 4 = 22	860 ÷ 5 = 172	54006 ÷6 = 9001

Long Division

Long division is time-consuming and uses up a lot of paper. This is one type of sum that nearly everyone prefers to work out on a calculator.

All the same, it does provide good practice in working with numbers in a more advanced way and most children enjoy the experience of being able to solve difficult sums without any electronic assistance.

example: **3425 ÷ 25 =**

$$\begin{array}{r} 0 \\ 25\,\overline{)3\,4\,2\,5} \end{array}$$

- How many times does 25 go into 3?
- No times. Put 0 above the 3

- How many times does 25 go into 34?
- One twenty-five is 25, so it goes once
- Put 1 above the 4
- Take 25 away from 34
- 4 take away 5 cannot be done. Take 1 from the next column (which leaves 2 in that column)
- 14 take away 5 is 9
- 2 take away 2 is 0. **34 – 25 = 9**

$$\begin{array}{r} 0\ 1 \\ 25\,\overline{)\,{}^2\!\!\!\not3\,{}^1\!4\,2\,5} \\ 2\ 5 \\ 0\ 9 \end{array}$$

- Bring down the 2 and put it beside the 9
- How many times does 25 go into 92?
- Three twenty-fives are 75, so it goes 3 times
- Put 3 above the 2
- Take 75 away from 92
- 2 take away 5 cannot be done. Take 1 from the next column (which leaves 8 in that column)
- 12 take away 5 is 7
- 8 take away 7 is 1. **92 – 75 = 17**

$$\begin{array}{r} 0\ 1\ 3 \\ 25\,\overline{)\,{}^2\!\!\!\not3\,{}^1\!4\,2\,5} \\ 2\ 5\ \downarrow \\ 0\ {}^8\!\not9\,{}^1\!2 \\ 7\ 5 \\ 1\ 7 \end{array}$$

- Bring down the 5 and put it beside the 17
- How many times does 25 go into 175?
- Seven twenty fives are 175, so it goes 7 times exactly
- Put 7 above the 5
- Take 175 away from 175. There is nothing left over

- The answer is 0137 which is **137**!

$$\begin{array}{r} 0\ 1\ 3\ 7 \\ 25\,\overline{)\,{}^2\!\!\!\not3\,{}^1\!4\,2\,5} \\ 2\ 5\ \downarrow \\ 0\ {}^8\!\not9\,{}^1\!2 \\ 7\ 5\ \downarrow \\ 1\ 7\ 5 \\ 1\ 7\ 5 \\ 0\ 0\ 0 \end{array}$$

Long division sums that involve dividing by numbers such as 15, 20, 25, 11 and 12, are not too difficult. In fact it is useful to know the multiplication tables for these numbers and long division provides good practice in working with them.

Problems can arise when you have to divide by other numbers and there is no reason why difficult examples should be given to young children – unless they ask for them!

$1 \times 15 = 15$

$2 \times 15 = 30$

$3 \times 15 = 45$

$4 \times 15 = 60$

$5 \times 15 = 75$

$6 \times 15 = 90$

$7 \times 15 = 105$

$8 \times 15 = 120$

$9 \times 15 = 135$

$10 \times 15 = 150$

You can write out one of the tables and then set some sums that involve using that table.

$$15\overline{)1\ 5\ 0\ 0}$$

$$15\overline{)1\ 5\ 0\ 0\ 0}$$

$$15\overline{)3\ 0\ 0\ 0}$$

$$15\overline{)3\ 0\ 4\ 5}$$

$$15\overline{)3\ 1\ 5\ 0}$$

$$15\overline{)1\ 4\ 8\ 5}$$

$$15\overline{)2\ 2\ 5}$$

Answers

$1500 \div 15 = 100$

$15000 \div 15 = 1000$

$3000 \div 15 = 200$

$3045 \div 15 = 203$

$3150 \div 15 = 210$

$225 \div 15 = 15$

$1485 \div 15 = 99$

141

Whole Numbers

The work covered on previous pages will, hopefully, have introduced your child to the fact that numbers can be fun.

This opens the way to learning something about the properties of whole numbers.

Prime Numbers

Prime numbers are the building blocks from which other numbers are constructed.

A prime number is a number that can only be divided by one and by itself (no one is really sure whether or not the number one should itself be considered a prime number – it is usually said to exist in a category of its own).

The sequence of prime numbers starts as follows:

(1), 2, 3, 5, 7, 11, 13, 17, 19, 23, 29, 31, 37, 41........ it is believed to go on forever. One of the remarkable things about the prime numbers is that they do not appear in any particular pattern. They seem to pop up more or less at random as you work through bigger and bigger numbers.

Square Numbers

A number multiplied by itself makes a 'square' number.

$$1 \times 1 = 1 \qquad\qquad 5 \times 5 = 25$$
$$2 \times 2 = 4 \qquad\qquad 6 \times 6 = 36$$
$$3 \times 3 = 9 \qquad\qquad 7 \times 7 = 49$$
$$4 \times 4 = 16 \qquad\qquad 8 \times 8 = 64$$

Three squared is written as 3^2.
Thus $3 \times 3 = 3^2 = 9$

Square numbers actually do make squares.

 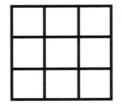

$1^2 = 1$ $\qquad\qquad\qquad\qquad$ $2^2 = 4$ $\qquad\qquad\qquad\qquad$ $3^2 = 9$

Multiples of 10

In our system of counting, 10 is the most important number.

It is therefore advisable to spend time specifically practising multiplying and dividing by 10.

example: **15 × 10**

$$
\begin{array}{r}
1\ 5 \\
\times\ 1\ 0 \\
\hline
1\ 5\ 0 \\
\scriptstyle 5
\end{array}
$$

- Ten fives are 50
- Put down 0 and carry 5
- Ten ones are 10. Add five makes 15
- The answer is **150**

Write out a series of sums like this:

$$
\begin{array}{r}
2\ 3 \\
\times\ 1\ 0 \\
\hline
\end{array}
\qquad
\begin{array}{r}
4\ 2 \\
\times\ 1\ 0 \\
\hline
\end{array}
\qquad
\begin{array}{r}
6\ 3 \\
\times\ 1\ 0 \\
\hline
\end{array}
$$

Your child will soon see that when multiplying by 10 you can simply 'add a 0' instead of working out the whole sum.

When multiplying by a hundred, add two noughts:

43 × 100 = 4 300

When multiplying by a thousand, add three noughts:

43 × 1000 = 43 000

When multiplying by a million, add six noughts:

43 × 1 000 000 = 4 300 000

Do the reverse when dividing by 10:

30 ÷ 10 = 3

120 ÷ 10 = 12

600 ÷ 10 = 60

Answers:
23 × 10 = 230
42 × 10 = 420
63 × 10 = 630

143

FRACTIONS

The more work that you do with whole numbers, the more you will come to see that they cannot be used to answer every mathematical question. Sooner or later, you have to confront the idea of parts of whole numbers i.e. fractions.

Young children often have problems with fractions and it is being taught about fractions at primary school that puts some people off mathematics for life. This means that you have to be very careful about how you introduce fractions. Most children are quite happy to talk about fractions and to draw shapes divided into different parts, but it is often preferable to leave sums that actually involve working with fractions until they are older (twelve or thirteen years old).

VULGAR FRACTIONS AND DECIMAL FRACTIONS

We do, in fact, use two distinct systems for describing parts of a whole number: vulgar fractions and decimal fractions.

Vulgar fractions (¼, ½, ¾, ⅔ etc.) are easy to understand but difficult to work with. Nowadays, it is only a small proportion of the adult population that is capable of working out sums that involve adding, subtracting, multiplying or dividing vulgar fractions.

Decimal fractions (0.5, 0.25, 0.875 etc.) are easy to use, especially as we have so much practice in using money, and metric measurements – but they are very difficult to understand.

INTRODUCING FRACTIONS

The idea of fractions is best introduced by talking about vulgar fractions. Children understand halves, quarters, thirds etc. from a surprisingly young age. It is quite fun to draw shapes and to divide them up into different fractions.

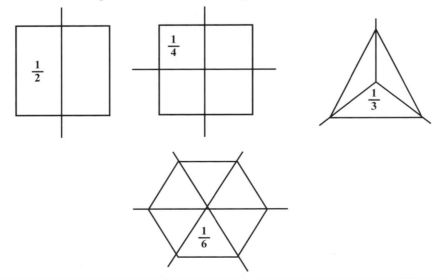

MONEY

It is difficult for a child to understand that the number 1.50 means one whole number, five tenths of a whole number and no hundredths of a whole number, and that this is the same as one and a half. However, £1.50 is instantly recognised as being one pound and fifty pence, or one and a half pounds.

Using money provides an ideal way for children to learn about decimals. They do not have to understand the theory in order to be able to work with them. Practical work with money is preferable to written work in the early stages. Counting out piles of old coins and making them into stacks of ten pences and pounds is the best way of understanding how money works.

Sums that involve adding up money are just as easy as sums that only use whole numbers, even though they require the use of decimal fractions! You simply have to remember to put the decimal point in the right place.

```
      £                    £                    £
    2 . 1 0              3 . 4 0              4 . 2 5
+   1 . 2 0          +   2 . 6 0          +   1 . 2 5
   ─────────            ─────────            ─────────
```

```
      £                    £                    £
    1 . 1 5              7 . 3 5              3 . 3 3
    5 . 4 5              1 . 4 0              3 . 3 3
    3 . 4 0              1 . 2 5              3 . 3 3
   ─────────            ─────────            ─────────
```

Answers:
£ 2.10 +£ 1.20 = £ 3.30
£ 3.40 +£ 2.60 = £ 6.00
£ 4.25 +£ 1.25 = £ 5.50
£ 1.15 + £ 5.45 + £ 3.40 = £ 10.00
£ 7.35 + £ 1.40 + £ 1.25 = £ 10.00
£ 3.33 + £ 3.33 + £ 3.33 = £ 9.99

TELLING THE TIME

The traditional clock face is derived from the mathematical principles developed in Mesopotamia several thousand years ago. It has proved to be a very popular means of showing the time, and learning to use it can teach a child a great deal about mathematics.

This does not mean that they should be made to learn to tell the time when they do not want to. Some children are not very interested in the time until they are quite old (anywhere between nine and sixteen!) and, in terms of its relevance to mathematics, it is often better if a child learns to tell the time later rather than sooner because they are then more likely to understand the mathematical principles involved.

The clock face uses fractions of a circle in order to represent the time. It is divided into twelfths and each of these twelfths represents an hour.

It is also divided into sixtieths and each one of these sixtieths represents one minute.

There are five sixtieths in a twelfth which has led to the minutes on the clock face being represented in multiples of five. As you see, the theory is quite complicated!

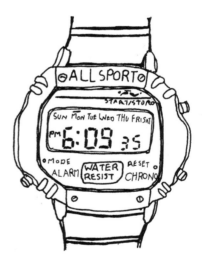

When a child becomes interested in the time, the simplest way for them to learn about it is for you to buy them a watch. Digital watches have their uses (for example they often have a good stopwatch function), but it is the traditional analogue watch that offers the best introduction to telling the time.

You have to be prepared to deal with a bout of persistent questioning but, generally speaking, a child armed with their own watch, who wants to learn how to tell the time, will master the art remarkably quickly.

Telling the time with a traditional clock face is essentially learning to solve a problem that involves fractions. One has to be able to recognise halves and quarters in order to take the first steps and then understand twelfths in order to work with the sequence: five past, ten past, quarter past, twenty past, twenty-five past and half past.

An approximate time can always be read by just looking at the hour hand.

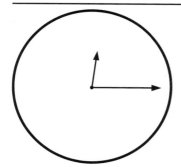

'Quarter past' - the big hand is a quarter of the way round the clock face.

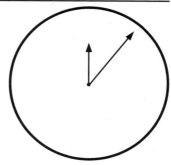

'Five past'. This is one twelfth of an hour.

'Half past' - the big hand is half of the way round the clock face.

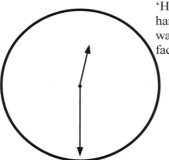

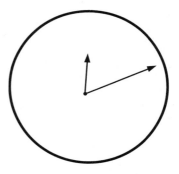

'Ten past'. This is two twelfths of an hour, which is a sixth.

'Quarter to' - the big hand is three quarters of the way round the clock face.

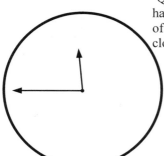

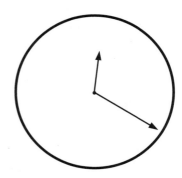

'Twenty past'. This is one third of an hour.

MEASURING

Measuring is not as simple as you might imagine.

In spite of all the efforts that have been made to establish a single system of measurement, the imperial and the metric systems are both still widely used.

IMPERIAL MEASUREMENTS
(Inches, feet, yards, miles, etc.)

Imperial measurements provide good practice in the use of vulgar fractions and make sense intuitively (everyone can understand that a foot is the length of an adult person's foot), but they are difficult to use.

Imperial Measurements
Inch: one twelfth of a foot

Foot: the length of the king's foot

Mile: 1000 double paces (Roman)

Metric Measurements
Metre:	*one ten-millionth of the distance from the equator to the North Pole.*
Kilometre:	*one thousand metres*
Centimetre:	*one hundredth of a metre*
Millimetre:	*one thousandth of a metre*

METRIC MEASUREMENTS
(Metres, centimetres, kilometres, etc.)

Metric measurements are not as intrinsically appealing as imperial measurements but they are easy to use and provide good practice in the use of decimal fractions.

WHICH IS BETTER?

Official policy has, for many years, been to try to make children only learn about the metric system. This is done in the mistaken belief that children become confused when confronted by two different ways of measuring.

This need not be the case: provided both systems are explained clearly and simply, children can actually benefit from understanding them both – it is similar to speaking two languages. (This cannot really happen in school, where chaos can erupt in a class if some children start measuring in inches and others measure in centimetres, but it is easy enough at home.)

PRACTICAL WORK

The best way to learn about measurements is to do a lot of measuring.

It helps if you have different things for measuring with: a ruler, a dressmaker's tape, a flexible steel rule etc.

Each has its own uses: a dressmaker's tape is good for measuring things that are curved, such as parts of the body; a flexible steel rule is good for measuring big things like pieces of furniture and rooms in the house; a ruler is good for measuring lines on the page.

THE RULER

The side of the ruler that shows imperial measurements can be very complicated.

Inches may be divided into eighths, tenths, twelfths or sixteenths.

Tenths are not a very good fraction of an inch. Five tenths make half an inch but a quarter of an inch is two and a half tenths, which is very difficult to work with.

Eighths are the easiest division of an inch to use. They allow measurements of half an inch, a quarter of an inch and an eighth of an inch to be made with ease.

Unfortunately this is not accurate enough in many situations, and the eighths have to be divided to make sixteenths.

Sixteenths are still not as small as millimetres and are sometimes divided to make thirty-secondths, which are too small for everyday use.

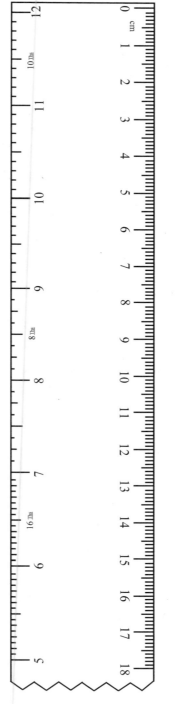

It is much easier to read measurements on the metric side of the ruler.

Millimetres provide as good a level of accuracy as one ever needs in normal circumstances.

Roman Numerals

A brief study of Roman numerals can help to give a child a different perspective on numbers.

I	1
II	2
III	3
IIII or IV	4
V	5
VI	6
VII	7
VIII	8
VIIII or IX	9
X	10
XX	20
L	50
C	100
D	500
M	1000

Roman numerals have an aesthetic appeal and they are still quite widely used on clock faces, to denote the year in copyright statements and on tombstones.

Roman numerals are thought to have evolved from a very primitive counting system: the numbers I, II, III and IIII represent the fingers on one hand; V is the shape of a hand with the thumb outstretched, and X is the shape of two hands crossed over each other.

Many children use their fingers to work out sums and are interested to learn that this was the basis of the Roman counting system.

Big numbers written out in Roman numerals look rather daunting, but they can still be fun to work out:

DC	600
DCI	601
MLXVI	1066
MCMXCIX	1999
MM	2000

Roman numerals do not lend themselves to calculation and you are not advised to try sums such as:

$$\begin{array}{r} \text{CLVII} \\ + \ \text{CCXLI} \\ \hline \end{array}$$

It is believed that the Romans worked out all their sums either in their heads or with an abacus, but never on a piece of paper.

Answer:
CLVII + CCXLI = CCCXCVIII

or: 157 + 241 = 398

Summary

Mathematics is an area in which many parents lack self-confidence and they do not believe that they can help their children to understand the subject.

This is a shame because it is the way that mathematics is taught in schools that causes so many problems. Parents have the opportunity to help their children overcome these problems.

Simply viewed from the perspective of good maths teaching, the best solution is not to send a child to primary school at all. They can then acquire a basic understanding of numbers as and when they are ready, and the idea that maths is difficult does not enter their heads.

Failing this, the best approach for parents of children who find maths difficult at school is not to mention anything to do with sums during term-time, but to spend half an hour per day doing sums during the holidays.

These sums should be of the sort described in this section: written by the parent specifically for the child and not taken from a pre-printed maths revision book.

The problem is a little more complex for children who really enjoy maths. They will find the work that they do at school insufficiently demanding. You can give them work to do at home but that will not make the maths lessons that they have to endure at school any more interesting.

There is often talk of schools 'fast tracking' bright pupils but all such schemes are fraught with difficulties and are probably best avoided.

Everybody has to accept a certain amount of tedium when they go to school and it is generally easier to bear being too good at a subject than being hopelessly bad. That is probably the best form of consolation that you can give to a child trapped in such a situation.

Mathematics is an area in which parents really do have to follow their own feelings. The main objective should be to ensure that children do not start to form a negative opinion of the subject before they have had a chance to master the basics. In the past, many problems have been caused by parents and teachers pushing children too hard because they are worried that they will suffer in some way if they do not keep up with everyone else. This is an erroneous belief. Children who are allowed to approach this subject in their own way will learn more, will learn faster and will have a better understanding of what they have learnt.

Parental Role in Education

Once a parent starts to understand the problems that are inherent within a school-based system of education, they are bound to want to do something to help their child to negotiate them:

Home Schooling

The simplest, and most radical, solution is to teach your own children at home, yourself. At present this is not an option chosen by a very large number of families, but, given that it represents the only available alternative to school, it is bound to become more and more popular (as it already is in the United States).

Home Schooling has many advantages, most of which revolve around the fact that it allows children to keep control over their own lives. This makes them happier, easier to live with and more motivated than they would be if they were having to go to school every day.

Home Schooling is particularly relevant to children up to the age of eight or nine: they can be seriously harmed by being forced through the primary school curriculum at too young an age, and being allowed to spend more time in the security of their own family confers benefits independent from any educational activities that they might pursue. This means that parents of young children are justified in at least considering Home Schooling as the preferred option.

Alternatively, it is something that parents can hold in reserve, in case things do not work out well for their children at school.

Home schooling obviously requires commitment, from at least one parent, but does not necessarily demand any special skills. The main requirements are sensitivity and patience.

The biggest potential problem is the parent being too dogmatic and rigid in their approach. Home Schooling is a pragmatic response to the practical difficulty of providing children with a good education: it need not be seen as an ideological statement or something that defines a particular set of values.

The Alien in My Desk   continued from page 26

Flexibility

Whatever choice you make for your child's education, flexibility is the key to success. Even parents who commit themselves to Home Schooling are unlikely to find that all their children will want to spend all their time being home taught. Some of them are quite likely to want to spend some of their years in education at school.

In the same way, the fact that a child goes to school does not mean that they no longer need help and support from their parents.

On the contrary, children who go to school are in extra need of support, and parents have to be very careful that they give appropriate help at the right times.

After School

A day at school can make a child tired and irritable and it is tempting just to let them watch television or play computer games when they come home. If you consider the situation from a young child's point of view, this is a disastrous option because it does not give them a proper break from one day to the next.

Care and attention on the part of a parent can help a child to establish a good rhythm to their school days. Here are some suggestions:

- Always be at home and available when school finishes.

- Do something to restore your child's spirits when they come in from school: food and drinks are the best for this.

- Do not ask questions about the school day (your child will tell you what has gone on if they are given a chance to unwind but may not want to be interrogated).

- Establish a pattern of doing something together in the evenings: drawing, gardening, cooking, crafts or going out for a walk, for example.

- Do not let school impinge on home life (no homework etc.).

- If your child wants to watch something on the television, watch it with them.

- Read aloud to your child. (This need not just be to young children; older children still enjoy being read to, or they can read to you if they prefer.)

Weekends

For most children, five days per week is too much time spent at school. This makes the weekends very precious and schoolwork should not be allowed to impinge upon them. (Some countries, such as France, only require young children to go to school four days per week: they can stay at home on Wednesdays and this gives a much better balance to their lives.)

At weekends, therefore, the emphasis should be placed on doing things that are enjoyable and which help a child to maintain a life that is independent of school. For example:

- Establish a routine that you follow each Saturday and Sunday during term time.

- Incorporate as many outdoor activities into this routine as you can: gardening, walking, cycling etc.

- Spend as much time as possible together as a family: do not become involved in too many clubs and suchlike.

- Encourage activities that help to broaden your child's social interaction. It is not normal for children to be forced into each other's company in the way that they are at school and it helps them if they can spend time with older or younger friends and relatives, grandparents, neighbours etc. at the weekend.

- Take your children with you if you have to go out (shopping etc.). Make sure that the outing is fun for them as well as for you.

- Have a project that you work on together at weekends.

The following chapters on gardening (*Page 163*), cooking (*Page 201*) and crafts (*Page 237*) contain ideas and suggestions for things that you can do with your children at weekends.

The aim is to provide a complete break from schoolwork and from everything to do with school. If you are successful your child will, hopefully, be able to face the next Monday morning with renewed enthusiasm.

Holidays

Parents who support their children during term-time will reap the reward during the holidays because they will find it relatively easy to re-establish a harmonious routine that actually allows them to enjoy being with their children, full-time, for a few weeks.

In particular, the holidays provide an opportunity to do things that would be inappropriate during the school term – such as arithmetic, writing and reading works of non-fiction.

At first glance, this may seem slightly pushy, but one has to remember that these activities can be enjoyable. When they are free from the pressure to succeed, children like doing sums and they enjoy working on paper. On the other hand, no one likes doing absolutely nothing, and it is unkind to children to expect them to go from constantly being told what to do at school to being able to organise all their own time during the holidays.

It is far preferable to suggest to your child that you sit down and work at something together, for a few hours, in the morning. This is when children are most wide awake and if they feel that they have done something really worthwhile at the start of the day, it tends to carry them through to the evening. You can do sums together, you can study history, geography, literature, poetry or drama: it is a good idea to base any work that you do around art and drawing. In fact, art and drawing offer a good starting point for working together *(see lessons page 272)*.

You can buy some new paints or crayons for the school holidays and spend a few days painting and drawing.

Of course, you can still be pursuing the activities that you normally do after school with your child – cooking, gardening, crafts, walking, playing games, etc. – it is really up to your child to decide. You simply have to present them with an attractive range of options.

Non-Resident Parents

Much of what has been said so far implies that a parent is living with their child all of the time.

Of course, that is not the case for many fathers or mothers: it is now quite common for a parent, in the aftermath of divorce, separation etc., only to have access to their child one day per week or on certain days of the year.

In these circumstances the parent concerned cannot have any direct influence over how a child is coping with school on a day-to-day basis – but they can make sure that they make the most of the time that they do spend with their children.

Parents in this situation often feel that they have to give their children special treats on the occasions that they are together, such as going out for a meal or going to the cinema or museums. This can become wearisome for everyone concerned, and it is far better to establish a routine that involves activities such as gardening, cooking, walking and making things, as outlined in the following sections.

Simple activities such as these give parents and children a chance to talk to each other and build a relationship within the confines of the limited amount of time that they have together.

(In particular, if you are able to start a garden with a child, you will find that they are always keen to keep their appointment to see you, because they will want to know how things are progressing in their garden.)

As an 'absent' parent it is easy to become resentful about the fact that children prefer to 'hang out' with their school friends at weekends rather than keeping up their visits to you. The ex-spouse is blamed for making access difficult. Arguments ensue and children are even less likely to want to visit their absent parent – the whole situation is too stressful.

The easiest way to come to terms with the situation is to look at it through the eyes of your child. It is not easy to cope with school at the best of times. Holidays and weekends have to be times in which to unwind and relax. If you create somewhere where they feel comfortable, and you manage to display infinite patience, eventually they will want to spend more time with you.

Grandparents

Much of that which applies to parents who do not live with their children also applies to grandparents. It is now common for grandparents to live well away from their grandchildren and to have no involvement in their day-to-day lives.

This can make it difficult for them to build up a good relationship with each other, especially if the children spend all their time watching television or playing computer games – activities which might not appeal to a caring grandparent!

The solution is not to start having arguments with the children's parents, telling them how they ought to bring up their children etc., but rather to take the initiative and introduce some constructive activities that your grandchildren can do with you, when they do visit.

This may require a little forward planning and preparation but it is worth the effort:

- Gardening is, once again, one of the best things that you can do. If time is limited, it is advisable to get things ready before your grandchildren arrive so that they can plant some seeds, or transplant some seedlings, themselves—just weeding or preparing the ground may not be very appealing to the uninitiated gardener.

- Drawing is something else that works very well, especially if you can buy some really good-quality crayons that you take care of yourself (so that they do not get lost or broken). Keep a folder of their work so that they can look through it each time that they come to visit.

- Reading aloud is one of the best ways of calming down children of any age. Have a selection of books, some of which are their old favourites and some new ones that you think they will like.

Grandparents sometimes forget that children have not changed with the advent of computer games and a frenetic modern lifestyle. Everything that worked in the past still works with today's children. Grandparents are often the people best placed to introduce a little sanity into a child's life and, when they make the effort to do so, they are always well rewarded.

Homework

If you ask children what they dislike most about school, the answer is often homework. Instead of doing something about this, parents and teachers continue to blindly insist that homework is necessary.

Actually, it tends to be parents who have the greater enthusiasm for homework – it simply represents extra work for teachers.

There is no rational justification for homework. Children spend far more hours at school than is good for them, or than is necessary to cover the school curriculum, and the idea that they have to do large amounts of work at home in addition, merely serves to point out that much of the time that they spend at school is being wasted.

People who have full-time jobs are not expected to do more work when they get home and, in the same way, children should not be expected to have to do homework when they come home from school.

Children need to be given some time to do what *they* want to do. If they want to spend their free time following up things that they do at school, that's fine. But they should have the choice and there should be no pressure.

If your child is being given homework that is intruding into their free time, then you have to be prepared to confront their school about the issue.

Generally speaking, teachers are normally plagued by parents who want their children to be given more homework. This is, presumably, because they are not prepared to spend a few hours each evening doing something constructive with their children and they want the school to assume control over every minute of their children's waking day. It is good for teachers to be confronted by the opposite viewpoint and to be told to keep schoolwork for school and to allow children to have a life of their own afterwards.

This is an important issue that has to be resolved as soon as it becomes a problem, because it is not reasonable to expect children to be able to cope with school once it starts to make inroads into their home life.

Supporting Your Child

It is all too easy to start ignoring what your child is saying to you about school.

This is a great mistake. Parents need to maintain respect for their children and always to take what they say seriously.

This is especially important when it relates to school. You do not really know what happens to your children when they are at school and you therefore have to be particularly alert to any clues that they might give you.

The time when this is most applicable is when they say that they do not want to go into school on a particular day.

Unfortunately, the normal response to this is firstly to try to persuade the child to go to school and only as a secondary consideration to try to find out what is wrong. This is not going to encourage a child to confide in you.

A better approach is to tell them that of course they do not have to go to school if they do not want to. If they decide not to go to school on a particular day, then make sure that you are at home to do interesting things with them. Over the course of the day, you are bound to find out why they did not want to go to school.

It makes children feel much more secure when they know that they have a choice about whether to go to school or not. Remember that school is not an easy environment in which to survive unscathed and children are constantly working out strategies for how to deal with it. Knowing that they do not have to go in to school every day, gives them an extra option: it does not mean that they will never go to school again.

In the same way, if your child gets into a situation of conflict with any member of the school staff you must be prepared to give them your full support. It is not a question of seeing whether or not your child has behaved well or badly.

In a school, it is the staff who have all the power. It is their responsibility if problems arise. No child would willingly become embroiled in a fight when the odds are so heavily stacked against them and it is your duty as a parent to point out to the member of staff concerned that they have to treat your child with consideration.

Single Parents / Two Parent Families

No special mention has so far been made about the respective roles of mothers and fathers or of the relative advantages of one and two parent families. This is because it is beyond the scope of any book to change the level of commitment that any particular parent is prepared to make towards their child.

This book is intended for parents who *do* want to play a positive role in their child's education and it is not really important whether that parent is a single parent or half of a two-parent family or an absent parent or whatever. From the child's point of view the important thing is that there is at least one person who cares.

In an ideal world every child would probably have two parents and four grandparents to whom they could turn for help and advice and who would all agree with each other, but children are not growing up in an ideal world and the amount of difference that one caring adult can make to a child's life is incalculable. It is the difference between something and nothing and, ultimately, that is all that really counts.

Support Groups

There are surprisingly few support groups for parents who do not wish to fully immerse their children in the school experience.

Education Otherwise is the most established group. It has members all over the country and is particularly well placed to help parents who are being harassed by the education authorities *(see useful addresses, page 313).*

The majority of people in Education Otherwise have opted not to send their children to school, but the organisation is open to anyone who is concerned about the way that children are being educated.

Taking responsibility for your own children's education can be slightly at odds with grouping together with lots of other parents to form a support group, and many parents who teach their children at home, or who play an active role in their children's education, prefer not to be part of any organisations.

In some ways this may be good but it does mean that the voice of those people who are very concerned about what is going on in schools, is hardly heard.

Problem Children

Some children are considered to be a problem before they ever go to school and it would be unfair to blame schools for the difficulties that such children find themselves in once they enter the education system.

Other children, however, appear to be quite normal and well balanced when they are young, and problems only arise once they go to school. In such cases it makes sense to consider that school itself may be the cause of the problem and parents should not look for solutions from within the school system – they have to sort it out themselves.

The most common difficulties arise from children not being able to cope with the early introduction to reading and writing. This causes frustration which can turn into aggression and a child can find themselves in a situation of conflict with staff and other pupils. Such children are quickly labelled as disturbed or as having learning difficulties and a path of failure is mapped out before them.

Another common problem occurs when children manage to keep up with the work, but find school itself too stressful. This can cause them to have difficulty sleeping at night, to wet the bed and to burst into tears at the slightest provocation, to have colds, headaches etc. and to feel generally unwell. They may start to make up excuses about why they do not want to go to school.

If your child displays these sorts of symptoms, and if you are convinced that they are the result of going to school, then the simplest solution is to withdraw them from school for a while. The sooner that you do this, the less long-term damage will result. You can teach your child at home for a year or two and try reintroducing them to the school system when they are older or, if the problem relates to a particular situation, you can move them to another school.

It is important to protect your child from being labelled a 'problem', and the sooner that you remove them from the situation that is causing them difficulty, the more likely it is that you will prevent this from happening.

Overall Strategy

The overall strategy for parents should be to retain responsibility for their children's education.

This does not only mean selecting a suitable school: in some cases it may involve parents teaching their children at home, full-time, and it should always involve parents spending a significant amount of time working with their children, pursuing educational activities.

In general, primary schools introduce reading, writing and arithmetic at too young an age, with the result that they make these activities, which should be enjoyable, something of a trial for many children. This means that parents who do send their children to school must work out a way of giving their children a complete break from all forms of bookwork in the evenings and at weekends.

School holidays provide a good opportunity to introduce children to those aspects of learning that they cannot experience at school.

Children who do not go to school should not be made to follow the school curriculum at home. Working at home allows a co-operative method of learning in which the child sets the pace: they will probably come to things later but will learn them quicker than if they were at school.

Parents need not be frightened of involving their children in the process of deciding whether or not they should go to school and which school they should go to. Children are remarkably astute and are able to make sound decisions when they are given all the relevant facts – especially when it concerns something that affects them so deeply.

Life is much easier for a child when their parent has a realistic attitude to school: school is not an ideal institution and it should not be allowed to encroach on home life through homework etc.

There are basic deficiencies in the school curriculum and parents who make the effort to compensate for these deficiencies by doing gardening, cooking, crafts, drawing, music, walking etc., with their children, at home, can help to make up for the inadequacies of a school-based system of education.

162

Continued on page 272

Gardening

GARDENING

Gardening is the most effective means of reconnecting children to the world of nature – something which is enormously important to them.

A hundred years ago the idea of including gardening, or any nature studies, in the school curriculum would have been ridiculous. The lives of children, even those growing up in city slums, were dominated and overshadowed by the forces of nature. The cycles of nature and the process of birth and death touched everyone's life on a daily basis. At that time the thing that children needed, in the way of help to improve their chances of a happy and useful life, was to learn to read and write. Illiteracy was a curse that increased the class divide and kept large sections of the population in poverty and destitution.

This state of affairs inspired the school system, which was dedicated to teaching every child, no matter how poor or how poorly-educated their parents might be, to read and write before they were forced out into the labour market.

Schools were very successful in this aim, but the situation today is completely different. Many people involved in education are still fighting the old battles and have not realised that the major problem *now* faced by most children is that they are growing up in a world almost completely divorced from nature.

Everyone has electricity, houses are always light and warm, water comes out of the tap, food comes from the shop, nobody walks anywhere (it is not safe), and life is full of electronic images generated by television, computer games and the internet. Even country children grow up in a bubble isolated from the natural world: it is difficult to walk in the countryside, wild flowers are disappearing, everything is fenced off, beauty spots are overcrowded, fields

are being sprayed and hedges are being ripped up. This is an incredibly bad situation. Children *need* to have an intimate connection with the natural world, it is their birthright and it is through interaction with nature that they will learn some of the most important lessons in life.

Schools try to redress the balance but they are not equipped to do the job: they have no option but to keep children in the classroom most of the time and nature is something that needs to be experienced, not discussed or read about in books. Children need to have a natural environment as part of their everyday lives so that they can witness, and be part of, the working of the natural world every single day of the year.

Fortunately, gardening is able to fulfil this role and must be a central part of the curriculum for the twenty-first century. By working with plants, children come to understand life and death, the waxing and waning of the seasons, the bounteous abundance of nature and the fragility of life. What could be more important than that?

MATERIALS

It is a peculiar aspect of our culture that, although we recognise the importance of having good tools and materials as a general principal, we do not think that it applies to children. We generally buy them tools that break easily and we put an inordinate amount of effort into trying to devise ways in which children can be encouraged to make use of waste packaging materials – such as using yoghurt pots, egg boxes and washing-up liquid bottles.

Whilst recycling is something that should be encouraged from the earliest years, beauty and aesthetics are also important. There is no reason why your children should not have materials at least as good as those that you use yourself.

In the garden, a sturdy trowel, a little fork and a watering can are the only tools your child will really need. A hoe and a rake may also be useful and you may need a spade or garden fork to prepare the ground in advance.

Do not be too ambitious. If you have a greenhouse, or are experienced at raising seeds in a propagator, then you can obviously help your child to raise their own seedlings indoors, otherwise it is probably best to begin by growing plants that can be sown directly into the soil or buying seedlings from a garden centre.

If you do not have much space, you will need a range of different-sized containers in which to grow plants. These can be purchased new or collected from car boot sales etc. A variety of unusual containers can enhance the beauty of a garden – demonstrating that good-quality materials do not necessarily involve spending a lot of money.

WINDOW BOXES, BACK YARDS AND BALCONIES

You do not need to have a garden in order to give your child a rewarding experience of growing plants out of doors *(growing indoor plants is covered on pages 183-194)*: window sills, back yards and balconies all provide good opportunities for growing things.

For very young children a window box may, in fact, be the ideal size of garden because it is small enough for them to look after on their own. It can contain a few vegetables that can be picked and eaten (lettuce and radishes for example), herbs that can be sampled from time to time (such as parsley and chives), and some flowers. The whole window box can be brought indoors in winter and some of the plants should survive right through the year.

Back yards and balconies also have specific advantages. If they are south or west facing and quite sheltered, they will be appreciably warmer than an open garden, which makes them ideal for growing vegetables like tomatoes, peppers and aubergines. They also provide a good site for flowering climbers and vines.

CONTAINERS

Window boxes do, of course, have to be the right size to fit the window sill that you are using: you can either make your own, out of wood, or buy them from a garden centre. Plastic boxes are good because they don't break when you drop them and they don't rot away. It is best to have containers (plant pots, bowls, buckets etc.) in a range of sizes, so that you can move plants from one pot to another as they get bigger. If possible, use containers that have holes in the bottom because this allows excess water to drain off during periods of heavy rain.

You can also use growbags. They are not very aesthetic but they can give a good crop of vegetables.

COMPOST AND FEEDING

The compost in the containers should be changed each year – if you are growing plants that live from one year to the next it is advisable to repot them each spring. If possible buy an organic compost, otherwise a normal potting compost can be used *(see page 183)*.

You will get better results with container grown plants if you give them some

sort of liquid feed – organic seaweed feeds are the best. You have to follow the instructions on the bottle.

WATERING

The only serious problem associated with growing plants in containers is that you have to remember to water them. If you forget for a few days in really hot weather, they will wilt badly and may even die. You have much less room for error than in an open garden.

WHAT TO GROW

Virtually anything can be grown in containers – especially if they are sited in a warm, sheltered spot. Potatoes can be grown in a large pot; lettuces will grow in any container – pots, tubs or window boxes – as will herbs such as parsley, chives, thyme, basil and mint. Flowers grow well in pots, especially if they are fed and watered regularly; and more demanding vegetables such as tomatoes and cucumbers will also do well, provided they are fed on a regular basis.

If you are restricted to a very small growing area it is probably best to buy seedlings and plants rather than growing them from seed: there are often hundreds of seeds in a packet and no one enjoys having to throw away seedlings once they have germinated.

A VEGETABLE PLOT

If you are fortunate enough to have a garden, then it is a good idea to give your child a small plot to look after on their own.

The most important factor to be taken into consideration is size. If you give them an area which is too big for them to manage, it will become overgrown with weeds and everything that they try to grow will be smothered. A young child of five or six years old should be able to manage a plot of about two feet by six feet (½ m by 1½ m). This can be increased in subsequent years: it is far better to have difficulty finding space to squeeze everything in, than to have too much room.

The next consideration is quality. Try to give your child a piece of ground that is free of weeds, has good-quality soil and which gets plenty of sun. If possible, it should be near the house or close to a source of water so that it can easily be watered in hot weather. Give the best part of your garden to your child and they will probably reward you by making it the most well cared for.

If you do not have a garden (or an allotment) then perhaps a grandparent or a friend will let you use a patch of ground in their garden. However, you should bear in mind that there is little point in starting a garden in a place where you never normally go because it will inevitably be neglected and will become a source of guilt rather than pleasure.

Vegetables make the natural starting point for a child's garden: children recognise the different vegetables and like to think that in time they will be able to eat them. Vegetables also mature rapidly (within one growing season), so that a child's efforts are quickly rewarded, and it is fascinating to watch one little seedling develop into a carrot whereas another one, that looks very similar, develops into a lettuce or some other vegetable.

ORGANIC GARDENING

At least half the educational value to be obtained from vegetable gardening is derived from using organic methods – i.e. not using any artificial fertilisers, weedkillers, pesticides or fungicides. This means that you have to work in harmony with nature in order to get the results that you want.

What does and what does not fall within the definition of being 'organic' is open to debate, and to a certain extent everyone has to make up their own minds as to what is acceptable. In my own garden I tend to be conservative and do not use any sprays and poisons at all, even though we lose quite a lot of produce as a result, and even though I know that the organic vegetables that we buy in the shops must have been treated with something to be so bug-free. However, this does mean that I do not have to worry that I may be poisoning a child when I see them helping themselves to the vegetables growing in the garden.

SOIL PREPARATION

Vegetables are very demanding plants that take a lot from the soil, and in order to get good results you need to have a soil rich in nutrients. If you are not a keen compost maker then it may be best to buy a large bag of organic compost and dig it into your child's vegetable plot. This may even prove to be one of the jobs that they enjoy most, as children seem to be fascinated by soil.

Whilst digging the compost in, take the opportunity to remove as many weed roots as possible.

COMPOST

In the long run, there are many advantages to making your own compost. Sometimes, people see a compost heap as a means of disposing of household waste, but this is a mistake because too many vegetable peelings do not make good compost – they just make a slimy mess.

The compost heap is an integral part of the garden itself. It is a means of returning to the soil all the nutrients contained in weeds, other plants that you pull up, dead leaves, grass cuttings (but not too many), and waste parts of the vegetables that you grow yourself.

The heap can be as big or as small as your garden allows. It can be in a special container or free-standing. Given enough time, everything will rot down eventually.

Once you have a reasonable pile, leave it to stand for a few months without adding anything more to it (start another one somewhere else), turn it over once or twice over the course of the summer and then spread it over the surface of your vegetable patch as a winter mulch. It is surprising just how much of it will disappear over the winter.

DESIGNING A VEGETABLE PLOT

Once you have prepared the plot, you can make a drawing of it so that you can plan out the crops you intend to grow – from the comfort and warmth of your home.

This may involve a process of negotiation. Some plants are easy to grow and give quick results whilst others are more difficult and may yield nothing to the novice gardener. Obviously it is your child who must decide what is to be planted, otherwise they will not feel any sense of responsibility for the plot, but you can lead them towards certain crops. The following pages describe vegetables that can usually be relied upon to give good results. Other vegetables may be a little too challenging for a novice gardener: members of the cabbage family are very susceptible to caterpillars; tomatoes, peppers and aubergines need high temperatures and plenty of sun in order to produce a good crop; courgettes, pumpkins and marrows need very rich soil and take up a lot of space; and celeriac never seem to grow very big. If you keep things simple, you will get good results and your child will want to try again the following year.

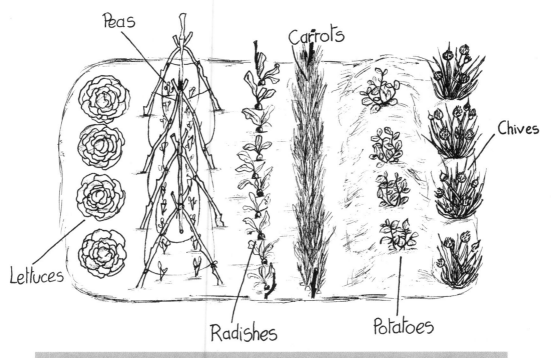

It is interesting to compare the design that you make for the vegetable plot with what you actually manage to grow. Occasionally, plants do not come up at all and have to be replaced with something else, whilst other vegetables seem to find their way onto the plot on their own.

Mustard and Cress

This is an old favourite with young children. It gives quick results and it can be grown either indoors or outdoors.

Cress itself has very small leaves and quite a peppery taste, and most people now prefer to grow rape (a mild-tasting variety of mustard), instead. Make sure that you buy the right seeds!

The simplest way to grow rape is to sprinkle seeds densely onto the surface of 1 cm (⅓″) of potting compost in the bottom of a small plastic container (containers in which you buy mustard and cress, or rape, from the supermarket are ideal).

They should be kept moist (by putting the tray in a polythene bag if necessary) and set in a warm place in the dark, until they start to sprout. You can inspect them several times a day, if you want, without doing them any harm. They should begin to germinate within three or four days.

Once this happens, take the tray out of the polythene bag and place it on a window sill in as warm a place as possible. The seedlings grow rapidly, bending towards the light.

If you want straight stems you will have to keep turning the tray round so that the seedlings have to bend back towards the window.

Providing you prevent the seedlings from ever drying out, and keep them warm, they will rapidly grow into the familiar 'mustard and cress' – long spindly stems with two thick, green leaves at the top – which can be cut and eaten.

This works best in summer when there is plenty of sunlight.

Outdoor sowings can be made throughout the summer; only sow a small area -15 cm x 15 cm (6″ x 6″) - at a time; make sure the ground is free of weeds; and water every day.

Mustard and cress can also be grown in ornamental containers, such as earthenware pigs and sheep.

Easy   Medium   Advanced

Onions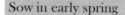

Onions are interesting because even though the onion is a bulb it is visible above the ground as it grows. This means that you can follow the development of your crop from day to day.

The easiest way to grow onions is from 'sets'. (A set is a very small onion that has been grown from seed the year before.) They are usually sold in bags of about a hundred, which is far more than you need, so either find a garden centre or nursery that sells them loose, or get a few from someone who has a large vegetable garden and has two or three to spare.

Plant the sets in the ground, with just the tips showing, in early spring. They do not mind cold weather. The roots develop first, as with all plants, but after several weeks a small green shoot will emerge from the tip of the onion set.

This rapidly develops into a tall green leaf and it isn't long before the onion bulb starts to swell out at the base.

The plants mustn't be allowed to become too dry or they will flower instead of producing an onion. On the other hand, it is only in very wet conditions that they are likely to suffer disease.

The leaves die back in mid to late summer and, as the onions themselves will be protruding above the ground, you can leave them in place to dry out in the sun. Pick them when you need to use them or, if you still have some left, when the leaves are completely dry.

Onion (Allium cepa)

The allium family includes onions, leeks, shallots, chives and garlic. It has been cultivated at least since ancient Egyptian times (3,000 BC) and probably originated in central Asia, perhaps in Iran or Pakistan.

Onions are mentioned in the Bible – the Israelites complained about not having onions when Moses was leading them to the Promised Land – and also in ancient Greek literature. Hippocrates recommended them for their medicinal properties in 430 BC.

Sow in early summer

Radish

Try to make some space for a few radishes, even if they are not vegetables that you normally eat. They are one of the quickest crops to grow and one of the first in the year to be ready to pick.

The radish is a member of the cabbage family but, as it is ready for picking a few weeks after it has been sown, it manages to avoid the scourge of the cabbage white butterfly which can easily blight any other cabbage crops.

Sow the seeds in the middle of spring. They don't mind fairly bad weather but do shrivel up if subjected to weeks and weeks of freezing cold winds, so don't make the mistake of planting them **too** early.

Radish seeds are quick to germinate and it is a great thrill when a row of seedlings first appears. As soon as the weather improves, the little plants grow rapidly and the roots start to develop into the characteristically red and white radishes. Pick them when they are small and they are exquisite – quite unlike those that you buy in the shops.

In theory you can grow several crops of radishes throughout the summer, sowing a new row of seeds every two or three weeks. In practice this can be difficult because the soil has to be kept damp all the time.

If it becomes too dry the plants will flower instead of producing edible radishes. It may therefore be better to use the space vacated by your early sowing of radishes for some other crop – such as French beans.

Radish (*Raphanus sativus*)

Black radishes were the first to be cultivated, and are known to have been part of the diet of workers on the Great Pyramid in ancient Egypt in 2780 BC.

In Europe, radish is now grown mainly as a salad crop, and the small, tender, red and white varieties are favoured. In Asia, radishes are grown as a major root crop, and are eaten cooked and sliced. Chinese radishes come in a wide variety of sizes and colours, including green and purple, and can be four feet long!

Easy   *Medium*   *Advanced*

Spinach

Spinach has acquired an undeserved reputation for being an unappetising vegetable. It is often characterised as being something that parents try to make their children eat because of its health-giving properties (cf. Popeye), but which children hate because it tastes horrid.

The fault does not lie with the spinach itself but in the way that it is processed. Tinned spinach is unpleasant, frozen spinach is slightly better, but fresh spinach from the garden is irresistible.

There are, in fact, two quite different vegetables with a similar taste, which are both known as spinach. True spinach, *Spinacia oleracea,* is difficult to grow and often flowers before the leaves are ready to be picked, unless it is kept in perfect conditions.

Perpetual Spinach Beet (*Beta vulgaris*), on the other hand, is very easy to grow. It is a close relative of beetroot and provides a good crop continuously from midsummer through to autumn, and even during the winter.

It has large, knobbly seeds that should be planted in a row, about 1 cm (½″) deep. Seedlings should be thinned to one every 7 to 10 cm (3″ to 4″), because the plants grow to be quite big. If you have a gap in your row you can plant more seeds, or transplant some of the seedlings that you removed during thinning. (You have to water transplanted seedlings frequently for the first few weeks.)

Apart from weeding and watering in dry weather, the spinach should need no further care. You don't pick the whole plant, just the outer leaves, so you get many crops off each plant. It is surprisingly useful to be able to go out and pick some spinach when you have no other vegetables available in the house, and you cannot help but be filled with a warm glow of parental pride when you see your children tucking into a nice plate of organic spinach!

Perpetual spinach is a member of the Chenopodiaceae family which provides almost as wide a diversity of vegetables as does the cabbage family, including sugar beet, beetroot, mangolds, and chard.

Perpetual spinach is closely related to wild beet which can still be found growing round the coasts of south and west Europe, North Africa and Asia. It has been cultivated at least since the times of ancient Greece and is mentioned by Aristotle.

Peas

Peas are a good crop to grow – they benefit the soil and can be eaten straight from the plant. You have to build a framework for the peas to climb up, which may seem to be a hassle, but it can make your little plot look like a real vegetable garden.

There are many different types of framework that you can make but it does not need to be too elaborate because most pea seeds now sold are for dwarf plants and will not grow higher than about 1 metre (3 ft) tall.

You can make a little conical shape with garden canes; you can use sticks cut from young trees or hedges; or you can use string.

Pea plants will germinate in cold weather, but if you plant the seeds in cold, waterlogged soil they will probably rot away without growing. If you want an early crop you will have to plant the seeds in pots on the window sill in February or March, and plant out the seedlings when they are about 7 to 10 cm (3″ to 4″) tall.

If you do not mind waiting, plant the peas directly into the ground in late spring, when the ground is warmer.

As the plants grow you must train them round the framework that you have provided, otherwise they may grow along the ground, smother other plants, and go mouldy. Once they start growing up the framework they will produce tendrils that wrap around the sticks, and hold the plants upright.

When they reach their full height the pea plants start to produce white flowers which develop into pea pods. The peas can be picked as soon as the pods fill out and become firm. Small peas are much sweeter and tastier than big ones, and therefore it pays to pick them early.

You cannot expect a very large pea crop from a few plants, but they are well worth growing just for the pleasure of eating pods fresh from the garden.

Peas (Pisum Sativum) are members of the Leguminosae family, which also includes beans, clover and peanuts. All these plants are very good for the soil because their roots have nodules that contain bacteria which are able to fix nitrogen directly from the air. Nitrogen stimulates plant growth and is also beneficial to the microbial life in the soil itself.

CARROTS

Carrot fly poses the biggest problem to anyone who wants to grow carrots. They lay their eggs on the young carrot and when the eggs hatch, the larvae burrow their way through the developing carrot root until it becomes more or less useless.

Possible solutions include covering your plants with enviromesh (a sort of fibrous material that lets in the light and water but not carrot fly); surrounding your plants with a two-foot high fence of clear plastic sheeting (the carrot flies fly along just above the ground and don't see your carrots behind their protective shield); or planting the carrot seeds late in the season (perhaps in the area where you have dug up your potatoes) in the hope that the carrot fly season will be over by the time the carrot seedlings appear above ground.

Alternatively, make sure that you eat your crop as it matures – if you do not let the carrots grow too big, the carrot fly larvae will not have time to hatch.

Carrot seeds are very small and have to be sown quite close together. This means that the seedlings have to be thinned out once they start to grow – one carrot every 7 to 10 cm (3″ to 4″) is enough, otherwise they crowd each other. Once they get going, carrots grow rapidly and do not need a great deal of attention. You just have to keep them free of weeds when the plants are small. You can start picking them when the carrot tops showing above the ground are 1¼ cm (½″) across. This allows those that you leave in the ground to grow even bigger. Carrots are normally quite happy to be left in the ground until early winter, although they don't grow much once the weather starts to get cold.

Carrot (Daucus carota) is in the same family as parsnip, celery and parsley. Hemlock, which was used to produce the notorious poison taken by Socrates, is also in this family, but, fortunately, carrot does not have any of its relative's poisonous characteristics. Although carrots have been grown for thousands of years, the orange carrot is quite a new invention. It was developed in Holland in the seventeenth century. Before that, white, red, yellow, purple and crimson carrots were grown throughout Europe, Asia and the Far East.

175

Potatoes

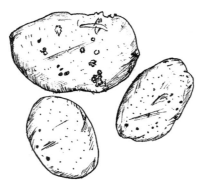

Plant in spring

Each potato plant takes up at least three square feet (⅓ m²) of ground but it is well worth growing at least two or three plants.

They grow very rapidly and are a source of interest in the early summer when there is not a lot to be seen in the vegetable garden. In addition there is nothing to compare to the taste of freshly harvested potatoes.

Seed potatoes are sold as disease-free and are therefore the best to grow. However, you may prefer to use potatoes that you already have in the kitchen. One problem is that potatoes are sprayed to retard the production of shoots. Also, potatoes are often washed before they are sold, which can reduce their resistance to fungal attack.

It is therefore a good idea to place your chosen potatoes on a cool window sill during late winter/early spring and to leave them there for a few weeks. They should start to produce little green shoots.

You can then select the healthiest-looking ones to plant out. A general guide for seeds is to plant them to a depth below the ground equal to their own length. This also seems to work for potatoes, so plant them 8 to 10 cm (3″ to 4″) below the surface.

Spring frosts pose the biggest threat to your getting a good potato crop and you have to protect the plants on cold, frosty nights. If the shoots are very small you can simply cover them over with soil. If they are slightly larger, cover them with a sack or pieces of newspaper – which can be removed in the morning.

Once above the ground, potato plants grow rapidly. They need to be watered in prolonged dry spells. If any of the potatoes themselves are visible they should be covered over with soil, otherwise they will turn green and should not be eaten.

You can harvest your crop any time from the end of June to October, depending on where you live and which variety you are growing. If the plants die back it is best to dig up the potatoes straightaway, to prevent them being eaten by slugs or mice whilst they are in the ground.

Potatoes (Solanum tuberosum) were grown in the high Andes up to 10,000 years ago but were first seen by Europeans in 1537 on an expedition to Colombia, led by Cieza de Leon.

Most European countries lay claim to bringing the potato from the New World. In England, Francis Drake is reputed to have brought potatoes back from Virginia, where he went to rescue Sir Walter Raleigh's colonists, in 1581.

Lettuce

Plant in spring

Not every child likes to eat lettuce, but most should enjoy growing it. Buy the plants (it's a much slower business if you try to grow them from seed) in late spring and plant them directly into the vegetable bed. They may need to be protected from slugs when they are little – if you don't like slug pellets, surround the young plants with soot or wood ash – but once established they will grow rapidly.

Lettuces often 'bolt' in hot, dry weather. This means that they flower instead of producing a nice firm heart. To prevent this, water them two or three times a day when the weather is hot and ensure that the soil they are growing in is always moist.

The lettuces are ready to pick a couple of months after planting and, like most vegetables, taste much better when taken directly from the garden.

There are many different varieties of lettuce, but if you buy plants from a local garden centre, they should be appropriate for your area and for the time of year.

Lettuce (Lactuca sativa). Wild lettuce is a winter annual which starts to grow in the autumn, survives through the winter and then grows rapidly through the following spring and summer to produce flowers and seeds before dying back in late summer. It is horribly bitter and the selection of less bitter varieties is thought to have been the first step in the cultivation of the lettuce that is eaten today.

French Beans

Sow after the last frost

French beans (*Phaseolus vulgaris*), also known as flageolets or haricots verts, are extremely useful plants in the vegetable garden. They must not be exposed to frost but can be planted right up to mid summer. This means that they can be put into ground vacated by other crops, such as radishes, lettuces or early potatoes, or they can be used to fill up an area in which something has failed to grow.

Make a little hole about 2 cm (1 inch) deep, drop in a bean seed and fill the hole with earth. Leave 8 to 10 cm (3 or 4 inches) between each plant. They should grow rapidly and will soon produce pale yellow flowers. These are self-pollinating, which means that the pods develop even when there are no insects about. The secret is to pick the pods when they are small. This is when they are most tender and have the best taste and it also encourages the production of new flowers.

In this way the 'fruiting season' can be extended right through to the autumn and your French beans will yield a high crop. In addition they will benefit the soil as, like peas, they are members of the *Leguminosae* family.

Chives

Once you have managed to establish a good clump of chives, you can go out and eat a few leaves whenever you want.

Chives grow well from seed but you will get quicker results if you start off with a few little plants. If you know anyone with chives in their garden they will probably be happy to give you a part of their clump, as one always has more than one needs: otherwise, garden centres normally sell chive seedlings in the spring.

When you plant your chives make sure that the area is free of weeds. In particular, remove any grass that may be mixed up with the chives that you have been given and also pieces of grass roots that may be in the soil. It is very difficult to remove grass from the centre of a clump of chives, so it is better not to let it get there in the first place.

You can plant out the chives quite early in the spring. The only thing that you have to do is weed round them from time to time and they will rapidly develop into a good clump. Each chive leaf has a tiny onion-like bulb at the base. These bulbs divide and produce new leaves and the clump spreads out in this way. You can start snipping off the leaves for salads as soon as you have a reasonable amount.

Chives have the added advantage of having very pretty purple flowers that give a touch of colour to your vegetable garden.

The leaves will die back in the winter but the bulbs remain and will re-grow the following year. If your chives start to take up too much space, you can divide the clump. This entails digging it up, separating it into smaller pieces, replanting some of these pieces and perhaps giving others away to (young) aspiring gardeners….

Chives *Allium schoenoprasum*
Chives are one of the few commonly-used vegetables that can still be found growing in the wild. Wild chives have a wide geographical range which extends from Ireland in the west to Japan in the east, and they even grow in Siberia. A closely-related species is found in North America growing from Alaska to Newfoundland.

  Easy   *Medium*   *Advanced*

HERBS

If you have space, it makes sense to grow a few herbs. Some are of southern European origin and require as much sun, and as dry a soil, as you can provide, whilst others will thrive in quite poor conditions.

LAVENDER

Lavender does best on dry soils with plenty of sun. English lavender has, however, been selected for its ability to grow well in a northern climate and it is worth giving it a trial in your garden, especially if you can find it a spot that does not become waterlogged in the winter.

PARSLEY

The only problem with parsley is getting the seeds to germinate. Once the plant starts to grow it can hold its own in almost any conditions.

Fresh seeds offer the best chance of successful germination and, if you do have some parsley growing in the garden, let a few plants flower so that you can collect seed for the following year. An even simpler technique is not to disturb the ground round your flowering parsley plants and in the spring they will be surrounded by hundreds of tiny seedlings which can be transplanted to a new site.

THYME

Thyme is useful in cooking, but it is also a very pretty ornamental plant that brightens up any part of the garden. It does not do well in exposed positions or in soils that are waterlogged over the winter.

SAGE

It may be better to buy sage plants rather than growing them from seed because each plant can grow to be quite big and can live for a few years. If you plant different varieties next to each other their leaves make an attractive display.

BASIL

Basil is frost-sensitive and has to be grown from seed each year, preferably indoors. It can be planted out in a sheltered spot that receives plenty of sun. Start picking individual leaves once the plants are 12-15 cm (5-6") high.

CORIANDER

Anyone who enjoys Indian food should try growing coriander because it tastes so much better from the garden than from the shops. It grows quite well in a sunny spot outdoors but you cannot stop it from flowering. This means that you have to make repeated sowings if you want to pick the leaves. You can collect coriander seeds from the plants that flower.

Flowers

It goes without saying that children like flowers, but they are not always the easiest plants to grow successfully: they can be choked out by weeds; the blooms are short-lived; and they sometimes do not seem to repay the work that is put into them. This means that you should not be too ambitious in your initial selection.

Start off with varieties that you feel quite confident of being able to grow and expand your collection in subsequent years.

Generally speaking, annuals have the greatest appeal to young children. The seeds are sown in spring, the seedlings emerge and grow rapidly to produce a highly-coloured mass of flowers in the summer, and then the plants die, leaving seeds that can be collected for the following year. Most annuals require specific conditions in order to thrive, and factors such as climate, soil conditions and how far north you live (some plants are very sensitive to day length), will determine whether or not a particular variety will prosper in your garden.

If you see one sort of flower growing in the gardens near where you live, you can be reasonably confident of having success with it yourself.

The biggest problem that you are likely to encounter with annuals results from being over ambitious – if you try to plant too large an area you are unlikely to be able to control the weeds and will end up with an unsightly mess. Restrict yourself to a small bed no more than 1 m x 2 m (3 feet by 6 feet) which your child will be able to weed and water on their own. Do not worry if the seeds of the different flowers get mixed up when you are planting them – flowers look beautiful when they are growing amongst each other.

Some of the flowers that do well in a child's garden are:

Night-Scented Stock *(Matthiola bicornis)*

This does not have particularly attractive flowers but because it is pollinated by night-flying insects it produces the most wonderful scent in the evenings, that can be smelt all over the garden.

Marigolds *(Calendula officinalis)*

Marigolds will grow well from seeds and provide a beautiful display of orange and yellow flowers that lasts for months. You can dead-head the flowers (this means cutting off the remains of the bloom once it has finished flowering) to extend the flowering season. The plants themselves are very hardy – they grow happily in the wild – and will manage to flower even if they are not particularly well looked after.

There is another variety – *Tagetes* – known as African or French marigold, which is often sold as a bedding plant. These are quite pretty but do not grow with the same abundance and exuberance as Calendula.

Snapdragons *(Antirrhinum)*

It is difficult to grow snapdragons from seed because the seeds are very small, but the plants are widely available in the spring in garden centres. In the case of snap-dragons, it may be worth making an exception to the rule of only growing flowers from seed because the flowers are so unusual. If you squeeze them at the back, the petals at the front open like a mouth – hence the name. This may not seem particularly wonderful to the jaded tastes of an adult, but it can literally provide a young child with hours of fun on a hot summer's day.

Candytuft *(Iberis)*

Candytuft is a remarkable plant. We have grown it in every garden that we have ever had and it has always managed to struggle through to produce a wonderful display of pink, white and purple flowers – sometimes in the face of drought, choking weeds and almost total neglect.

Simply sprinkle the seeds on the surface of the earth and cover them over with a thin layer of soil. They obviously prefer to be looked after properly. Weed them two or three times when the plants are small; water them in hot weather; and thin them out a little if the seedlings are too densely packed together. You will be rewarded with a brilliant mass of flowers that lasts on and on through the summer.

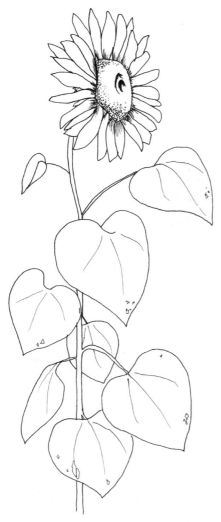

Cornflower *(Centaurea)*

Cornflowers are grown for the incredible shade of blue of their blossoms – there is nothing quite like it. You can get other colours of cornflowers but somehow that seems to miss the point – cornflowers should be blue.

The plants are easy to grow – they are considered a weed in wheat fields – but can be rather straggly. You should, therefore, plant them at the back of the bed or in amongst other plants – such as marigolds. They can easily grow to one metre (3 ft) tall and, if they not supported by other plants, should be held up with a stake.

Sunflower *(Helianthus)*

This spectacular plant cannot help but be a favourite with any child. Its rapid growth, absurd height and outrageous flower appeal to everyone's sense of anarchy.

The young seedlings are very susceptible to slugs, however, and one year we lost all of our sunflower seedlings (over 40 plants) to this pest.

This is only a small selection of the flowers that you can grow. Others might include nasturtium, larkspur, poppies (especially Californian poppies) and marguerites.

GROWING TROPICAL PLANTS

Growing tropical fruit plants from seed can make an exciting addition to a child's experience of gardening and is also something that children who do not have access to an outdoor garden can enjoy. It is a remarkable fact that the fruits that we buy in our supermarkets are capable of producing new plants: they are healthy, vibrant, living things despite having been transported halfway around the world and stored in refrigerated units for weeks on end.

In fact, no matter how much gardening one has done, it is always an amazing experience to see a seed germinate and produce a little shoot. This wonder is increased when the seed is taken from an orange, an avocado, a mango or any other similar species and starts to produce one of those exotic plants that normally grow only in the tropics.

All the plants dealt with in this section have to be grown indoors. Some of them, such as citrus plants, can be put outside during hot summer weather but all of them are sensitive to cold and will suffer badly even if kept in unheated rooms in the house during the winter months.

Consequently it is important not to grow more plants than you can accommodate in the warmth throughout the year.

Most of the seeds are best started off in 8 cm (3″) pots – plastic pots are just as good as earthenware ones, and less expensive. The pot has to be stood on a saucer and put in a warm place. (They can be kept in the dark but then they tend to be forgotten, with the result that they dry out and the seed fails to grow.) All seeds like to be kept moist while germinating, so every time that the water in the saucer dries up, it should be replenished. This is preferable to keeping the soil constantly sodden, because it is closer to the natural cycle of rainy and dry periods.

Potting Compost

The most difficult question concerns the nature of the soil or compost that you put in the pot. Soil from the garden is not suitable for houseplants, and if you use it you cannot expect good results.

The simplest solution is to buy potting compost from a garden centre – any all-purpose variety will do. It is free from pests, diseases and weed seeds, it contains a good balance of nutrients and its soft, friable texture provides the ideal medium for roots confined to a pot.

It does, however, have two disadvantages. The first is that it is made of peat. Peat is a finite resource that is being depleted for the short-term benefit of the nation's gardeners. The second is that it is not organic. The nutrients that it contains are chemical, factory produced fertilisers and additives.

This has led to people trying to find an alternative. You can buy potting compost based on coconut fibre, or sterilised organic compost, or you can try to make your own from rotted-down turf. The trouble is that none of these works very well.

In view of the educational benefits to be derived from growing plants and the small amount of peat actually used by a child to grow indoor plants, it would seem to be acceptable to let them use normal potting compost. It is always best to try to avoid imposing one's own passion and prejudices on one's children and, even if you are a committed organic gardener, it is better to buy your child a bag of potting compost for their plants rather than making then try to cope with an alternative that does not work as well.

Repotting

Repotting is an essential part of indoor plant care. The plants should be allowed to grow to a size where the roots fill the pot that they are in, but do not become too densely tangled. It is hard to tell when they have achieved this condition, but little roots coming out of the holes at the bottom of the pot give some indication.

Soak the plant that is to be repotted for an hour or two before starting work, as this helps to prevent root damage when you pull the plant out of the pot. This is usually best done by tipping the pot upside down (over some old newspapers if indoors) tapping it on the base and gently pulling on the stem of the plant. Hopefully, roots and compost will all come out as one neat unit and can be placed directly into a new pot slightly larger than the old one. The new pot should have some potting compost in the bottom when you put the plant in, and then be carefully topped up with compost until it is 2 cm (¾″) below the rim. A little root disturbance does the plant good and stimulates growth.

Repotting ensures that the roots continue to receive air and nutrients and that they do not become unmanageably compacted.

In the long run, the size of the pot will determine the size of the plant. Plants that have the potential to grow into huge trees will not grow more than a few feet tall if their roots are limited to a smallish pot. Therefore once a plant has reached the size that you think is big enough, you do not have to repot it into a larger container but you can still remove it from its pot, shake off as much of the old compost as you can, loosen the roots a little, and then replace the plant in the same pot, packing new compost around the roots. This exercise is an excellent tonic for an old plant.

In general it is a good idea to repot a plant once a year. Spring is the best time to do it because it is at this time that the plant prepares for its major period of growth.

Seedlings are an exception. If you plant several seeds in one container and a few of them grow, you will have to transplant them into separate pots once they each have two or three proper leaves.

Pruning (or Stopping)

Children often do not like the idea of cutting branches off plants that they have carefully nurtured from seed, but you do have to prune (or stop) tropical plants that you grow.

In particular, avocado plants and citrus plants have to have their growing tips snipped off (stopped) regularly when they are young to prevent them developing into tree-like plants with thick trunks and a few branches pressed against the ceiling.

Stopping and pruning encourages the development of a bushy shape, which helps to make the plants concerned look attractive.

Leaf care

Plants are not designed to grow indoors and one of the adverse effects of living in an environment free from wind and rain is that their leaves become coated in dust. Regularly cleaning is therefore necessary: the shiny, lustrous appearance of the dusted leaves will reward you for your efforts. In addition, citrus leaves give off a wonderful, aromatic smell when their leaves are rubbed, so your room will be filled with the exotic scent of orange, lemon, grapefruit or kumquat every time you clean the leaves.

Some plants – banana for example – are adapted to living in tropical forests that have high levels of humidity and their leaves dry out in a centrally-heated house. The remedy is to spray them regularly with a fine water spray.

Lemon
(Citrus limon)

Citrus

There are several good reasons for growing citrus plants (orange, grapefruit, lemon, lime, etc.): the fruit is readily available; the seeds germinate quite easily; and the plants are attractive, grow well in pots and withstand fairly cold conditions.

There are differences between the members of the citrus family. Oranges are reputed to be the most sensitive plants and lemons the most hardy.

Put the seeds in a three inch (8 cm) pot of potting compost. Keep them warm and ensure that the soil is moist by constantly topping up the saucer beneath the pot with water. A high proportion of the seeds should germinate. Transplant the seedlings into separate pots and keep watering. Citrus plants are evergreen and, if it is warm enough, will grow all year. Normally, however, they grow in summer and remain fairly dormant throughout the winter. In their natural state they are likely to experience summer droughts and it does not do them much harm if you forget to water your mature plants for a while.

Citrus plants can be quite vigorously pruned. You can snip off the growing tips if the plant is getting too tall, and you can cut off branches to keep the plant the shape that you want it to be. Citrus grow well in containers and can be put outdoors in the summer especially from the second year onwards.

The plant should flower after a few years – and the flowers have an incredible scent – but you are unlikely to get any usable fruit.

Kumquat (Fortunella) is one of the more obscure members of the citrus family but the fruit is often available in supermarkets and its seeds germinate just as readily as those of other members of the family.
Its leaves have a particularly interesting scent and that in itself makes the plant well worth growing.

Easy   *Medium*   *Advanced*

Like apples and pears, citrus trees have been grown for thousands of years for their fruit. In that time people have bred and selected all the different varieties that we know today. These varieties cannot normally be reproduced from seeds, but have to be maintained by taking cuttings from a parent tree. Thus all the trees of one variety of orange or lemon will probably have come from one original parent tree.

Seeds produced by these offspring will have different properties from their parents and, consequently, do not usually produce edible fruit.

This should not put you off, because there is always a remote chance that you *may* get some good fruit, and in any event you will have a beautiful plant that is well worth growing simply for ornamental purposes.

CITRUS

Citrus plants originated in the Malaysia/Indonesia regions but have been cultivated since early times. They were used medicinally in ancient India and spread through all the early civilisations of the Middle East and the Mediterranean.

Christopher Columbus took them to the New World where they quickly became established as the main fruit crop of North America.

Grapefruit
(*Citrus paradisi*)

AVOCADO

Avocado is the tropical fruit seed most commonly planted and grown by children. There is something very appealing about the large, smooth, dark brown avocado stone.

Many books suggest that the stone be pierced with cocktail sticks, suspended over a jar of water and kept in the dark. After a while a root should grow down from the stone into the water and the jar can be placed on the windowsill. A shoot will grow and the avocado can be potted.

This sounds like an interesting technique but it is not always successful. The water in the jar can become green and slimy and the stone can be very slow to produce a root.

It is better to simply plant the stone in potting compost and keep it warm and  moist. Sometimes they have to be left for months, but one can expect a success rate of over ninety per cent using this method. Once the first shoot appears above the ground, the plant grows very rapidly. Its natural inclination is to grow tall and upright like a tree. Most people prefer their houseplants to have a more bushy appearance and to achieve this with avocados you have to keep pinching off the tip of the most prominently-growing shoot. You can be quite ruthless as there are plenty of reserves in the stone. You can safely cut off the tip of each new shoot for several weeks before any proper leaves have been formed at all, without doing any harm.

The plant itself, however, is quite delicate and is easily killed by neglect. It must not be allowed to dry out in hot weather and must not be waterlogged in cold weather. It can be killed by frost.

Avocado stones germinate best when left to themselves. If you find seedlings growing in your compost heap, you can lift them out and carefully place them in a pot of potting compost. The experience doesn't seem to do them any harm and they continue to grow vigorously.

Easy   *Medium*   *Advanced*

As a word of warning, do not assume that young children are only attached to their animal pets – they can be just as devastated by the death of a carefully-nurtured plant. Avocados are particularly annoying because once they go into decline – which can be triggered by cold, drought or being waterlogged – they seem unable to recover: they linger on for weeks or even months getting worse and worse until they are completely dead. Nothing is able to reverse the process and they respond to neither conventional nor alternative remedies.

This is unusual, because most plants have remarkable powers of recovery and will regrow from the tiniest fragment of healthy root or stem.

One solution is to have several avocados, so that not all of your child's affection is concentrated on one plant. Once you *have* found a spot in your house where the avocado is happy, it will continue growing for years and its vibrant appearance and large, elegant, oval-shaped leaves will provide a great deal of pleasure.

Avocado (Persia americana) – also known as Alligator Pear and Love Fruit – originated in Central America and was a popular food amongst the Aztecs of Mexico when the Spanish arrived there in the 1500s. In its natural state the avocado is an evergreen tree growing to 20-60 feet high depending on the variety.

Star Fruit *(Averrhoa carambola)*

Star fruit is not a very popular fruit in this country but, nevertheless, it is often available in supermarkets. It has a delicious taste and texture – unlike some of the other less common tropical fruits.

The seeds look similar to lemon pips. They germinate easily if put in some potting compost and kept warm. The plants are very pretty, having delicate, pale-green leaves. They are frost sensitive, especially when young, and should be kept in the warmest room in the house.

In their natural environment they grow to a height of 8 m (25 ft) but their sensitivity to cold means that they do not grow vigorously in a temperate climate, even when kept indoors, and they do not need much pruning.

Passion Fruit

This is another fruit that has not traditionally been much used in this country, but which is now readily available in supermarkets.

It is unusual in that it is actually grown from seed commercially (most fruits are grown from cuttings), and this means that you have a good chance of success if you decide to plant it.

The seeds are slimy and coated with gel, but don't let this put you off: simply tip the glutinous mass into some potting compost. They should germinate in two to three weeks – you must keep them warm and damp – and you can then transplant the seedlings. Use 8 cm (3″) containers, fill them with potting compost and plant two or three seedlings in each pot, being careful to harm the roots as little as possible.

The young plants are delicate and can easily be killed by being too cold or too wet, but with any luck quite a few should survive.

The passion fruit plant is a type of vine and grows very rapidly in hot weather, so you will have to provide a framework up which the plants can climb. A lightweight wooden trellis pushed into the growing pot serves very well.

The plants produce tendrils that can be wrapped around the trellis, and they look quite spectacular in the height of summer. You have to cut off the tips of shoots that grow too big (the plant will grow six metres (20 feet) per year in the tropics!), and this will encourage the plants to be bushier and less straggly.

The plants will lose a lot of leaves in winter if they get cold, but this is not necessarily a disaster and they should grow back the following spring.

In theory they will produce flowers, and even fruit, after two to three years, but we are still waiting for our plants to do so.

Passion Fruit Passiflora edulis
A Spanish missionary who thought that its beautiful flowers symbolised the Passion of Christ gave the passion fruit its name.
It is a vigorous, climbing, evergreen vine, native to the tropical forests of Central and South America.

Easy   Medium   Advanced

Mango

The mango has an enormous seed and throwing it away always seems a terrible waste. An alternative is to plant it in a large pot of potting compost. The seed should be laid on its side just below the surface and the pot placed somewhere warm and kept moist.

Warmth is in fact the most important factor and you stand the best chance of success if you plant the seed in summer. The seed is even more likely to germinate if you have a greenhouse or conservatory in which to stand the pot.

The real thrill when growing a mango comes when the first shoot appears above the ground. It starts off as a small purple arch which gradually unbends to reveal soft, dark purple leaves which rapidly grow to a length of 8 to 10 cm (4″ to 5″). As they grow their colour changes from purple to green and they develop the waxy surface typical of many tropical plants.

The mango plant is evergreen: it produces new leaves throughout the year and can live for many years in the house. It is sensitive to frost and must be kept in the warmest room on cold winter nights, but it does have powers of recovery and will grow back even when the leaves are badly damaged by cold.

Unfortunately, there is no chance of a container-grown mango flowering or producing fruit. You have to content yourself with enjoying the plant's beautiful foliage.

Mango *Mangifera indica*
This handsome, evergreen tree is native to India and south-east Asia and is so common in the southern hemisphere that it is sometimes called the apple of the tropics.
Under ideal conditions, it can grow to a height of fifty feet (15 metres).

PINEAPPLE

Pineapple plants are unusual in that they can be grown from the rosette of leaves at the top of the fruit.

This crown of leaves can be cut off together with about half an inch (1½ cm) of the pineapple and kept, with the cut section uppermost, for two or three days in a warm place to dry out. The cut section can then be dusted with rooting compound (although this is not essential) and placed in a pot of compost. The pot need only be big enough to accommodate the base of the crown, but the compost does need to be well drained. Mix sand with the compost if you have some, or put pebbles or pieces of broken china in the bottom of the container.

The next stage is the most critical, because the plant needs to produce roots from the cut-off base if it is to survive. The danger is that it will rot and die before it has a chance to root properly. The best way to prevent this is to give the plant bottom heat. This means resting the pot on a heat source such as the top of a fridge, a water heater, a boiler or a propagator, if you have one. This keeps the soil warm all the time and is the surest way of promoting root development. The soil should be moist, but it is better for it to be too dry than too wet.

Once roots have become established the leaves grow rapidly, especially in hot weather, producing a large evergreen plant with long, sword-like leaves. It does not like frost but can stand quite low temperatures and should survive well in the house throughout the year. To get a really big plant, with the chance of a fruit being produced, you need to be able to put it into a hot, humid greenhouse over the summer months.

Pineapple – Ananas comosus

Pineapple is native to South America and was widely grown in tropical America before the arrival of the Europeans.

Christopher Columbus first saw pineapples on the island of Guadeloupe in 1493.

They rapidly became popular in Europe where gardeners learnt to grow them in the hothouses attached to stately homes.

☞ *Easy*   ☞☞ *Medium*   ☞☞☞ *Advanced*

GINGER

We have found ginger to be a surprisingly easy plant to grow. It offers many advantages to young children: the root is edible; the shoots grow rapidly (over an inch (2½ cm) per day in hot weather); it grows well in a pot; it doesn't grow too tall (never more than four feet); and its leaves smell of ginger.

Everything depends on finding a good piece of root ginger in the supermarket or wholefood shop. The root should not be dry or withered, but firm with pale green buds visible on the surface. It does not have to be particularly big – two inches (5 cm) of root is sufficient.

Put the root into a large pot of potting compost (just beneath the surface) in the spring or early summer. Keep it warm and moist and in full sunlight. Warmth is important: ginger does not like frost or cold nights and grows best if the soil in its pot does not have a chance to get cold. As a result it should be kept in the warmest room in the house, near to a window where it can receive plenty of sun.

After a few weeks, green shoots appear above the surface. These develop into leaves and stems that rapidly grow to a height of about four feet (1.2m). In hot weather a new shoot can appear each day. In late summer and autumn, ginger is one of the most beautiful of house plants as well as being an interesting talking point.

The stems die back in the winter when all the strength of the plant returns to the root (or rather the rhizome, which is part of the stem). Some of the roots can be harvested after a successful growing season (although we have never done this with our plant!).

Ginger – Zingiber officinale
Ginger has been one of the staple ingredients in Chinese cuisine for millennia, and has been cultivated in Britain from as early as 1605. It is used in curries and is a popular ingredient in many cakes and biscuits.
It is also a traditional Indian medicine.

Banana

Banana seeds are rock hard, and for this reason you are extremely unlikely to find them in the fruit that you buy from the supermarket. Over the years, varieties of bananas have been selected that do not produce any seeds at all, and these are the ones that are grown on banana farms and sold in the shops. This means that the only practical way to get a banana plant is to buy one.

They are available at garden centres and are not too expensive. All edible bananas come from the *Musa* family and these are the plants that are usually sold in this country.

Before you do go ahead and buy a banana plant you must carefully consider whether or not you have enough room. They are big plants – they can easily grow to two metres (6 ft) in height and their leaves spread out to form a circle of one and a half metres (5 ft) in diameter. They need to be kept free of frost all year round, which means that the room your plant is in must be heated, and they also like to have as much sunlight, and to be as warm as possible, throughout the summer.

Banana plants need to be watered regularly, and in addition you should spray the leaves with a fine water spray twice a day from April to September. (Do not worry if this makes black/brown patches appear on the leaves, they are perfectly normal.)

In addition to the possibility of getting fruit, there is the further incentive to growing banana plants in that they are keen to reproduce. Young plants, known as 'suckers', grow up around the base of the parent plant. These can be cut off and repotted – the secret of success is to be quite ruthless.

Remove the plant from its pot and cut off the sucker from the main plant with a sharp knife, being sure to get some root as well as the stem and leaf. Repot the parent as well as the new plant, and in this way you will soon have a small jungle.

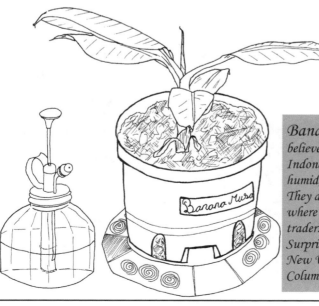

Bananas (Musa sapientum) are believed to have originated in the Indonesian islands. They thrive in hot, humid, jungle-like conditions.
They are now most prolific in East Africa where they were taken by Indonesian traders one thousand years ago. Surprisingly, there were no bananas in the New World before the arrival of Columbus.

Easy   *Medium*   *Advanced*

Animals

The previous sections have dealt with gardening and with the growing of indoor plants and have shown that children can learn much about the world of nature through working with plants. However, it cannot be denied that children have a special affection for animals: many children even prefer the company of animals to that of people.

This presents parents with a difficulty: we live in a society that does not allow space in which animals can live happy and contented lives and it is difficult to find a way of allowing children to have satisfactory relationships with animals.

Pets may appear to be the simplest solution, but this is not necessarily the case. If a pet has to be kept in a cage, then it is difficult to see how it can be happy, and if a child feels that they are contributing to their pet's unhappiness, they will be miserable – which is not the purpose of keeping a pet.

Dogs and cats do not need to be kept in cages and this in itself makes them the most suitable pets, but you do have to think carefully before taking on responsibility for such long-lived animals.

One of the problems associated with keeping pets is the intensity of the attachment that a child can form for an animal. In a more natural environment a child would be able to spread their affections over a range of animals, and would become accustomed to the births and deaths that are such a regular feature of animal life. When children 'lose' a pet cat or pet dog they can be completely devastated, and the experience can scar them for life. Of course children cannot, and should not, be protected from death, but encouraging them to focus all their love on an all too mortal animal is not being fair to them.

Some people are able to look after many animals with the result that their children do not become too attached to any one in particular, but for most people this is not a feasible option – animals require space, attention and money if they are to be properly cared for.

The solution to the conundrum of how to let your children have contact with animals without being damaged by the experience is to maximise the amount of time that they spend with wild animals, and this is where the garden once again comes into its own – because any garden, no matter how small, will be home to all sorts of wild animals.

You can make your garden animal-friendly by growing plants that attract birds, butterflies, bees etc.; you can have a small pond to attract frogs and toads; you can refrain from using toxic chemicals; and you can put out food for animals such as birds and hedgehogs. These creatures may not seem to be very exciting or lovable, at first, but watching them day in, day out does give a precious insight into animal life.

Birds

Birds are the easiest wild animals to observe. If you have space in your garden put up a bird table outside a window that you use regularly. This allows your child to sit and watch the birds whilst getting on with something else at the same time.

If you do not have a garden, food placed on a balcony or on a window sill is just as acceptable to the birds.

- Put food out regularly. It may take a while for your local bird population to recognise your bird table as a regular source of food, so you have to be patient.

- Supermarkets and garden centres sell seed mixtures suitable for wild birds and you can supplement this with scraps left over from the kitchen.

- Peanuts attract all sorts of birds – especially tits – but should not be put out in the spring because the chicks can choke on them.

- It is in winter that your efforts will be most appreciated.

- Put out a bowl of water, as well as food. On cold days, when it freezes, keep replacing the ice with fresh water.

Be Like The Bird

Be like the bird, who
Halting in his flight
On limb too slight
Feels it give way beneath him,
Yet sings,
Knowing he hath wings.

Victor Hugo

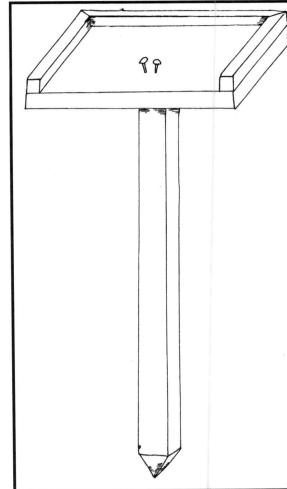

The Bird Table

Birds appreciate a simple, uncluttered bird table that gives them a clear sight of everything around them and from which they can make a quick exit when they feel threatened.

It is quite simple to make a bird table similar to the one shown here.

The top should be about 45 cm x 30 cm (18″ x 12″) in size (it can be made from a single piece of plywood) and needs to be bordered on three sides by beading to stop the birds from knocking the food onto the ground. The fourth side should be left clear so that the bird table can be swept clean from time to time.

The base of the pole can be soaked in creosote, to help extend its life in the soil, but if the table itself is left untreated, it will be more appealing to the birds.

You will soon start to recognise regular visitors: robins, blackbirds, thrushes, tits, sparrows and starlings are the birds that you are most likely to see.

By watching birds one becomes aware of the way in which they relate to each other and the way in which their behaviour changes over the course of the year: in the winter they are interested in little more than staying alive, but as soon as spring arrives they mark out territories, fight each other, sing loudly and start to build nests. In the summer they work frantically to keep their chicks fed.

In some respects there are parallels to be drawn with human life.

Frogs and Toads

Amphibians are another class of animals that can be studied at close hand in the garden and, while it must be admitted that frogs and toads are unlikely to occupy the same place in a child's affections as a pet dog, they are surprisingly endearing creatures when one has regular contact with them.

They can be encouraged to take up home in your garden by providing them with a source of water. This can be as simple or as elaborate as you wish. An old sink kept topped up with water and stocked with a few water plants provides a good habitat for aquatic insects and may well attract visiting frogs.

If you are able to be a little more ambitious, and have space for a pond in your garden, you will definitely be able to attract permanent amphibian residents.

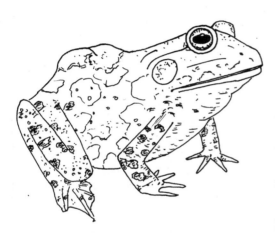

Frogs and toads have shown that they are able to adapt and survive in the modern urban environment. Your pond does not need to be deep enough for them to hibernate in (something that they do in cold areas): they seem to be able to find places to over-winter and if your frogs disappear in the autumn, don't despair, they are quite likely to return in the spring.

Similarly, you may find that you do not get frogspawn in your pond even though you have frogs living in your garden. This is because frogs try to return to the place where they themselves developed as tadpoles, to lay their own eggs.

Life Cycle of the Frog

This leads onto the fascinating subject of the frog's life cycle which should form part of every child's education. The development of a tadpole into a frog is obviously something that they should be allowed to observe at first hand: merely reading about it is not the same thing at all.

Keeping tadpoles indoors is not to be recommended because they eat each other. Observing them becomes a rather gruesome experience when their numbers go steadily down. However, when they are outdoors, in a reasonably well-stocked pond, their survival rate is much higher, and one has the pleasure of eventually seeing the emergence into the world of tens of tiny frogs.

If you do not have any frogspawn in your pond in the spring then you may be able to get some from a friend. In the South, frogspawn first appears in January or February; in the North it is later.

Pond Life

Irrespective of whether or not you have frogs and toads in your pond, it will provide an interesting insight into the working of nature as a whole. A pond is a more or less self-contained environment, and if one sits beside it and just watches what is going on, one can learn a lot about how the world of nature operates.

Insects dominate pond life and although few people feel much empathy with the insect world, watching them rushing around the surface of a pond is remarkably reminiscent of watching people rushing from one place to another as they go about their daily lives.

Water does have a therapeutic quality, even when it is not flowing, and a pond provides a place where a child can go and be peaceful and feel in harmony with the natural world. It can give them a chance to reflect and to be on their own for a short space of time.

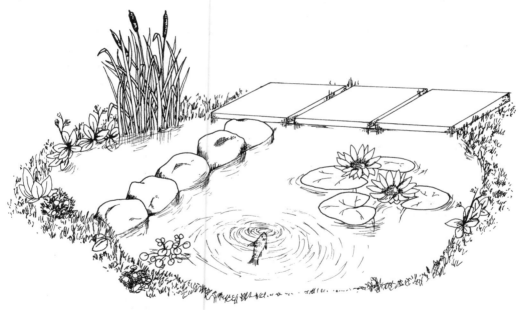

Farming

Another way in which people interrelate with animals is through farming. The way in which animals are treated on farms is a subject that arouses considerable passion, and it is difficult to say how much children should be told about farming practices.

Ultimately, it is hypocritical to *use* animal products whilst being disapproving and ignorant about how the animals involved are being treated However, as children are largely unable to determine whether or not they do use animal products in their own lives, it may be best to put the issue of animal husbandry to one side, until they are older.

Pets

To return briefly to the subject of pets. It is easy to become too intense when talking about animals and their rights and to imagine that animals feel everything in the same way that we do. There is no doubt that animals do respond to care and affection and that children do, often, feel a genuine bond with their pets. Who is to say that the love that they bestow upon them does not in itself enhance the life of the animal concerned?

Children can, of course, become very upset when a cherished creature dies, and you must do what you can to prepare them for this event.

When a child has had a chance to consider all the implications of owning and looking after a particular pet, and remains undeterred, it would seem unkind not to let them have their way.

You must make sure that they look after their pet as well as they possibly can: that they feed it well, give it plenty of exercise, provide it with a chance to be outdoors and make sure that it has a variety of experiences every day. If they do all this their pet is sure to reward them by bringing them a great deal of pleasure.

You must also bear in mind, of course, that if, for any reason, your child loses interest in their pet, then the responsibility to provide this level of care will fall upon you.

Cooking

Introduction

Diet represents one of the biggest challenges facing the next generation. As things stand at the moment, those of us living in the 'Western world' have the opportunity to eat better than anyone has ever been able to do before.

Fresh fruit and vegetables are available throughout the year, coming from all over the world. As well as being able to enjoy locally-grown crops, such as grains and vegetables, we also have the opportunity to eat exotic tropical fruits such as bananas, pineapples and citrus fruits. This produce is not only available in abundance but also virtually all year round. Food is rarely in short supply and we have an enormous choice about what we choose to eat.

The paradox is that, in the midst of all this abundance, the diet of most western people is getting worse and worse. We are developing habits that threaten our health and that of our children. The problem is usually referred to by the simple term 'junk food'.

Junk Food

'Junk food' is food that is high in sugar and saturated fats; it is processed food that contains huge numbers of additives. It is tinned food, packaged food, pre-cooked food. It is food produced on factory farms. It is genetically-modified food. It is food soaked in pesticides and herbicides. It is food sold by fast-food restaurants. It is fizzy drinks, packets of crisps and chocolate bars. It represents a massive proportion of what we eat.

Junk food has not existed long enough for us to know what precise long-term effects it will have on our children, but all the evidence suggests that it is likely to be catastrophic.

Children brought up on junk food are in danger of having teeth and digestive problems, a greater suscep-tibility to cancer and a tendency to obesity.

The tragedy is that we do not have to eat junk food and we do not have to feed it to our children. It is not cheaper than proper food – it is more expensive. However, we consider it to be more convenient (hence the term 'convenience food').

This leads to the heart of the problem. Whereas for most people in the world, life revolves around a home in which someone cooks and prepares food, we in the West have developed a lifestyle that revolves around our work.

Everything, including the care of our children and the running of our homes, has to take second place to the activity of going to work and earning money. Amongst other consequences, this has led to a state of affairs in which we no longer have time to cook. Somewhere along the line we have lost sight of the fact that cooking and eating are basic to life and we have come to accept a culture in which we buy a large proportion of our food pre-cooked and tampered with in various ways. We know that this food contains preservatives which effectively neutralise its nutritional value, colours that mask its insipid pallor and flavourings that disguise its lack of taste.

We have terrible suspicions about the farming techniques used to produce this food, we are dubious about the factories where it is processed and we have suspicions about how fresh it is when it finally reaches the shops. However, we put all these doubts and fears to one side because we have convinced ourselves that we do not have time to do our own cooking.

With this lack of time has come a lack of ability and many people, especially young people, no longer feel able to cook – they have no option but to eat a packaged offering from the supermarket almost every single day of their lives.

Once again, the solution to this problem lies in education – but it is not an education that can easily be provided at school.

Cooking at School

Cooking lessons in school are a major logistical exercise and do not work very well. Every child has to be provided with cooking utensils, ingredients and access to a cooker. There has to be a high level of staffing to ensure that children aren't unintentionally (or intentionally) set on fire and, even then, it is not possible to give everyone the attention that they need, when they need it.

At the end of the lesson everyone is exhausted but, instead of being able to sit down together and enjoy the fruits of their labours, the children have to rush off to their next lesson. This is a very unnatural way to be introduced to the art of cooking and it is not surprising that few people cite their school cookery lessons as a major inspiration in their lives.

Cooking at home

Cooking is best learnt at home. A child has a sense of belonging in their own kitchen, which is necessary for a cook. Here the natural rhythm of preparing, cooking and then eating the food can take place uninterrupted. The one-to-one interaction between child and adult in the home increases the chance that the cooking will be a success: failures in cooking are very dispiriting and can put off a potential cook for years. Also, it allows the child to be involved in deciding what to cook and when – an important matter for all cooks.

Even if you do not have time to do much cooking yourself and have little free time to devote to working with your child, cooking should be near the top of the list of things that you do together.

If you can cook together once a week, you will find that you will both benefit: it is a good bonding exercise – preparing a meal requires a great deal of co-operation!

Sometimes people think that cooking is not worthy of being included in a proper educational curriculum. There have been times in the past when boys were not taught to cook at all and only those girls who were not bright enough to do well in academic subjects were given a serious amount of cookery tuition. This reflects a gross misunderstanding of the real purpose of education. Reading, writing, arithmetic, languages, science, history, geography, etc. are only worth studying when one is sure that the skills that are really important have already been taken care of.

Cooking is the foremost of these skills and all other education is practically useless if someone cannot even prepare food for themselves.

Advantages of Cooking, for Children

Being able to cook provides a great boost to a child's self-confidence. It is a very real and potent form of empowerment, and allows children to feel much more in control of their day-to-day lives.

It is not necessary that they should cook every day (that would rapidly become a chore), but it is important that they know that they can prepare their own food when they need to.

Another advantage of learning to cook is that it provides a much better education about what is and what is not good food than any amount of lecturing or reading on the subject. Someone who cooks does not take long to develop an appreciation for good-quality ingredients.

In addition, cooking is an activity that is indisputably useful. Too many of the activities that we encourage our children to pursue are essentially ways of wasting time (watching television, computer games, half the time that they spend at school etc.) and then, in later years, parents complain that their children are lazy and cannot apply themselves to the realities of life. Cooking is the ideal antidote to this syndrome: children can prepare a meal and the fruits of their action are immediately apparent, and can be appreciated by everyone. It engages a child in a worthwhile activity in the most direct way possible.

Recipes Included in This Book

In selecting the recipes for this book we have avoided restricting ourselves to the simple biscuit and cake recipes that people often associate with children's cooking. Instead we have concentrated on recipes that use fresh ingredients and which allow children to help in the preparation of complete meals.

This may involve a little more work and pre-planning but it should also prove to be more rewarding.

We have not given indications about how old children should be before attempting the various recipes, because experience is more important than age. Young children are not expected to be able to follow these recipes and produce a meal on their own – most of them are too demanding for that. However, it should be within the scope of most children to be able to help in the preparation of these meals (and perhaps be able to follow the recipes on their own when they have worked through them with you once or twice).

It is not easy to learn to cook from a book and, although we have tried to make the recipes as clear as possible, it is recommended that you work with your child the first time that they attempt them.

Cooking With Children — Basic Rules

- Children up to the age of five or six cannot usually cook things on their own – they have to work with you.

- If you can think of little jobs to give them while you are cooking it will help to keep them involved and interested. These could include chopping up vegetables, weighing ingredients or washing-up.

- Obviously a young child's help will slow you down and might try your patience, but it is better to have them working with you than letting them become bored and frustrated because you are not giving them enough attention.

- Older children can cook on their own – perhaps with a little help from you in reading the recipe, getting the ingredients together, making sure the scales work etc.

- The recipes that have been included here have all been tried and tested and found to work well.

- One of the worst experiences for any cook is when things go wrong and (in extreme cases) all the food has to be thrown away. This happens to everyone from time to time and, as a parent, you have to offer what consolation you can when it happens to your child. It may put them off cooking for a while, but hopefully the rewards of being able to prepare their own food will entice them back into the kitchen before too long.

- When cooking with several children at the same time you can only give each one a limited amount of attention so, if any of them wants to cook something in particular, it might be best to help them to do it when the kitchen is not otherwise in use – in the middle of the afternoon for example.

- Most cookery involves the use of heat and it is the source of heat that is the biggest potential source of danger to a child. You have to make sure that they are familiar with the way that your cooker works, what things they are allowed to do on it and what things they are not. You should try to be available to help with the cooker, even when your child is a fairly experienced cook.

- Some recipes involve cooking in a pre-heated oven. Following a recipe can be a slow, painstaking affair and knowing that the oven is switched on and not being used adds to the stress. For this reason we have not indicated a particular stage in each recipe when it is appropriate to light the oven. It would be helpful if you could keep a check on progress and light the oven when you think that it is close to being needed.

Safety with Children

In some ways the kitchen is a safer place for a child when they are working in it than when they are excluded from helping and are unaware of what is happening.

All the same, common sense must be used to make everything as safe as possible. Extra care must be taken if you have several children in the kitchen at once, because you cannot be constantly aware of what they are all doing.

- The cooker is the greatest source of danger. Make sure your children understand how it works, and arrange with them what they are and are not allowed to do – light the rings, light the oven etc.

- Take things in and out of the oven yourself until you are sure that your children know how to handle hot objects.

- Keep a fire blanket handy near the cooker, and if they are old enough, tell them how to use it.

- Likewise with a fire extinguisher.

- Don't leave pan handles sticking out over the edge of the cooker.

- Don't have flexes or leads hanging over the edge of work surfaces – children can pull the appliance onto their heads.

- If the work surfaces are too high, have something solid and stable for the children to stand on.

- Make sure your children know how to handle knives – never pick them up by the blade, never play with them and put them somewhere safe when they have finished using them.

- Scissors can be as dangerous as knives. Try to have a place where they are kept and return them to this place after use.

- This applies to all the utensils and kitchen tools. Your kitchen should be tidy, which may present a problem to some cooks but it is an essential requirement when cooking with children.

- Use aprons. Make sure that they are fastened on properly. Aprons not only protect a child's clothes but also let them know that they are engaged in a special activity and this makes them more aware of what they are doing.

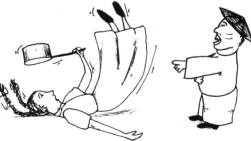

BREAD

Bread has been the staple food of all western civilisations for the past three thousand years. By a stroke of good luck it also provides the easiest way to get a child involved in cooking.

If you make the bread dough then even the smallest child can help to form it into interesting shapes for baking.

making the Dough

This basic recipe is included for the benefit of those people who do not normally make their own bread. Every baker has their own variation. You can use different flours, different types of yeast, and experiment with a variety of sweeteners and seeds.

Ingredients (sufficient for 3 loaves):
1½ kg (3 lbs) wholemeal flour
10 ml (2 level teaspoons) salt
30 ml (2 tablespoons) sunflower oil
1 packet fast-action yeast
850 ml (1½ pints) warm water (approx.)

> *Note: You can make less bread by reducing all the ingredients, providing you keep the proportions more or less the same.*

Method:
1. Sieve the flour and salt into your biggest mixing bowl. Rub in the oil. Add the yeast.
2. Pour the water into a pan, heat it up to about 37°C (i.e. until it feels very warm to the touch).
3. Gradually add the warm water until you get a dough which is easily malleable but not sticky. If the dough is too sticky, add more flour. If it is too dry, add more water.
4. Knead the dough for ten to twelve minutes. The dough is now ready to be made into shapes prior to baking *(see page 210)*.
5. Put the loaves in tins, or the shapes on an oiled baking sheet, and brush a little oil on the tops.

6. Cover and allow the loaves to rise until they double in size (ensure that they are in a warm place).
7. Bake them in a hot oven, gas 7 (220°C / 425°F) until they are brown underneath and sound hollow when tapped (10-15 min for small shapes and 20-30 min for loaves).
8. Remove from tins and leave to cool on a wire rack.

  Easy *Medium* *Advanced*

Ingredients – more information

Flour. *There are many different types of flour. Organic, wholemeal flour is the best for bread-making. Organic flours are often still marketed under the name of the farm or area where they are produced and they can be very different from each other. If you are not having any success with one brand, then try switching to another. Big companies and supermarkets blend their flours, which results in a more standardised product.*

If you find wholemeal bread too heavy you can use 85% flour instead, or mix white flour with the wholemeal. The more white you use, the lighter the bread will be.

Conversely, you can mix in a small proportion of rye flour which will make the bread even heavier. Wheat allergy is much more common than is generally accepted and even quite a small proportion of rye flour can make bread more acceptable to some children.

Baking wheat-free bread is probably beyond the scope of the novice cook – other grains do not have the bread-making properties of wheat flour.

Yeast. *Yeast is a living organism and, in order to succeed as a baker, you have to understand its needs.*

When making bread, yeast needs air. That is why the dough has to be kneaded. When yeast does not get enough oxygen it makes the dough sour – sourdough bread. The yeast also has to be kept warm. Like all living organisms it grows best at a temperature of about 37°C (98°F). Above this temperature it dies.

The yeast releases carbon dioxide as it grows. This gas is trapped by the dough and forces it to expand or 'rise'.

Yeast is available in various different forms and, if you prefer, you can use fresh yeast or dried yeast instead of fast action yeast (but make sure that you follow appropriate instructions, you cannot use them in the same way as fast action yeast).

Oil or Margarine. *This ingredient is optional but it does help to improve the texture of the bread and provides extra nutrients for the yeast – hence helping the bread to rise.*

Water. *It requires a certain amount of practice to determine how much water to add – too little and the bread is dry, too much and it won't cook. However, there is room for error: you don't have to get the amount right, down to the last drop.*

Salt. *Salt is not an essential ingredient. Most people prefer their bread to contain some salt but in excess it can be harmful rather than beneficial. Add enough to suit your own taste.*

Making the Loaves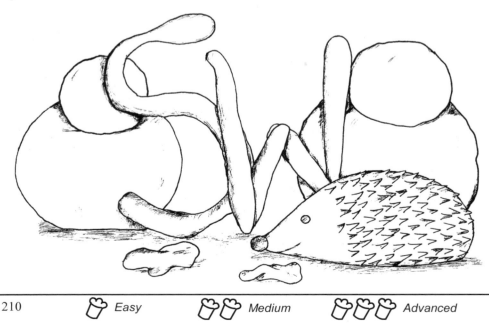

It is at this stage that you can involve your child (or children). Give them each some dough to model into a shape suitable for baking.

It is not necessary to give a child a large lump of dough. They tend to prefer to concentrate on making complex shapes out of smaller pieces. If they have too much time, the dough gets cold and the end result is not very palatable.

Here are some things that they might like to make:

Prickly Hedgehogs. Make a round ball, pull out a snout at one end, snip all over the back with the tip of a pair of scissors. You can use raisins to make eyes. This works well in that it looks like a hedgehog, but if it is in the least overcooked the spines on the back become hard and painful to eat.

Letter Shapes. Every child enjoys forming the initials of their own name. Thin strips of bread dry out very quickly and to be appreciated at their best, shapes like this should be eaten straight away .

Cottage Loaves. Make two balls of dough, one bigger than the other. Stick the smaller one onto the top of the larger one with the aid of a drop of water.

Buns. Make buns of varying shapes – round, cylindrical, flat, square, etc. If you slit them along the top with a knife, it helps them to rise. You can also roll the dough into a cylindrical shape and tie it into a loose knot, or you can place smaller pieces of dough (cubes, balls, etc.) next to each other on the baking tray (so that they are touching) and they will merge together as they rise to produce interesting shapes.

Plaited Loaf. If you are any good at plaiting you can make a plaited loaf. Make a flat, oblong shape. Divide it into three, lengthways, and plait the three strands together.

Buns

This recipe can be used to make dough for 8 buns.

Ingredients:
175 gm (6 oz) plain strong white flour
175 gm (6 oz) strong wholemeal flour
2½ ml (½ tsp) salt
½ packet rapid action dried yeast
5 ml (1 tsp) sugar
45 ml (3 tbsp) sunflower oil
200 ml (7 fl oz) tepid water
beaten egg to glaze (optional)
sesame seeds, poppy seeds or oat flakes to garnish (optional)

Method:
1. Sieve the flours into a bowl.
2. Add the salt, the yeast, the sugar and the oil. Mix them together with your fingers.
3. Heat the water, add to the flour and mix to a dough. Turn it out onto a clean, floured work surface.
4. Knead for 5 – 10 minutes.
5. Return the dough to the bowl, cover with cling film or a clean tea towel and leave it to rise in a warm place until it has doubled in size. (This should only take 30 minutes to an hour if you have managed to keep the dough warm.)
6. Divide the dough into eight pieces, make them into roll shapes and place them on a well-greased baking tray.
7. Cover the tray with cling film or a tea towel and leave the buns to rise again for another 30 – 60 minutes.
8. Preheat the oven to gas 6 (200°C / 400°F).
9. Glaze the buns with egg and dust with flour or sprinkle with seeds or oat flakes.
10. Bake for about 20 minutes – until the buns are lightly brown and sound hollow when tapped on the underside.

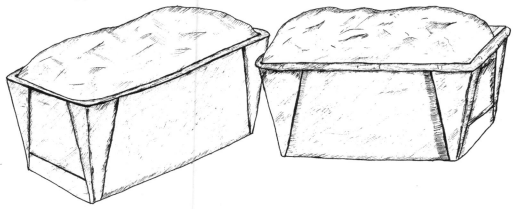

Bean Sprouts

Bean sprouts have been an important part of the Eastern diet (especially in China and Japan) for over 5000 years. They are tasty and very healthy. They are also easy to grow and do not need to be cooked, which makes them ideal for children.

Many seeds can be successfully sprouted – not just beans. Mung bean sprouts are the most common but alfalfa sprouts are just as easy to grow. You can also experiment with aduki beans, lentils, peas, chick peas and wheat.

Sprouts are healthy because the germinating seed converts its starch reserves into vitamins and amino acids as it starts to grow.

How to Sprout

The cheapest way to sprout seeds is in a glass jar. Seeds can swell and grow to ten times their original size, so use a largish jar.

1. Soak 125 gm (4 oz) of seeds in water overnight. This allows the seeds to swell and speeds up germination.

2. Drain this water off and put the seeds in the jar. Secure a piece of muslin or cheesecloth over the top of the jar with a rubber band.

3. Leave the jar on its side on the draining board. It is important that the seeds are well drained – otherwise they may go mouldy instead of sprouting!

4. Rinse twice per day, using warm water if possible. Drain carefully each time and keep the jar on its side.

5. The ideal temperature for germination is 13-15°C (55-70°F). In most houses, this makes the kitchen the best place to sprout seeds. Germination should be visible within a day or two.

6. Different seeds take different amounts of time to become ready for using, but the longest time is about six days.

Warning.

Never use seed sold for planting – it may have been coated in insoluble fungicides and pesticides (including mercury compounds) and could be bad for your health.

Always use food-quality seed. Health food shops sell seed specifically for sprouting – it is often organic. Fresh seed germinates better than old seed.

Light or Dark?

Sprouts that one buys in the shops are sprouted in the dark. This gives them their characteristic white colour. At home it is usually easier to sprout seeds in the light. One can keep an eye on them and one remembers to rinse them regularly.

Sprouts grown in the light will not be as big as those grown in the dark and will be slightly green in colour but this does not affect their nutritional value.

How to Cook

Many sprouts make an excellent addition to a salad (especially alfalfa sprouts) but they can also be steamed or stir-fried. Mung bean sprouts, cooked in a wok, are a traditional part of Chinese cuisine.

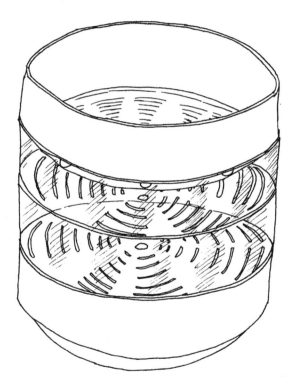

If you find that you enjoy growing bean sprouts, you might consider buying a bean sprouter. They come in various shapes and sizes. This one has trays on which you can sprout different seeds. It is made of tinted plastic to reduce the amount of light that reaches them. The trays have holes that allow the seeds to drain freely. This makes the task of rinsing the sprouts much simpler.

SALAD

These salads can be served with a main meal, or as a lunchtime dish with a warmed baguette or wholemeal bread.

To warm a baguette, cut it into two halves, wrap each half in cooking foil and put it into an oven on a low heat.

TOMATO PASTA SALAD

Serves 4

Ingredients:
175 gm (6 oz) dried pasta shapes
225 gm (8 oz) cherry tomatoes
(or 2 quartered ordinary tomatoes)
10 black olives
8 chopped fresh basil leaves (or 1 tablespoon dried basil)
A few chives, well chopped (optional)

Dressing:
30 ml (2 tbsp) olive oil
7 ml (½ tsp) cider vinegar or red wine vinegar
15 ml (1 tbsp) tomato paste
1 ml (¼ tsp) ground black pepper
(or 2 twists of the pepper mill)
1 ml (¼ tsp) salt—(optional)

Method:
1. Bring a large pan of water to the boil and cook the pasta according to the time indicated on the packet. (To prevent the cooked pasta from being sticky, add 2½ ml (½ tsp) of any vegetable oil to the water before cooking.)
2. Drain it through a sieve over the sink and then rinse it with cold water. Drain again and put into a serving bowl.
3. Cut the cherry tomatoes into halves and add to the pasta along with the olives and basil.
4. In a mug or small bowl mix together the olive oil, vinegar, tomato paste and black pepper and pour over the salad. Mix well.
5. Sprinkle the chives over the salad and serve.

Easy   Medium   Advanced

CUCUMBER AND TOMATO SIDE SALAD

Serves 4

Ingredients:

½ large cucumber or 1 small cucumber

2 tomatoes

2 spring onions or 15 ml (1 tablespoon) chopped
   chives

15 ml (1 tablespoon) chopped fresh parsley

Dressing:
25 ml (5 tsp) olive oil
juice of ½ lemon
1 small garlic clove

Method:

1. In a small bowl, mix together the olive oil, lemon juice and crushed garlic clove.

2. Peel and cut the cucumber lengthways into four pieces. Carefully scrape out the seeds and discard. Chop up the cucumber lengths into small pieces. Place in a salad bowl.

3. Wash and cut up the tomatoes and the spring onions (or chives) into small pieces and add them to the salad bowl.

4. Add the salad dressing and stir well. Serve.

TOFU AND CARROT SALAD WITH RAISINS

Serves 4

Ingredients:

175 gm (6 oz) block tofu

2 large carrots

125 gm (4 oz) raisins

freshly ground pepper

1 tablespoon chopped chives

Dressing:
5 ml (1 tsp) soy sauce
30 ml (2 tbsp) orange juice
2½ ml (½ tsp) dry mustard
2½ ml (½ tsp) brown sugar

Method:

1. Cut the tofu into small pieces and put into a salad bowl.

2. Peel or scrape the carrots, grate them into the salad bowl and add the raisins.

3. In a little bowl or cup, mix together the soy sauce, orange juice, mustard and sugar.

4. Pour this over the carrot and tofu mixture.

5. Add a little black pepper (two twists of a pepper mill).

6. Gently mix it all together with a fork.

7. Sprinkle a tablespoon of chopped fresh, or dried, chives on top and serve.

Potatoes

If you have managed to grow your own potatoes you will probably just want to eat them boiled with a little salt and butter, at first, because this is the way that they taste best.

However, here are three other potato recipes.

Fantail roast potatoes

Serves 4

Ingredients:

1 kg (2 lb) potatoes
30 gm (1 oz) melted butter or margarine

Method:

1. Put a large pan of water on to boil.
2. Peel and cut the potatoes in half.
3. Cut fine slits in the rounded top of each one, being careful not to cut right through to the flat base, so that each potato stays intact.
4. Boil the potatoes for 5 minutes. Meanwhile melt the butter or margarine in a small pan over a low heat.
5. Turn off the heat, lift the potatoes out of the pan with a slotted spoon and allow to drain.
6. Stand them on a greased tray and brush them all over with the melted butter or margarine. Put them in an oven preheated to gas 6 (200°C, 400°F).
7. Cook the potatoes for about 45 – 60 minutes, until they are golden and crisp on the outside and tender on the inside.
8. Serve at once.

Baked (Jacket) Potatoes

Baked potatoes are delicious served with a filling, or as part of a meal. They are also amongst the easiest things to cook. You simply have to scrub the potatoes clean, prick them with a fork and put them in a hot oven (gas 7, 220°C, 400°F).

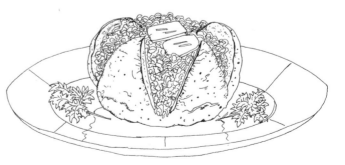

They take between ¾ - 1½ hours to cook, depending on their size.

 Easy   *Medium*   *Advanced*

Bombay potatoes

Serves 4

Ingredients:
750 gm (1½ lbs) potatoes
30 ml (2 tbsp) groundnut or sunflower oil
1 medium onion, chopped
2 cloves of garlic, chopped
10 ml (2 tsp) ground cumin
10 ml (2 tsp) ground coriander
2½ ml (½ tsp) turmeric
1 ml (¼ tsp) cayenne pepper
5 ml (1 tsp) salt
5 ml (1 tsp) garam masala
freshly ground black pepper
30 – 60 ml (2-4 tbsp) chopped fresh coriander, to serve

Method:

1. Peel and cut up the potatoes into 1 cm (½″) cubes.
2. Warm the oil in a medium-sized saucepan over a moderate heat. Add the onion, cover and cook for 5 minutes.

Note: A bulb of garlic is made up of several cloves or segments. Remove 1 clove, peel off the skin and chop it up finely. (If you always use the wrong side of the chopping board for garlic and onion it will prevent other food, that is chopped up on the right side of the board, from absorbing the taste.)
Alternatively, you can use a garlic press.

3. Add the garlic, cumin, ground coriander, turmeric and cayenne pepper and cook for 2 minutes, stirring from time to time.
4. Add the potatoes and stir well to coat them with the onion, garlic and spices. Add a teaspoon of salt and pour in 150 ml (5 fl oz) of water.
5. Bring to the boil, then cover and cook over a gentle heat until the potato is just tender and most of the water has disappeared (about 10-15 minutes).
6. Stir in the garam masala. Taste the mixture. If necessary add more salt, some black pepper and, if you want a hotter dish, some more cayenne.
7. Serve warm or cool, sprinkled with chopped coriander.

Brown Rice

Serves 4

Ingredients:

350 gm (12 oz) short grain or long grain brown rice (organic if possible).

Method:

1. Wash the rice thoroughly under running water.
2. Place it in a saucepan with one litre (2 pints) of cold water.
3. Bring to the boil and cook until the rice is tender (30-40 minutes). You can add more water if needed.
4. When the rice is cooked, turn off the heat and tip the rice into a colander or sieve, hold it over the sink and pour a kettle of recently boiled water over it.
5. Put the rice back into the pan, replace the lid, and it will keep warm for up to 20 minutes.

White Rice

Ingredients:

The ratio is 1 rice to 1½ water.

This means that if you have one mug full of white rice, you will need one and a half mugs full of water; 2 mugs of rice will need 3 mugs of water.

15 ml (1 tbsp) olive oil

Method:

1. Measure out the water into a pan and bring to the boil.
2. Meanwhile gently heat the oil for 15 seconds in a flame-proof casserole that has a tight-fitting lid. Add the rice and fry it gently, stirring frequently with a wooden spoon, until the water in the other pan is boiling.
3. When the water is boiling, turn off both heat sources and pour the boiling water into the casserole filled with the rice. This creates a lot of steam and is best done by an adult.
4. Put the lid on the casserole and place it in the oven, gas 3 (160°C or 325°F), for about 15 minutes.
5. Remove from the oven and put to one side. Keep covered and it will stay warm for up to 20 minutes.

Chick Pea Soup with Fried Bread

Serves 5-6

Ingredients:

2 carrots
1 large potato (about 175 gm (6 oz))
3 tomatoes
1 medium onion
1 clove garlic, peeled and crushed
50 ml (3 tbsp) olive oil

5 or 6 thin slices of bread

10 ml (2 tsp) each of cumin, coriander and *mild* paprika
1¾ litres (3 pints) water
2 vegetable stock cubes
5 ml (1 tsp) dried mixed herbs
2 400 gm (14 oz) cans chick peas
salt and pepper

Method:

1. Wash the carrots, potato and tomatoes and cut into large chunks. Set to one side.
2. Peel and chop the onion and garlic.
3. Heat the oil carefully in a large flameproof casserole that has a lid, and add the onion and garlic. Cook on a low heat for a few minutes, until the onion is softened. Stir the mixture with a wooden spoon so that it doesn't burn.
4. Add the spices and cook for approximately 3 minutes.
5. Add the vegetables and stir for a few minutes so that they are all coated with the onion and spice mix.
6. Carefully add the water, vegetable stock cubes and mixed herbs.
7. Bring to the boil, turn down the heat, cover and simmer for twenty minutes.
8. Add the washed and drained chick peas and cook for another fifteen minutes.
9. After making sure that the vegetables are cooked, turn off the heat and let the mixture stand for five minutes, to cool down a little.
10. Purée the soup until it is quite smooth with a hand-held liquidiser, blender or food-processor. *An adult should be available to help with this.*
11. Taste it and add salt and pepper if necessary.
12. **Fried Bread:**
    Thinly spread both sides of each slice of bread with margarine, and fry gently in a large frying pan over a **low** heat, turning the bread over after a few minutes, to cook the other side.
13. Reheat the soup if necessary and serve.

Italian Meals

Pasta

Serves 4-5
Ingredients.
1 large onion
4 medium-sized carrots
200 gm (½ lb) tofu
30 ml (2 tbsp) olive oil
5 ml (1 tsp) olive oil for pasta
    water
2 x 400 gm (14 oz) cans
    chopped, peeled tomatoes
375 gm (12 oz) dried pasta
A little freshly ground pepper
125 gm (4 oz) hard cheese

Method:

1. Peel the onion. Cut in half and chop into quite small pieces.

2. Wash, peel and slice the carrots into thin rounds. Rinse and cut the tofu into 1 cm (½ inch) cubes.

3. Warm the olive oil in a flameproof casserole that has a lid.

4. Add the onion carefully and cook on a low heat until just softened and beginning to brown (about 5 minutes).

5. Add the chopped carrots and tofu. Stir with a wooden spoon or spatula, cover, turn down the heat and let them cook for about 5 minutes.

6. Add the chopped tomatoes with their juice. Stir well, replace the lid and put it in the oven, gas 4 (180°C, 350°F) until the carrots are cooked.

7. Pour 1½ litres (3 pts) of water into a big pan and bring to the boil. This will be used for cooking the pasta.

8. Tip the pasta carefully into the boiling water. Add ¼ teaspoon of salt and a teaspoon of olive oil. The oil helps to prevent the pasta from sticking together.

9. Turn up the heat, stir the pasta once, and then cook it on a medium to high heat according to the directions on the packet.

10. To see if it's cooked, carefully remove a piece with a fork and bite it. It should be tender but not too soft.

11. Drain the pasta in a colander over the sink and then tip it out into a large serving dish. Take the sauce from the oven, pour it over the pasta.

12. Grate the cheese over the meal before serving (optional).

13. Serve and eat immediately.

  Easy Medium Advanced

Pizza

Pizza has become one of the world's most popular dishes, and has travelled far beyond its native Italy.

Almost any ingredient can be put upon a pizza, and they are ideally suited to large families in which people often have different tastes. Simply decide which part of the pizza will belong to whom and vary the 'toppings' accordingly – it is quite possible to have three or four different versions on the same base.

The Base

Serves 2-4 people (makes one 30 cm (12″) round pizza)
Ingredients:
(These quantities can be doubled if two pizzas are required)
225 gm (8 oz) strong, plain flour
2½ ml (½ tsp) salt
2½ ml (½ tsp) fast-action dried yeast
15 ml (1 tbsp) olive oil
120 ml (4 fl oz) warm water

Method:
1. Sift the flour into a large bowl and add the salt and dried yeast.
2. Make a well in the centre and pour in the oil. Gradually work in the warm water until the mixture is soft and malleable.
3. Turn out onto a floured surface and knead for five to ten minutes. The dough should be smooth: if it is at all sticky, sprinkle with flour, and continue to knead until it comes away easily from your fingers.

Place the dough in an oiled bowl, then cover with cling film, or a dampened tea towel. Leave to rise in a warm place for 40-45 minutes. When risen, remove from the bowl and knead gently for a minute or so.

continued overleaf

Making the Pizza

Method:
1. Roll out the dough into a fairly thin circle, and place in a round pizza pan. (Alternatively the pizza could be rectangular, and cooked on a normal baking tray.)
2. Make sure that the dough covers the entire surface of the pizza pan or tray, and turns up to form a shallow rim around the edge.
3. Spread the tomato paste over the base.
4. Since the choice of toppings is up to you, the list below describes how to prepare various ingredients: of course, you don't have to use them all on one pizza.

Toppings:
The following is a list of the toppings which we have found to be particularly successful, but you can experiment with different combinations.
(The quantities are only meant to be rough guidelines. They can be increased or reduced depending on the sort of pizza you have in mind.)

45 ml (3 tbsp) tomato paste or passata

1 courgette	1 onion or shallot
½ medium-size block tofu	1 to 2 cloves garlic
sweetcorn – 1 tin or 300 gm (10 oz) frozen	5 ml (1 tsp) capers
frozen peas – 1 tin or 250 gm (9 oz)	200 gm canned tomatoes or 2 fresh
5 to 7 mushrooms	tomatoes
½ tin or jar artichoke hearts	75 gm (3 oz) any hard cheese
½ red or yellow pepper	1 handful black or green olives
125 gm to 175 gm (4 to 6 oz) fresh spinach	10 ml (2 tsp) dried oregano

Courgette
Wash and peel the courgette, cut into thin slices and lay them upon the pizza.

Tofu
Although not a traditional ingredient, tofu works well as a pizza topping, and is sold in wholefood shops and supermarkets. Cut half a medium-size block into thin strips and then place them upon the base.

Peas and Sweetcorn
If tinned, drain, and sprinkle over the base. If frozen, add the desired amount to a small pan of water, cook until soft, drain and then sprinkle over the base.

Mushrooms
Button mushrooms are the most widely available, although other sorts will do equally well. If necessary, remove the outer covering, slice, and lay upon the base.

Artichoke Hearts

These can be bought in jars or tins. The tough outer layer should be removed before you slice them and place them on the pizza.

Peppers

Red or yellow peppers are sweeter than green ones, and a half or a quarter of one of these can be washed, thinly sliced or cut into small pieces.

Spinach

Spinach is delicious upon pizzas and can be bought tinned, frozen or fresh. Fresh leaves are highly superior and are well worth the extra preparation. If the stems are thick then rib the leaves with your fingers or a sharp knife and cook in a very small amount of water until the spinach has turned dark green and shrunk to at least half its original size.

Onions

Remove the outer skin of a small onion or shallot, cut into small pieces, or thin slices, and lay them on the pizza.

Garlic

Garlic is very strong, and does not appeal to all tastes. Only one or two cloves should be used, and the finely-cut pieces scattered with a sparing hand over the pizza.

Capers

Capers are bought in jars (the smaller, French varieties are preferable) and a teaspoonful or two should be quite sufficient, as they also have a strong taste.

Tomatoes

Tomatoes are a classic topping, and can be used sliced or cut into pieces.

Cheese

Any hard cheese with good melting properties will do, and should be grated or sprinkled over the pizza. It is interesting to note that although often considered a staple ingredient, cheese need not be used at all.

Olives

Either black or green olives can be used, and are sold tinned, in jars, or fresh.

Oregano

A little oregano sprinkled over the finished pizza will give it an authentic Italian taste.

When you are happy with your toppings, put the pizza into the oven at gas 7 (220°C, 425°F), for twenty to thirty minutes. Take out when the base is golden brown or, if you are using a baking tray, when the crust comes away from the edge.

Chinese Cooking

Cooking with a Wok

The wok is one of the distinctive features of Chinese cookery. It was developed in a society where heat for cooking was a scarce commodity and it allows food to be cooked very efficiently. The heat is most intense in the bottom of the wok and less intense at the sides, so ingredients can be moved around (usually with big chopsticks) to ensure that everything is cooked at the same time. Slower-cooking ingredients can be added to the wok first and quicker-cooking ones added later.

Ingredients:

Vegetables: If you have a vegetable garden, a wok offers the best way of cooking your home produce.

If you are buying vegetables, make sure that they are as fresh as possible (organic vegetables from a local grower would be best). A typical selection could be **an onion, two or three carrots, a parsnip, broccoli, cabbage and some spinach,** but any vegetables will do.

Oil: Olive oil is not suitable because cooking with a wok involves high temperatures that cause olive oil to break down. You should therefore use **soya oil, peanut oil or corn oil** if possible.

Sesame Seeds, Cashew Nuts

Tamari (Wheat-free soya sauce)

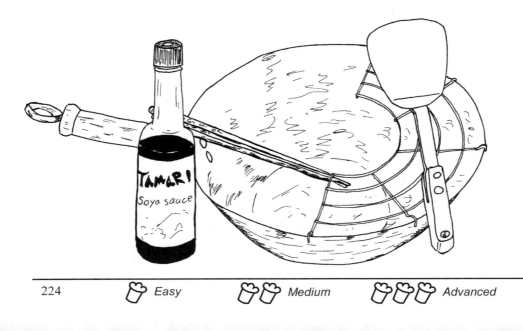

Easy   Medium   Advanced

Method:

1. Chop up all the vegetables. This is what takes the time. They are often cut into matchstick-thin strips but it doesn't really matter what shape you cut them into as long as the pieces are thin.

2. The secret of success with a wok is heat, so place the wok on a hot ring (turned up high) and add four tablespoons of oil. *An adult should be available to help with this.*

3. After about a minute, start to add the vegetables, stirring gently all the while. Begin with the onions, then the parsnips, broccoli, carrots, and cabbage, and finish with the spinach. Cover with a lid.

4. Remove the lid and stir the vegetables from time to time. Turn the heat down if they start to stick to the wok. Remove from heat when vegetables are cooked *(10 to 15 min)*.

5. Gently roast the sesame seeds and the cashew nuts in a dry frying pan until they are slightly brown. Sprinkle them over the cooked vegetables in the wok.

6. Sprinkle two or three teaspoonfuls of tamari over the vegetables and serve.

Tofu

Tofu is an important ingredient in Chinese cooking.

An interesting way in which to use it is to chop it into cubes about 1 cm (½″) square and add it to the wok with the vegetables.

The tofu takes up the taste of the vegetables and is delicious.

There are different ways of making tofu which result in it having different consistencies. If possible buy fresh tofu because it is firmer than the tofu which has a long sell-by date.

Mexican Cooking

Red Bean Chilli

Serves 6
Serve with brown rice *(page 218)*
and guacamole *(page 227)*.

Ingredients:
2 large carrots
1 medium onion
2 cloves garlic
45 ml (3 tbsp) olive oil
10 ml (2 tsp) cumin seeds
    (or 2 tsp ground cumin)
5 ml (1 tsp) *mild* paprika
2½ ml (½ tsp) chilli powder
    (or hot paprika)
2½ ml (½ tsp) powdered cinnamon
5 ml (1 tsp) dried thyme or oregano (or 2½ ml (½ tsp) of each)
500 ml (18 fluid ounces) passata (tomato purée)
1 x 425 gm (15 oz) tin chopped tomatoes
2 x 400 gm (14 oz) tins red kidney beans, washed and drained
15 ml (1 tbsp) lime or lemon juice

Method:
1. Wash and peel the carrots and chop into strips or thin rounds.
2. Peel and chop the onion and garlic into small pieces.
3. Gently heat the oil in a large flameproof casserole that has a lid, add the onion and garlic, cover and fry gently in the oil until the onion is softened but not brown (about 5 minutes).
4. Add the spices and herbs and cook for a couple of minutes.
4. Add the chopped carrots to the pan. Stir and cook for 2 minutes and then add the passata, tinned tomatoes and beans.
5. Simmer, with a lid on, for 20 minutes, or put it in the oven on gas 4 (180°C, 350°F) for 20 minutes.
6. Check that the carrots are cooked, and add the lime or lemon juice just before serving.

   Easy   *Medium*   *Advanced*

While the chilli is cooking, you can prepare the guacamole.

Guacamole
Serves 6

Ingredients:
2 medium tomatoes
1 medium onion
4 large ripe avocados
10 ml (2 tsp) ground coriander
10 ml (2 tsp) ground cumin
juice of 1 lime (or lemon)
1 ml (¼ tsp) salt

Method:
1. Chop the tomatoes and remove the seeds. Peel and chop the onion into small pieces.

2. Peel the avocados and mash in a medium-sized serving bowl.

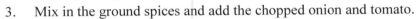

3. Mix in the ground spices and add the chopped onion and tomato.

4. Add the lime juice and the salt.

5. Mix well and serve.

Corn (maize) is the main cereal crop grown in Mexico and meals are traditionally served with corn taco shells or with corn tortillas. They are difficult to make oneself but are widely available in supermarkets.
Hot chilli sauce is the preferred condiment to accompany Mexican food.

Indian Cooking

This meal consists of a curry, a side dish of dahl (lentils), rice and chapatis. You will also find a variation of dahl that can be made if you have more time.

If you are in a hurry you can leave out the dahl and chapatis – the curry and rice is a balanced meal in itself.

Ground spices are available from supermarkets. The essential ones are: ground cumin, ground coriander, ground turmeric, mild paprika and chilli powder.

There are also many authentic Indian spice pastes ('curry pastes') available. They have a distinctive flavour, but they can easily overwhelm the vegetables if you use them too generously. It is better therefore to use traditional spices which can be varied according to the recipe. If you can't find a particular spice just make the meal without it.

Vegetable curry with chick peas

Serves 4

Ingredients:

1 large onion
1 clove garlic
30 ml (2 tbsp) oil
10 ml (2 tsp) ground coriander
5 ml (1 tsp) ground cumin
5 ml (1 tsp) ground turmeric

450 gm (1 lb) potatoes, chopped into small pieces
400 gm (12 oz) can chick peas, washed and drained
175 gm (6 oz) can tomatoes including juice
juice ½ lemon
5 ml (1 tsp) brown sugar
a little salt and pepper (optional)

Method:

1. Peel and chop the onion and garlic.
2. In a large, heavy saucepan or flameproof casserole, gently heat the oil and add the onion, the garlic and the spices.
3. Fry gently for a few minutes and add the potatoes and chick peas, stirring until they are all coated with the spice mixture.
4. Add the tomatoes and break them up with a wooden spoon.

Easy   Medium   Advanced

5. Add about 150 ml (¼ pint) water. Bring to the boil and then reduce the heat, cover and simmer for about 15 minutes until the potatoes are soft but not mushy.
6. Add the lemon juice, sugar and a little salt if necessary, according to taste.

Simple dahl (lentils)

Ingredients:

125 gm (4 oz) red lentils
1 onion
30 ml (2 tablespoons) oil
5 ml (1 tsp) ground cumin
2½ ml (½ tsp) turmeric

5 ml (1 tsp) garam masala (optional)
450 ml (¾ pint) water
1 vegetable stock cube
15 ml (1 tbsp) lemon juice
30 ml (2 tbsp) fresh coriander (optional)

Method:
1. Rinse and soak the lentils in cold water for about an hour before you need them. Strain off the soaking water before use (if you are in a hurry, do not soak, just put the lentils in a sieve and rinse well under cold running water).
2. Peel and chop the onion. Gently heat the oil in a medium-sized saucepan and add the onion, cumin, turmeric and garam masala. Cook gently for 5 minutes, until the onion is soft.
3. Carefully add the soaked lentils together with 450 ml (¾ pint) of water and the stock cube. Bring to the boil, reduce heat and simmer until the lentils are cooked (about 30 minutes).
4. Add the lemon juice and serve hot (with the chopped fresh coriander sprinkled on top).
5. This dahl may be thinned by adding a little more water.

Special dahl with cauliflower

Ingredients:

same ingredients as for simple dahl, plus
500 gm (1 lb) cauliflower
30 ml (2 tbsp) oil

⅓ block creamed coconut
15 ml (1 tbsp) curry paste
125 gm (4 oz) frozen peas

Method:
Make the simple dahl, then while the lentils are cooking:
1. Wash the cauliflower and break it up into small florets.
2. Heat the oil in a medium to large pan. Add the creamed coconut and the curry paste. Cook for 3 minutes and add the cauliflower florets. Stir until the cauliflower is coated with the mixture.
3. Add 150 ml (¼ pint) water, bring to the boil, turn the heat down, cover and simmer for about 5 minutes, until the cauliflower is just beginning to soften.
4. Add the frozen peas and cook for a further 5 minutes on a medium heat.
5. The cauliflower should now be cooked. Remove from the heat.
6. Add to the cooked dahl, stir well and cook together for a further 2 minutes.

See overleaf for chapati recipe

Chapatis

Makes 6 chapatis

Ingredients:

150 gm (5 oz) chapati flour (wholemeal flour mixed with a small amount of white flour can be used)

1 ml (¼ teaspoon) of salt

90 ml (6 tablespoons) water – approximately

Method:

1. Sift the flour with the salt into a large bowl.
2. Add water until a soft dough is formed.
3. Knead well with the fist for about 5 minutes.
4. Divide the dough into 6 balls.
5. Roll out each ball on a floured board, using a rolling pin, to form a thin pancake shape.
6. Set a thick iron pan or hot plate on a medium heat (a frying pan can also be used).
7. Cook the chapatis one at a time in the pan. Turn them over with a spatula when the edges start to curl or until smoke comes from underneath. Cook both sides. You may need help with this process of cooking the chapatis. It can work quite well if one person rolls the chapatis while the other person cooks them.
8. Ideally, the chapati puffs up like a ball as it cooks and then collapses. (This can be encouraged by briefly holding the cooked chapati over a gas flame, but this is not easy and should *only* be done with the help of an adult).
9. Spread a little margarine or butter on one side of each freshly-cooked chapati, and stack them, buttered sides together, in a warm oven until they are all cooked.

Baking

The following pages contain recipes for cakes and biscuits. In some ways, they are easier to follow than recipes that involve chopping up vegetables. They might provide a good starting point for a child who wants to do something on their own – with only the minimum of help from their parent.

SCONES

Ingredients:

225 gm (½ lb) plain, organic, wholemeal flour (if you want lighter scones use a mixture of wholemeal and white flour)

5 ml (1 tsp) of baking powder

1 ml (¼ tsp) of salt

50 gm (2 oz) sugar

50 gm (2 oz) butter or margarine

25-50 gm (1-2 oz) washed and drained sultanas or raisins (optional)

150 ml (¼ pint) milk or water

Method:

1. Sieve together the flour and baking powder. Add the salt and sugar.
2. Add the butter or margarine. Cut it into small pieces and rub it into the mixture using the tips of your fingers. (Ideally you shouldn't get any of the mixture on the palms of your hands.)
3. Add the raisins or sultanas.
4. Mix to a soft dough by adding the liquid gradually. A soft dough is a dough that is as soft as it can be without being sticky. If your dough *is* sticky, add some more flour.
5. Knead the dough lightly, to ensure that it has a uniform consistency, and roll it out to a thickness of ½ inch (1 cm).
6. Turn on the oven – gas 7 (220°C, 425°F).
7. Cut into rounds with a cutter 2-2½ inch (5 cm) in diameter. Place the rounds on a lightly greased baking tray.
8. Bake for 10-15 minutes or until they are golden brown underneath. Put the cooked scones on a wire tray to cool.

Scones are best eaten fresh and are delicious with butter, jam or whipped cream.

Birthday cake

This is a very simple cake recipe which even those with little baking experience should be able to make. Once you have mastered the basic instructions try adding different ingredients. For example, if you add 10-15 ml (2-3 tsp) of cocoa powder at Stage 4 you will have a chocolate cake; 60 gm (2 oz) of chopped walnuts added at Stage 5 will make a walnut cake.

Ingredients:
125 gm (4 oz) margarine
125 gm (4 oz) sugar
2 eggs
175 gm (6 oz) flour
5 ml (1 tsp) baking powder

Method:

1. Beat together the margarine and the sugar in a large bowl until the mixture is thick and creamy.
2. Crack the eggs into a cup, beat well and add slowly to the mix.
3. Sieve the flour and baking powder into the mixture.
4. Stir well with a wooden spoon until all the ingredients are thoroughly mixed together and turn into a small, lined, 17 cm (7″) diameter cake tin.

Tip 1: Line the base of the tin with greaseproof paper – it will make it easier to remove the cake when it is cooked. Stand the empty tin on a piece of greaseproof paper, draw round it and then cut out the circle 2½ cm (1″) bigger than what you have drawn. Lightly grease the inside of the tin. Place the greaseproof paper in the tin and flatten it into shape, pressing the extra paper up around the sides of the tin. Lightly grease the inside of the greaseproof paper.

Tip 2: How do you tell when the cake is cooked? : Don't open the oven door during the first 20 minutes or the cake may sink. After this time, you can open the oven door, slightly withdraw the shelf on which the cake is sitting, and stick a thin knife or cake skewer into the top. If it comes out clean i.e. with no sticky cake attached, then the cake is cooked. If there is cake mixture on the knife, gently push the shelf back inside the oven, close the door and wait another 7 – 10 minutes. N.B. Always use thick oven gloves before withdrawing the shelf.

    Easy   *Medium*   *Advanced*

5. Put it an oven preheated to gas 6 (200°C, 400°F).
6. Cook for about 25 – 30 minutes.
7. Remove the cake from the oven and place on a wire rack to cool.
8. When the cake has cooled, sprinkle sifted icing sugar over the top.

When the cake is being made for a special occasion, mix a teaspoon of fresh lemon juice or fresh orange juice with icing sugar to make a stiff mix, spread it over the top of the cake and decorate it with a few fresh flowers – buttercups and daisies look very pretty.

Lemon Oat Biscuits

Makes 20 – 25 biscuits
Ingredients:
125 gm (4 oz) rolled oats
50 gm (2 oz) flour
50 gm (2 oz) sugar
1 ml (¼ tsp) salt (or less)
2½ ml (½ tsp) baking powder
50 gm (2 oz) butter or margarine
30 ml (2 tablespoons) (approx.) fresh lemon juice

Method:

1. Mix together the oats, sieved flour, sugar, salt and baking powder in a large bowl.

2. Add the butter or margarine and cut into small pieces.

3. With the fingertips, rub the margarine into the other ingredients until the mixture looks and feels like fine breadcrumbs.

4. Gradually add the lemon juice and, with clean hands, mix to a dry paste. Add 5-10 ml (1-2 teaspoons) of water if the mixture is too dry.

5. Roll out to a thickness of ½ cm (¼"), cut into rounds with a 5 cm (2″) biscuit cutter, place on a greased baking tray and bake for 15 minutes in the oven – gas mark 4 (177°C, 350°F).

Tip: Rolling out a dry mixture can be difficult. Try placing it between 2 sheets of greaseproof paper and then rolling it out until it is the required thickness.

6. Remove carefully from the baking tray – the biscuits might be crumbly because there is no egg in the mixture – and lay on a wire rack to cool.

RASPBERRY BUNS

Makes 10 – 15 buns

Ingredients:
250 gm (8 oz) wholemeal
   flour
5 ml (1 tsp) baking powder
75 gm (3 oz) margarine
75 gm (3 oz) sugar
A little finely grated lemon rind
1 free-range egg (optional)
A little milk or water
Raspberry (or other) jam

Method:

1. Sieve flour and baking powder together into a bowl.

2. Coarsely chop the margarine and, with the fingertips, rub it into the flour until the mixture is the consistency of fine breadcrumbs.

3. Add the sugar and lemon rind.

4. Beat the egg and add it to the mixture (leaving a tiny amount of egg to be used for brushing over the buns before they go in the oven). Stir well. Add sufficient milk or water to form a soft dough.

5. Turn out onto a floured board or piece of greaseproof paper and form into a long roll (see picture). Slice into 10 – 15 pieces.

6. Turn each piece on its side on a greased baking tray and make a well in the centre of each with the end of the handle of a wooden spoon.

7. Brush milk or the remaining egg over the top of each one.

8. Fill each well with a small amount of raspberry jam – not too much or the jam will ooze out in cooking and burn on the tray.

9. Sprinkle all the tops lightly with caster sugar.

10. Bake for 20 minutes in an oven gas 6 (200°C or 400°F).

11. Cool on a wire rack.

Preferably use organic or untreated lemons. Wash their skins with water and dry, before grating.

    *Easy*   *Medium*   *Advanced*

Apricot and Almond Tart

Ingredients:
150 gm (5 oz) margarine
125 gm (4 oz) brown sugar
finely grated rind and juice of 1 lemon
2½ ml (½ teaspoon) almond essence
1 egg yolk (optional)
175 gm (6 oz) wholemeal flour
5 ml (1 teaspoon) of ground cinnamon
50 gm (2 oz) ground almonds
5 - 7 large dessertspoonfuls of apricot jam

Method:

1. In a large bowl mix together the margarine and the sugar until the mixture is smooth and creamy.
2. Grate in the lemon rind, cut the lemon in half and squeeze in its juice.
3. Add the almond essence and the egg yolk. (The flan is just as nice without these 2 ingredients. The egg yolk is added mainly for colour and not for binding.)

> *Tip:* When grating a lemon, use the finest holes on the grater and grate off only the thin yellow skin on the lemon's surface (called the zest). The white layer underneath, called the pith, is very bitter.

4. Add the flour and the cinnamon, sieved together.
5. Finely grind the almonds and add to the mix.
6. Mix it all together with your hands and knead gently. If the mixture is too moist, add some flour. You can put the covered bowl and mixture into the fridge for half an hour, to make it firmer, but if you are in a hurry just add a little more flour.
7. Divide the dough into two pieces. One piece should be twice the size of the other piece.
8. Press the larger piece into a lightly-greased, flat, fluted dish – about 23 cm (9″) wide. Alternatively you can halve it and put it into 2 separate, smaller flan tins. This way the flans will be smaller and will cook quicker.
9. Spread with apricot jam.
10. Divide the remaining piece of dough into 5 balls and, with floured hands, roll each ball out until you have 5 long, thin strips. Divide each strip into two and lay the ten strips across the flan to create a lattice shape (see picture). Press down the ends.
11. Bake for 25 – 35 minutes (or 20 minutes if you have made 2 smaller flans) in an oven gas 3 (160°C, 325°F) until the jam has started to bubble and the pastry is golden brown.
12. Remove from the oven. Remember that jam keeps its heat longer than pastry, so let it cool for about 20 minutes before cutting it up and serving.

ALMOND BISCUITS

Makes about 30

Ingredients:
175 gm (6 oz) flour
5 ml (1 tsp) baking powder
pinch salt
75 gm (3 oz) caster
    sugar
50 gm (2 oz) ground
    almonds
150 gm (5 oz) margarine
1 ml (¼ tsp) almond
    essence
15 blanched almonds

Method:

1. Sieve the flour and baking powder into a mixing bowl.

2. Add the salt, sugar and ground almonds. Mix thoroughly.

3. Add the margarine, chop it up and rub it into the flour using the fingertips until the mixture looks and feels like fine breadcrumbs.

4. Add the almond essence and knead well with your hands, adding a little more flour if the mixture is too moist.

5. Roll out to a thickness of about ½ cm (¼″), cut into rounds with a scone cutter. Place half a blanched almond on each.

Instead of buying blanched almonds, you can blanch your own. Bring a small pan of water to the boil. Turn off the heat and put the almonds in the hot water. Allow them to soak for five to ten minutes, drain and plunge into cold water for one minute. Carefully slip the skin from each nut and prise it in half.

6. Place on lightly greased baking trays and bake in a moderate oven, gas 3-4 (160-180°C, 325-350°F), for about 15 minutes. Remove from the oven.

7. They will be quite crumbly when hot so let them rest for a moment on the tray before carefully transferring them to a wire rack to cool.

Easy   Medium   Advanced

Crafts

RED PAINT BLU

Introduction

In the same way that gardening gives a child a connection with the world of nature, and cooking enables a child to make sensible decisions about their diet, crafts help children to make sense of all the man-made things that surround them in their everyday lives.

These things can be a source of great distress and confusion for a child. Individual children are subjected to a considerable amount of advertising and peer pressure that tells them that they are somehow defined by the things that they own, and that happiness will come from having more toys, more clothes, and more of everything in general.

Few children know how to cope with this materialistic philosophy and they need to be given practical ways to deal with it. By doing crafts they learn how to transform simple materials into things that are beautiful and useful to them in their daily lives. This gives them a clearer understanding of the true value of everything and helps them to be able to discriminate between those items that they do like and those that they are simply told to like.

Which Crafts?

It is important that you do not attempt craft projects that are too difficult for your child to complete.

This means that you must carefully select projects that enable them to build up their skills step by step. We have included, in the following section, instructions for projects that involve sewing, knitting, embroidery, papier mâché and making things with paper, all of which should provide a good introduction to the art of craft.

We have not covered woodworking because it requires specialist tools and cannot easily be done indoors (the crafts that we have included can be done in the living room or round the kitchen table and are particularly suitable for winter evenings or rainy days).

Some ideas for woodworking are mentioned elsewhere: making a bird table *(page 197)*; making wooden animals *(page 11)*; and making stilts *(page 14).*

Boys and Girls

The idea that crafts are gender specific is erroneous: girls enjoy woodwork and boys enjoy knitting and sewing. Individual children often do have personal preferences for different crafts and, if possible, they should be encouraged to pursue these, even if it does mean going against commonly-held ideas about what boys should be doing and what girls should be doing.

The important thing is that each child enjoys the craft work that they do and is proud of the items that they make.

Materials

In order to be successful in encouraging children to do crafts, you have to make sure that the very best materials are available to them. These could include:

- Embroidery silks
- Good, sharp scissors – a collection of different sizes (including left-handed ones if necessary)
- Needles, needle-threaders and thimbles
- A selection of different-coloured pieces of felt
- Knitting needles in a range of sizes
- Knitting wool
- A good selection of different papers and sheets of card in different colours, textures and thicknesses
- Craft knife with replaceable blades
- A selection of different glues. Stick glues (such as Pritt) can be used by children of almost any age. Solvent-based glues have to be treated with care.
- A workbox to keep everything in

You do not have to buy all these things at once, but when you do buy something for a particular project make sure that it is of good quality and keep anything that you have left over for use at a later date: it is much easier to do crafts when you have a well-stocked box of materials upon which to draw.

Sometimes children's crafts are portrayed as an area in which second-best will do: in fact craft books for children often suggest that children make things from items retrieved from the rubbish bin, such as packaging materials, egg cartons, washing-up bottles etc. Occasionally, these items might be ideal for a particular purpose, in which case they should of course be used, but to suggest to children that these things should make up the bulk of their craft materials gives them completely the wrong message.

By buying a child the best materials you are demonstrating that you consider the activity worthwhile and your child's time to be precious. You are also giving them a chance to make something that is beautiful – which cannot be done with plastic bottles.

Good materials are not cheap but they are considerably less expensive than the things against which they are competing for your child's time and attention, such as toys and computer games, and can safely be considered a sound investment.

Note: If you are not experienced at doing crafts it is important that you try making each of the items yourself, on your own, before you make them with your child.
Children find it very dispiriting when their craft project goes wrong and the person who should be helping them cannot tell them what to do.

Seasons table

One of the easiest ways of introducing crafts to a child is to have a seasons table. This is simply a small area of the living room or kitchen (a window sill, a table, a work surface, a tray or the top of a cupboard) on which you display items that you find on your walks and also things that you make.

The secret of a successful seasons table is to keep it looking interesting – add new things regularly and remove things as they get old. If possible, drape a backdrop of coloured material behind.

Here are some ideas:

- **Early spring**: backdrop of brown, earth colours
  branches with catkins (or with berries left from the winter);
  bulbs in a pot

- **Late spring:** yellow or white backdrop
  branches with spring blossom; spring flowers; catkins

- **Summer:** a choice of many colours for the backdrop
  summer flowers; bark boats with leaf sails

- **Autumn:** orange/red/yellow colours for the backdrop
  branches with berries; chestnuts; pumpkins; gourds; teasels;
  conker web *(see page 245)*; hazelnuts; fir cones

- **Winter:** white backdrop
  fir cones, branches with berries

Items you may like to use at one time or another during the year could include:

- Moss
- Lichen
- Large piece of interestingly-shaped wood
- Old bird's nest
- Sheep's wool
- Seasonal grasses
- Crystals
- Pebbles
- Unusual stones
- Feathers....

Gnome

Little gnomes can be made from scraps of felt and tiny amounts of sheep's wool (this can be bought in small quantities from craft shops). They can decorate the seasons table and can be used to bring presents on birthdays and special occasions.

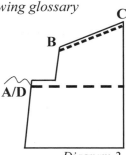

You will need:

- 10 cm x 7 cm (4″ x 3″)
-     piece of felt
- Sheep's wool (size of
-     a cotton wool ball)
- Needle and thread
- Tracing paper or greaseproof paper
- Scissors
- Pencil

Diagram 1

Instructions:

1. Trace *Diagram 1*, cut out the traced template and pin it onto the felt.

2. Cut round this template.

3. Remove template and pins.

4. Make a large knot in your thread and sew a row of running stitches from D to A *(see sewing glossary page 309),* leaving a length of thread at the end *(Diagram 1).*

5. Thread the needle with another length of cotton. Fold the felt in half, so that D meets A and B meets B and backstitch together, along line BC. This forms the top of the gnome's hood *(Diagram 2).*

Diagram 2

6. Turn the felt inside out, so that the row of stitches you have just sewn is on the inside, and stuff in the sheep's wool.

7. Pull up the running thread tightly, at A.

8. Rethread your needle with this thread, and join point A to point D with a small stitch. Fasten off tightly, cut the thread and you have a tiny gnome. (To make the gnome stand up properly, cut level any protruding wool.)

Snowflakes

A child can make paper snowflakes as soon as they are able to use scissors.

They can be hung on threads or stuck to the window at Christmas time, and can also be used to make Christmas cards *(see page 243)*.

You will need:

- Medium-thickness (80 gm) white paper
- Small, sharp, pointed scissors
- A drawing compass or an upturned mug

Instructions:

1. Set your compass at about 4 cm (1½″) and draw a circle on the paper. If you don't have a compass you can draw round an upturned mug.

2. Cut out the circle *(Diagram 1)*.

3. Fold as shown in *Diagrams 1, 2, 3 and 4*.

4. Cut into a diamond shape *(Diagram 5)*.

5. Carefully cutting through all the thicknesses, snip away small wedges of paper *(Diagram 6)*, taking care always to have some folded paper showing at the edges – or you will end up with 8 separate pieces of paper.

6. Now unfold the diamond shape and you have a snowflake *(Diagram 7)*. By snipping in different places you can create endless variations.

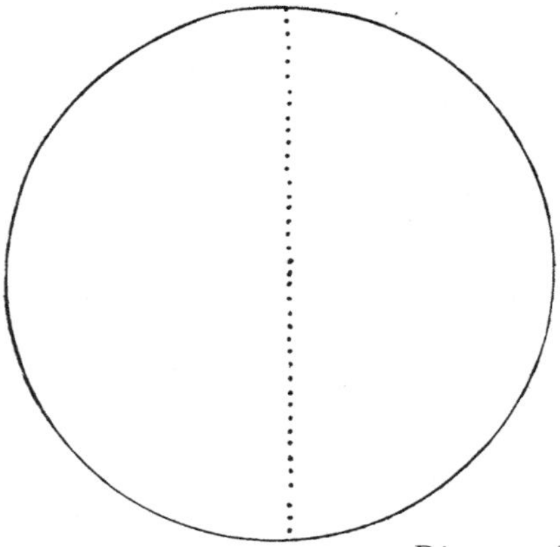

You can create further variations by using different types of paper; drawing larger and smaller circles and by cutting off less at step 4 so that you produce a kite shape instead of a diamond shape.

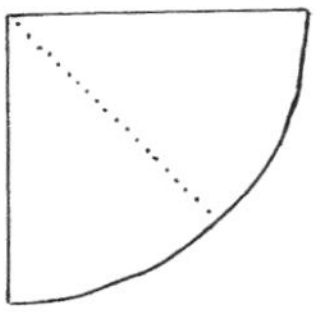

Diagram 1

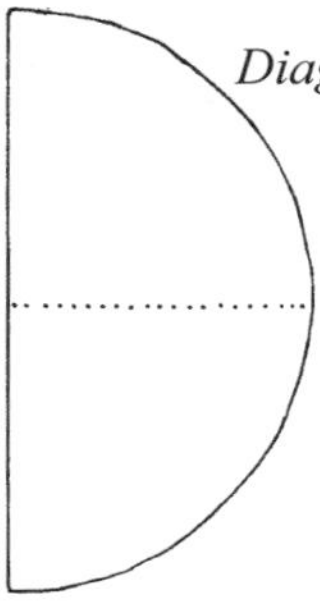

Diagram 2

Diagram 3   *Diagram 4*

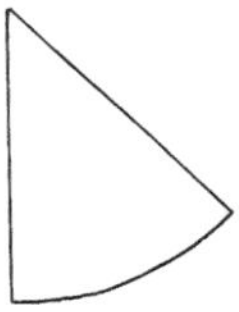

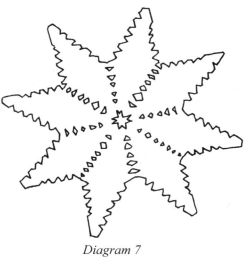

Diagram 7

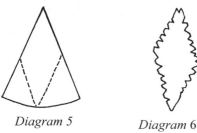

Diagram 5   *Diagram 6*

𝄄 Easy   𝄄𝄄 Medium   𝄄𝄄𝄄 Advanced

GREETINGS CARDS

Making Christmas and birthday cards for friends and relatives provides a child with an opportunity to demonstrate their artistic skills in a practical way.

It simply involves your child drawing a picture on the front of a piece of folded card, and you writing a greeting inside.

Providing that they have good quality crayons and card, or thick drawing paper, this can be remarkably effective and will enable your child to produce cards that are treasured for years by their recipients.

You can buy individual sheets of 180 gm white paper – 50 x 65 cm (20" x 26") from good art shops, but it is more economical to buy a pack containing 50 sheets.

It is essential to use good quality paper for this sort of work, and it is much easier if you always have a ready supply to hand.

SNOWFLAKE CHRISTMAS CARD

You will need:

- Heavy-quality coloured paper (180 gm) or similar weight coloured card (you can use dark green or cherry red)
- Pritt or paper glue
- A gold, or silver, steel point, metallic ink pen
- Several paper snowflakes *(see page 242)*

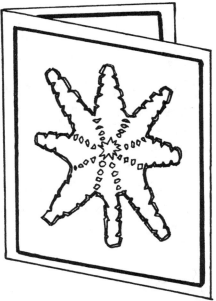

Instructions:

1. Cut the paper or card into 21 cm x 12 cm (8½"x 5") pieces. Fold each one in half.

2. Stick a snowflake onto the front of the card.

3. Draw a border with a gold or silver pen round the front and inside of the card.

4. If you are very careful you could also outline the snowflake using one of the pens, but keeping the card as simple as possible and not overdoing the use of the gold and silver pens gives the best results.

Wrapping Paper

It is surprisingly easy to make striking and effective wrapping paper from simple materials such as brown paper, or white lining paper, and potato prints.

Potato Prints

You will need:

- A few potatoes of different sizes
- Small amounts of water-based or acrylic paint in several different colours
- A few old saucers or plates
- A sharp knife
- Several large sheets of brown wrapping paper or white lining paper

Instructions:

1. Cut a clean potato in half.

2. With a pencil or fine pointed crayon, draw a design onto one of the cut halves.

3. Using the knife, cut away the potato around the design to a depth of about ½ cm (¼″).

4. Dip the cut half into one of the saucers of paint. Wipe off excess paint on the rim of the saucer.

5. Press it repeatedly in several places on a sheet of paper.

6. When the first prints are dry you can either wash and dry the potato and use it for another colour, or make another shape and print an alternating or overlapping design on the paper.

Tips:
When working with young children, it may be better if an adult does the work that involves using a knife.
Don't make your designs too complicated. Simple designs, such as those shown, are easier to cut out and are more effective.

Conker Web

This makes an attractive decoration to hang from the ceiling or in the window.

You will need:

- One medium to large conker
- 8 wooden cocktail sticks, each with one sharp end cut off
- Several 1½ m (5 ft) lengths of brightly-coloured wool
- A bradawl or hand drill

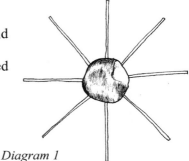

Instructions:

1. Using the bradawl or hand drill make 8 small holes in a circle around the conker.

Diagram 1

> *Note: Children under the age of about seven years old may need help in making these holes.*

2. Insert the pointed end of a cocktail stick into each hole *(Diagram 1)*.

3. Using one of your pieces of wool, start to wrap it carefully around each cocktail stick in turn *(Diagram 2)*.

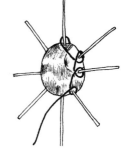

4. As you go round the conker keep the woven threads pushed down towards the body of the conker, so that the weaving has no gaps in it.

Diagram 2

5. Continue in this way until you reach the end of your first piece of wool.

6. Fasten another length of different-coloured wool to this end with a small knot. Keep this knot at the back of your work.

7. Continue weaving in this way, joining in a new length of coloured wool when an old one has run out, until you are about ½ cm (¼″) from the ends of the cocktail sticks *(Diagram 3)*.

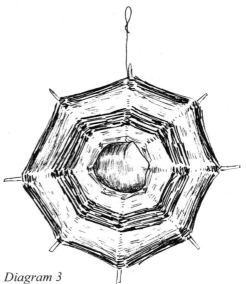

8. Fasten off the wool by making a small knot round the cocktail stick, leaving a length of about 20 cm (8″) with which to hang it up.

Diagram 3

Pompom

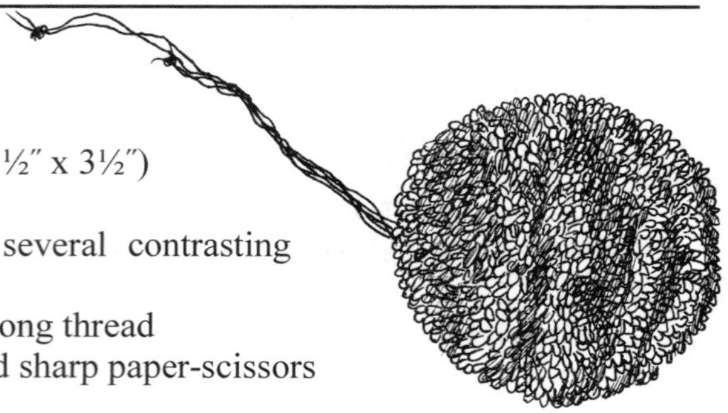

You will need:

- 2 pieces of card 8½ cm x 8½ cm (3½″ x 3½″)
- A drawing compass
- 15 gm (½ oz) wool in one or several contrasting colours
- 1 m (3 ft) button thread or other strong thread
- A large-eyed blunt wool needle and sharp paper-scissors

Instructions:

1. Using a compass draw 2 circles of 4 cm (1½″) radius on the cards.
2. Using the same central point, draw another circle of 1½ cm (¾″) radius within the larger circle (*Diagram 1*).
3. Cut out both discs and also cut out the inner circles. Place one disc on top of the other.

Diagram 1

4. Cut the wool into 2 metre (6 ft) lengths, thread the wool needle with one of them and begin to wind it round the 2 discs (*Diagram 2*), keeping the winding as even as possible. You can use your fingers if a needle is not available.
5. Continue with successive lengths, tucking in the ends, as you work, under the closely-wound wool, until you have used it all. Save a 1 metre length of wool for hanging.

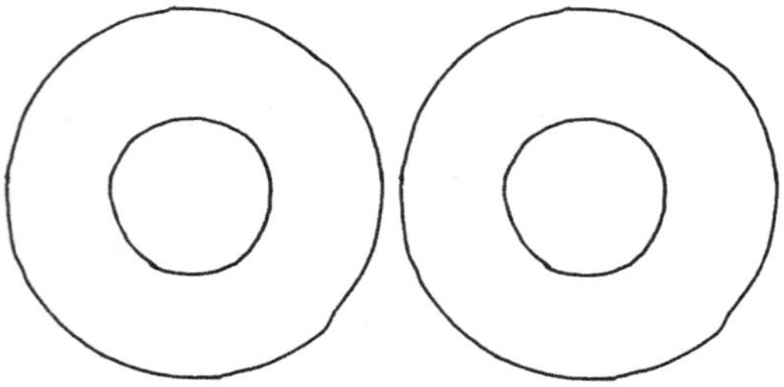

Depending on when you change colour, you can make your pompom striped, coloured in quarters or even half one colour and half another. You can make pompoms in virtually any size and using any type of wool. Adjust the size of the circles, but keep roughly the same ratio of outer circle to inner circle i.e. 2:1

Diagram 2

6. Snip round the perimeter of the ball, through all the thicknesses of wool, in between the 2 cardboard discs (*Diagram 3*).
7. Pass the length of button thread between the now exposed edges of the cardboard discs and fasten the thread round the central core of the pompom with a tight double knot.

Diagram 3

8. Next fasten the 1 metre length of wool round this central core. This can be used for hanging up the pompom.
9. Carefully snip away, then remove, both cardboard discs, taking care not to cut the thread.
10. The pompom will now fall into a ball shape. Fasten the ends of the length of wool so that it makes a loop.

⚊ *Easy*   ⚊ ⚊ *Medium*   ⚊ ⚊ ⚊ *Advanced*

JACK-O'-LANTERN

You will need:

- 1 pumpkin – any size, but rounder ones are easier to work with

- A sharp knife

- A pencil

- A large spoon

Instructions:

1. With a pencil, draw a zigzag line around the upper third of the pumpkin.

2. Using a sharp knife cut through the pumpkin along this line, and continue until you have cut all the way round. You will have to push your knife in quite deeply to cut through the fibres that hold the pumpkin together.

3. Carefully ease off the top. This will act as the lid. If your pumpkin has a stalk, don't use this to help prise off the lid because it might snap. (If this should happen you can glue it on again later.)

4. Scoop out the seeds and fibres from the inside and discard.

5. Following your own design or copying from the picture above, draw eyes, nose and mouth on the pumpkin, and then cut out the shapes with the knife. (This sounds easy but it does require a little care and patience to get the pieces to come away cleanly.)

6. Place a night light inside and your Jack-o'-Lantern is complete.

Note 1. Do not put the lid on while the candle is lit, or the inside of the lid will burn.
Note 2. You may have to widen the eyes, nose and mouth from the inside to allow more light through.
*Note 3. If you stand the Jack-o'-Lantern in a cool place it will keep for almost a week, but it **will** go mouldy very quickly after about 3 days, if kept indoors.*

Bookmark

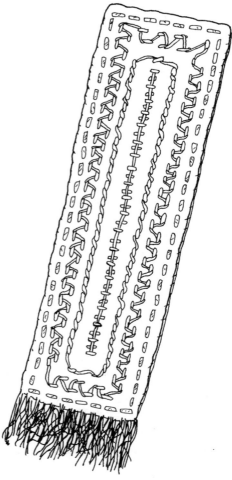

This bookmark can be attempted by quite young children – aged 5 and upwards. You will need to show them the different steps and stitches.

You will need:

- A piece of binca (24 holes per 10 cm) (approx.) cut to 24 cm long and 10 cm wide (9½"x 4")
- A variety of coloured embroidery threads
- Large-eyed, blunt needle – it should pass easily through the holes
- A 20 cm x 10 cm (10" x 4") piece of patterned fabric, preferably cotton, for backing
- White cotton thread
- Sharp, small-eyed embroidery needle
- Pins, scissors

Binca is a stiffened, open-weave cotton fabric that is available from craft shops and some fabric shops.

Instructions:

1. Cut a piece of binca 24 cm long and 10 cm wide (9½"x 4").

2. Turn under a 1 cm (½") edge round 3 sides, leaving one of the short sides raw.

3. Measure 5 cm (2") up from the raw edge and, using the larger needle and doubled white cotton thread, sew a row of backstitch from side to side *(see sewing glossary page 309)*. The 5 cm (2") below this line will later be frayed to make a fringed end for the bookmark.

4. Select 3 or 4 colours that you want to use and thread your larger needle with a 1m (1 yd) length of one of the colours.

5. Using a running stitch **(A)** and starting at the outer edge – where you will initially be sewing through 2 thicknesses – sew round the perimeter of the fabric, sewing *within* the backstitched line when you come to it. Finish off on the reverse side of the bookmark, weaving through the back of the stitches you have just sewn, several times, so that the thread is secure and won't come undone.

🏃 *Easy* 🏃🏃 *Medium* 🏃🏃🏃 *Advanced*

6. If you do 'offset running stitches' on two consecutive rows **(B)** you can then weave another coloured thread through them **(C)**. Half cross stitch **(D)** also works well, whereas full cross stitch *(see page 262)* can be a more difficult concept for a small child. Both **E** and **F** are easy stitches that produce attractive results.

7. When all the rows of stitches have been sewn, cut out a piece of material 20 cm x 10 cm (8″ x 4″). Fold under and pin a small hem all the way round so that it is the same size as the bookmark (not including the fringe). Place the wrong sides together then, using the smaller needle, stitch the lining to the binca all the way round the edge, using over-and-over stitches *(see sewing glossary page 309)*.

> *Note: When you reach the row of cotton backstitches that you sewed at the beginning (Point 3), switch from over-and-over stitch to backstitch.*

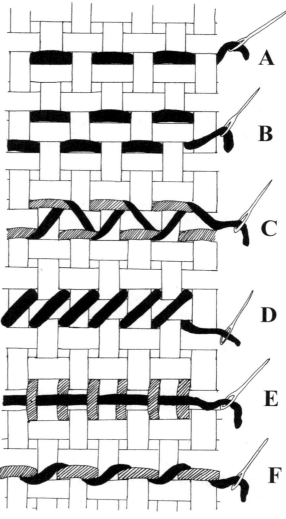

8. To make the fringe, carefully pull away one row at a time of the crossways binca threads using the large needle and starting at the raw edge. Carry on in this way until you reach the horizontal row of cotton backstitches.

9. Lay a damp cloth on top of the bookmark and press both sides with an iron, set on medium heat.

> *Always make sure your hands are clean before and during sewing: the natural oils in them cause the thread and fabric to become soiled.*

Weaving on a card

Card weaving is interesting because you are weaving the front and back of the item at the same time. You can experiment with different-coloured wools – lengths of fine wool in the colours of the rainbow, or pastel shades, give a beautiful effect.

You can also vary the size, using the full length of the card to make a pencil case or half the length to make a purse.

Pencil Case

You will need:

- A piece of *extremely* thick, rigid card 12 cm x 27 cm (4½" x 10½")
- 10 m (30 ft) of strong navy wool or thick cotton (it must not break)
- Approx. ten 2½ m (8 ft) lengths of different coloured wool
- A large darning or wool needle (optional)
- Three 10 cm (3½") lengths of embroidery thread
- A large button
- Pencil, scissors

Instructions:

1. Draw 14 small notches at each end of the card, making sure that they line up with each other. Cut them out *(see picture)*.

2. Draw a line across one end of the card, about 6 cm (2¼") from the bottom.

3. Leaving a 13 cm (5") end, wind the strong wool or cotton over and over the card until you have 14 threads on each side, connecting all the 28 notches. This is the 'warp' thread.

4. Fasten both the starting and finishing ends around the nearest warp thread with a tight knot.

5. Starting at the very top of the end of the card that is furthest away from the pencil line, weave a length of wool over and under alternate warp threads, going round and round from the front to the back of the card *(see picture)*. Make sure that the woven strands are close together.

Tip You can either weave with your fingers or with the help of a darning needle threaded with the wool.

     Easy   Medium   Advanced

6. When the length of wool begins to run out continue weaving with it to the edge of the card and then fasten it to a new length of wool with a small knot, leaving a 20 cm (8″) end on both threads. These will be sewn in when you have finished.

7. When you reach the pencil line, start to weave on one side only. This will eventually be the flap of the pencil case.

> *Tip: When weaving the flap don't pull the wool too tightly at the sides because it will cause distortion.*

8. Finish weaving about 1 cm (½″) below the top of the card. Make a loop with your wool round the last warp thread, pass the weaving wool through it and pull tight. Sew this end in later.

9. Turn the card over and cut the warp threads halfway between the top of the card and the line of weaving.

10. Double knot these warp threads together – each one with its neighbouring thread – keeping close to the weaving. Do this to the threads on the top of the flap and also to the threads at the top of the opening. Pull the card out of the weaving.

11. Sew in the knotted warp threads and also the ends of the wool by weaving them around the top or up the sides of the work. It is easier if you put your hand inside the case when you are doing this.

12. Turn the weaving right side out. Thread a wool needle with a 1 m (3 ft) length of coloured wool and sew a row of blanket stitch along the bottom of the pencil case *(see sewing glossary page 309).*

13. Sew another row of blanket stitch around the opening at the top of the pencil case *(see picture).*

14. Plait the three lengths of embroidery thread together.

15. Make a loop by fastening the ends of the plait onto the underside of the flap with a few small stitches.

16. Finally sew on the button, and the pencil case is finished.

Felt Crown

To fit a head of 54 cm (21″) or smaller.

This adjustable felt crown can be decorated or left plain. It is simple to make and is much more hardwearing than a paper version.

You will need:
- 2 long strips of felt 47 cm x 10 cm (18½″ x 4″) in contrasting colours
- 1 short strip of felt 18 cm x 8 cm (5½″ x 3¼″)
- Piece of elastic 16 cm x 3 cm (5½″ x 1¼″)
- Tracing paper (or greaseproof paper)
- A piece of cardboard (maybe the back of a cereal packet)
- Needle and sewing thread in colours that match the felt
- Scraps of glittery braid, paste jewels etc.
- Non-toxic fabric glue
- A piece of white chalk or tailor's chalk
- Scissors
- Soft pencil for tracing
- Pins

Instructions:

1. The template for this crown is on *page 312* – it is a template for *half* the crown. Trace the template using tracing, or greaseproof paper and transfer the shape onto a piece of cardboard.

2. Cut it out.

3. Place this cardboard template on one of the long pieces of felt and draw round it with white chalk or tailor's chalk. When you reach the line CD, flip the template over to make one continuous piece 42 cm (17″) long and draw round the template again. You will then have one complete side of a crown, with 7 points.

4. Cut out and repeat on the other long piece of felt.

⅄ Easy   ⅄⅄ Medium   ⅄⅄⅄ Advanced

5. Fold the third, shortest, piece of felt in half lengthways. Slip the piece of elastic inside, pin together the two long sides of felt, then sew them together using over-and-over stitch *(see sewing glossary page 309)*. Remove the pins *(Diagram 1)*.

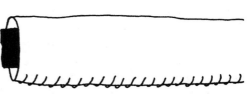

Diagram 1

6. Sew a row of backstitch *(see sewing glossary page 309)* along one of the ends, making sure that you sew through both layers of felt and the elastic between them *(Diagram 2)*.

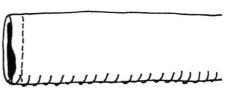

Diagram 2

7. Bunch up the felt at the other, open, end until it is the same length as the elastic (16 cm). Sew a row of backstitch along this end. This piece will go at the back of the head.

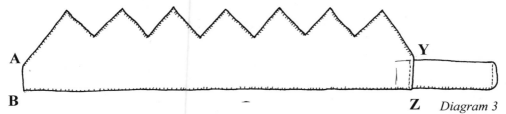

Diagram 3

8. Place the 2 pieces of felt crown together and pin and sew them together using small over-and-over stitches *(Diagram 3)*. Leave both ends of the crown open (AB and YZ). The elastic will go here.

9. Place one end of the felt-covered elastic in one of the open sides (AB or YZ) and backstitch through all 5 thicknesses *(Diagram 3)*.

10. Measure the crown on the child's head, and according to the size, push the other end of the felt-covered elastic into the open end of the crown (i.e. if you want the crown smaller, push the elastic in a long way; if you want it larger, don't push it in quite so far). Backstitch together the open sides, once again through all five thicknesses.

11. As the child's head grows you can adjust the crown's size by unpicking the stitches, letting out a little of the elastic and sewing it up again.

12. You can decorate one or both sides of the crown with sewn-on felt shapes, beads or glittery braid.

Knitting

Knitting is rapidly becoming a forgotten skill. Whereas at one time most women and many men (knitting is reputed to have been invented by fishermen and in some communities remained an exclusively male preserve) could knit with ease, it is now seen as a slightly cranky activity. This is a pity because, above everything else, knitting is very enjoyable. One can derive a great deal of satisfaction from knitting a garment, even though one knows that a similar item can be bought from a shop for little extra expense.

Children in particular like to knit. The fact that they can actually create a proper item out of a length of wool is almost a magical experience for them.

Most children can learn to knit fairly quickly at about 6 years old. Start with something small and simple, such as a scarf for a teddy. As with all craft projects it is important to finish each item that you begin, otherwise discouragement soon sets in. Few children will fail to finish a little scarf, which should only take a few hours' work in total.

They can then progress onto making a scarf for themselves and a doll's jumper. By then they will have mastered the essentials of knitting and can decide for themselves what they want to try next – they could knit a jumper or even experiment with four-needle knitting and make some socks.

The following instructions have been made as clear as possible, and have been successfully tested by some very inexperienced knitters, but the easiest way to learn how to knit is for someone to show you, and if you have any difficulty following them it may be a good idea to seek help from a friend who knows how to knit.

Casting on

Casting on is the most difficult aspect of knitting and there are various different methods of doing it. The method shown here is relatively simple and works well.

Tip: The ball of wool should be at your right side, and the wool is carried by the right hand, unless you are left-handed, in which case the instructions can be reversed. However, some left-handed people are quite at ease knitting in a right-handed way, provided they learn the right-handed method from the beginning.

Easy   *Medium*   *Advanced*

1. Make an ordinary slip-loop 20 cm (8˝) from the end of the wool and push one needle through this loop. Pull the loop up so that it fits closely round the needle, but is not too tight. This will be the first stitch.

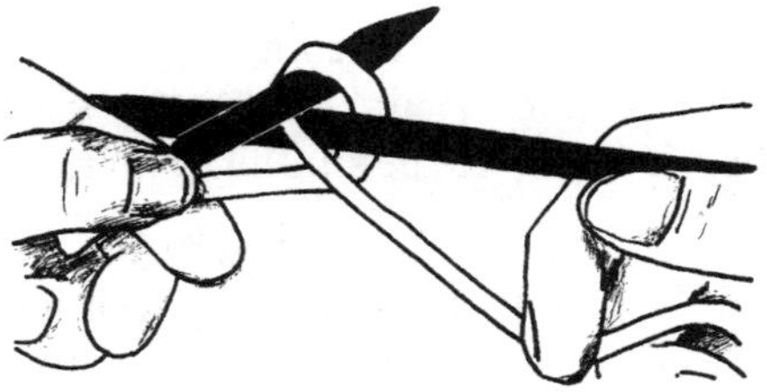

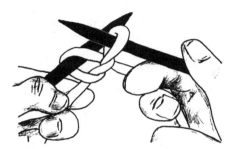

Diagram 1

2. Hold this needle in the left hand. Take the second needle and the length of wool that is attached to the ball, in the right hand. Push the right needle up through the loop on the left needle, so that the right needle comes *under* the left one *(Diagram 1)*.

3. Lift the wool that is attached to the ball, over the point of the right needle, from left to right.

4. Draw the right needle back towards yourself from under the left needle, and when the point has emerged carrying a stitch, place it on top of the left needle *(Diagram 2)*.

Diagram 2

5. Bring the point of the left needle round on top of the right needle, insert it up through the loop on the right needle, then draw the right needle out and away *(Diagram 3)*. There are now 2 stitches or loops on the left needle.

6. Continue in this way until you have the required number of stitches on your left needle.

Diagram 3

7. Always keep the length of wool that you are knitting with, underneath and at the back of the needles.

Plain Knitting

There are 2 basic knitting stitches – plain and purl. Plain knitting is usually abbreviated to 'K' in knitting patterns.

Before you begin a garment it is a good idea to do some practice knitting to get used to the stitches. You can always pull out your work and start again if it all goes wrong.

1. Cast on 10 stitches.

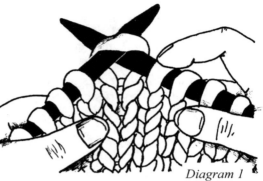

Diagram 1

2. Hold the needle with the stitches in the left hand. Insert the right needle up through the first stitch on the left needle, so that the right needle comes under the left one (just as you did when casting on) *(Diagram 1)*.

3. Pass the wool round the point of the right needle, from left to right. Draw the point of the right needle back out of the stitch and round to the front of the needle, making sure that you still have a stitch on the right needle *(Diagrams 2 and 3)*.

Diagram 2

4. Slip the first loop off the left needle. There should now be 9 stitches on the left needle and 1 stitch on the right needle.

5. Continue to work into every loop in this way, until there are 10 stitches on the right needle and none on the left needle.

6. Turn the work, placing the needle with all the new stitches into the left hand, with its tip pointing to the right.

7. Work another row exactly as you did the last one, remembering that in plain knitting the wool is always kept at the back of the work, and that every row is the same.

Diagram 3

🏃 Easy   🏃🏃 Medium   🏃🏃🏃 Advanced

Purl Knitting

You can now learn purl knitting. This is done into the *front* of the stitches. (It is abbreviated to 'P' in knitting patterns.)

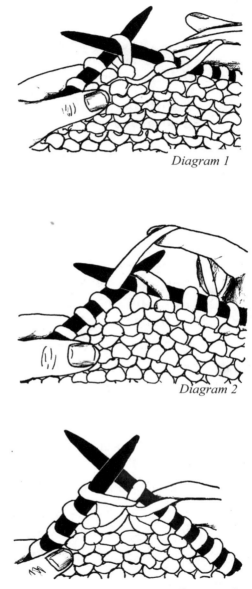

1. Cast on another 10 stitches (or continue on the piece of plain knitting you have just done). Take the needle with stitches in the left hand, and keep the wool at the *front* of the work.

2. Holding the left needle horizontally, push the right needle through the top of the first stitch on the left needle, *from the right to the left of the stitch,* keeping the right needle in front of the left one *(Diagram 1).*

Diagram 1

3. Now pass the wool round the point of the right needle, from right to left *(Diagram 2).*

4. Repeat the action described in Step 3 of plain knitting i.e. draw the point of the right needle back out of the stitch making sure that it emerges with the loop still round it *(Diagram 3).*

Diagram 2

5. Place the right needle behind the left needle, then slip the first stitch off the left needle.

6. Work into each stitch on the left needle in the same way, until all the stitches are transferred to the right needle.

Diagram 3

Stitches

Garter Stitch

Garter stitch is another name for plain knitting stitch. Knitting something in garter stitch also means to knit every row in plain knitting (i.e. no purl knitting). It forms ridges on alternate rows.

Stocking Stitch (abbreviated to st.st.)

Stocking stitch is one row in plain knitting and the next row in purl knitting.

Slip Stitch (abbreviated to sl.st.)

1. Hold the needle with the stitches in the left hand.

2. Push the point of the right needle up through the front of the first stitch on the left needle, from left to right, and draw the loop off the left needle on to the right needle, without knitting it.

Casting off

This should be done *loosely*.

1. Put the needle with the stitches on in the left hand, and knit the first two stitches in plain knitting.

2. Push the point of the left needle, *from left to right*, through the front of the first-knitted of the two stitches on the right needle

3. Hook this first stitch over the second stitch and then over the point of the right needle. Let this stitch drop in between the needles. One stitch has now been cast off.

4. Plain knit (K) the next stitch from the left needle, making two stitches again on the right needle and, as before, slip the first one over the second.

5. Continue in this way until only one stitch remains on the right needle.

6. Break off the wool from the work, leaving about 15 cm (6″) of wool hanging loose.

7. Slip the last remaining stitch loosely off the needle and draw the end of the wool through this last stitch. Pull tightly.

8. Thread the end through a wool needle and sew it neatly into what you have knitted. (A wool needle is like an ordinary sewing needle, but it has a blunt point.)

⼈ *Easy*   ⼈⼈ *Medium*   ⼈⼈⼈ *Advanced*

Knitting Patterns

Here are some abbreviations that you may come across.

K.........Knit   *P.........Purl*

st.........stitch   *sts.........stitches*

K2 tog.....Knit 2 stitches together. (You do this by putting your needle into the second of the next 2 stitches as if you were going to knit it first, and then immediately through and into the first stitch. You then treat them as one stitch and knit them in the usual way. This is also called decreasing and is abbreviated to dec.)

K2 P2   ...Knit 2 stitches, purl 2 stitches.

Inc........Increase. (This is done by beginning to knit a stitch and just before you slip the stitch off the needle, at the last step, you move the point of the right needle round to the back of the stitch, put it into the back of the stitch, put the wool round the needle again, pull the right needle through and slip off the loop. In this way you have knitted twice into one stitch and will have 2 stitches instead of just the one, on the right needle.)

Teddy's scarf

You will need:

- 25 gm (1 oz) of double knitting wool
- 1 pair 4 mm (Size 8 UK, 5 US) knitting needles

Instructions:

Using the method explained above, cast on 14 sts.

Knit 40 rows in garter stitch (every stitch and every row in plain knitting).

Cast off and then sew the end into the work with a wool needle.

When a young child is learning to knit, each stitch is a potential disaster or triumph, and it is important that you sit next to them and watch what they are doing all the time. In this way you can correct any mistakes as soon as they occur and avoid the necessity of having to 'pull the work out'.

After a little practice, a child starts to understand how knitting works and will know for themselves when they go wrong. They can then be left safely to work on their own.

Child's scarf

This is a single-coloured scarf for a child age 6 – 8 years. For a 8+ year-old child, cast on 32 stitches and follow the pattern in exactly the same way.

Tip: If you want a striped scarf you can change colour every few inches. At the end of a row break off the wool you have been using, leaving a 20 cm (8″) length. Begin to knit the row using the new wool, also leaving a 20 cm (8″) length. When you have finished the scarf, knot these two ends together, and sew them into the scarf with a wool or darning needle.

You will need:

- 100 gm (4 oz) chunky or very thick wool
- 1 pair 6½ mm (3 UK, 10½ US) knitting needles
- Crochet hook (optional)

Instructions:

1. Cast on 24 sts.
2. Knit 4 stitches, purl 4 stitches. Repeat this sequence until you reach the end of the row.
3. Continue in this way (knit 4 sts, purl 4 sts) until the scarf is 1 metre (3 feet) long.
4. Cast off loosely.

To make the fringe:

Cut 48 lengths of wool 16 cm (6″) long (if you are making the larger scarf, you will need to cut 64 lengths of wool). Fold each one in half and, using a crochet hook or your fingers, push the folded end through one of the stitches at the end of the garment. When half-way through, push the two cut ends through the loop you have made. Pull tightly.

Repeat along both ends of the scarf. You should have a fringe of 24 lengths on both ends of the scarf (or 32 lengths if you are making the larger scarf).

Doll's Jumper

The pattern is for a 40 cm (16″) doll or a medium-sized teddy bear. The jumper is worked in one piece and is knitted in garter stitch i.e. every row and every stitch is plain knitting.
You start with the front.

You will need:

- 25 gm (1 oz) of chunky or aran wool
- 1 pair 5 mm (6 UK, 8 US) knitting needles
- Stitch holder or spare needle

Instructions:

1. Using the 5 mm needles cast on 25 sts.

2. Work 7 cm (2 ¾″) in garter stitch
   (every row and every stitch in plain
   knitting) (approximately 18 rows).

3. *Shape sleeves:* Cast on 8 sts., knit
   to the end of the row. Cast on another
   8 sts at the beginning of the next row.
   (41 sts now on needle.) Continue in
   garter stitch until the work measures
   10 cm (4″).

4. *Divide for the neck:* Knit 14 sts, turn
   the work and, ignoring the remaining
   stitches on the needle, continue to work
   on these first 14 sts until the work measures
   15 cm (6″).
   Break off the wool, leaving a 30 cm (12″) end.
   Leaving a 20 cm (8″) length, rejoin the wool at the centre, cast off 13 sts, and knit
   to the end of the row.
   Continue to work on these last 14 sts until this second side is the same length as
   the first side.

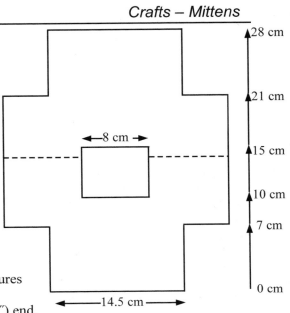

5. *Joining the 2 sides:* Knit a row of the 14 sts so that you finish the row on the neck
   side. Turn the work round, cast on 13 sts. Turn the work round again and continue
   to knit the 14 sts from the stitch holder or spare needle. (You should now have 41
   sts on your needle again.)
   Continue straight until work
   measures 21 cm (8¼″).
   Cast off 8 sts at the beginning of
   the next 2 rows (25 sts now on
   needle).
   Work straight on these remaining
   25 sts until work measures 28 cm
   (11″).

6. Cast off.

To make up:
Sew together side and sleeve seams
using the ends of wool left over from
casting on and off.
Turn jumper inside out. Turn up 2
cm (¾″) at the bottom of each sleeve
and fasten in place with a few small
stitches on the inside of the sleeve.

Cross Stitch

Cross stitch is one of the most widely-used embroidery stitches. It gives a very pleasing and professional-looking result.

It is not the easiest of stitches to master and a little practice may be necessary before you are able to produce consistently neat work. Despite this drawback, children of 9 or 10 usually enjoy cross stitch because of the wide range of designs it enables them to make.

Step by step diagrams for cross stitch are shown here.

Although some books will tell you to sew a row of half cross stitches, then to work back over them, a neater result can be achieved if you sew each cross stitch separately.

There are many simple and beautiful items that can be made incorporating a cross-stitch design.

They are particularly effective in Christmas and greetings cards.

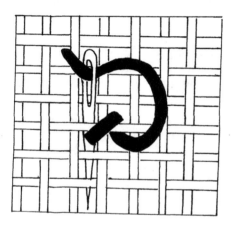

Note: Embroidery silks come in 6 strands. Unless otherwise stated, cross-stitch embroideries should be worked in 2 strands. This means that you will have to cut off the required length of thread, unwind 2 strands and work with these 2 together. Keep the other 4 strands in a safe place and use 2 more strands when required.

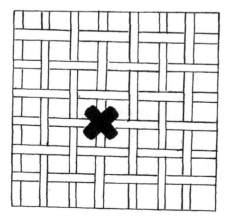

Embroidered Cross-Stitch Cards

You will need (for 1 card):

- One piece 10 cm x 10 cm (4″ x 4″) of Aida fabric (53 holes per 10 cm approx.) in blue, white or cream

- Several lengths of dark green, red and yellow embroidery silks

- A piece of dark green, white or cream card - 21 cm x 12 cm (8½″ x 5″)

- A piece of thick paper in the same, or matching, colour - 10½ cm x 12 cm (4½″ x 5″)

- Small amounts of non-toxic fabric glue and paper glue

- A gold, or silver, metallic point pen

- Scissors and a sharp craft knife

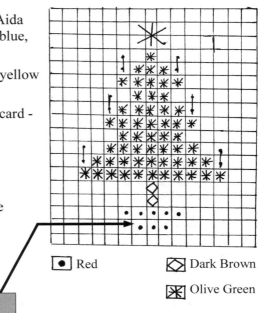

⊡ Red	◇ Dark Brown
	✳ Olive Green

First Stitch

Instructions:

1. Find the middle point of your piece of Aida fabric by folding it lengthways, opening it out and then folding it widthways. When opened out, the intersection of the two folds is the middle point. It is important to know this so that the finished embroidery will be in the centre of the fabric.

2. Mark the top of the piece of fabric with a pin or coloured thread.

3. From the centre of the fabric, count 7 holes down and 1 hole to the left, and starting with 2 strands of the red silk, work your first cross stitch (*see Diagram*).

4. Follow the chart above, changing colour when necessary. When joining in and finishing off your coloured thread it is better just to leave a long end, which can be worked in later, rather than having a knot. A knot will give an uneven surface to the finished work, which will show up if you are using it in a card.

5. To sew the candles, take one strand of red silk and sew a vertical line at the end of each branch (see picture). Take a single strand of yellow silk and sew a vertical line at the tip of each of the red candles. The star should also be sewn with a single strand of yellow silk.

6. Press the finished design on the reverse side using a medium-hot iron and damp cloth.

Making the card:

1. Fold the card *(Diagram 1)*

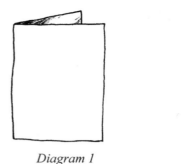

Diagram 1

Diagram 2

2. Using a sharp craft knife carefully cut out a window in the front of the card, *just larger than the size of your finished tree (Diagram 2)*.

Diagram 3

3. Squeeze a *small amount* of fabric glue round the front edge of the finished fabric *(Diagram 3)* and stick it to the inside of the front of the card *(Diagram 4)*, so that the embroidery shows through the window *(Diagram 5)*.

Diagram 4

4. Lay the piece of paper over the reverse of the fabric, and glue it onto the inside of the card *Diagram 6)*.

Diagram 5

Diagram 6

5. Outline the perimeter of the card and the perimeter of the window with a gold or silver pen, and write your greeting on the inside.

More Designs

Here are some more, simple cross stitch patterns which you can use for birthday cards etc. You can also frame the embroideries using small frames bought from a craft shop.

Ladybird

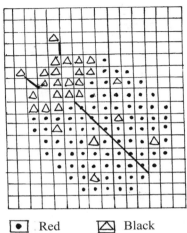

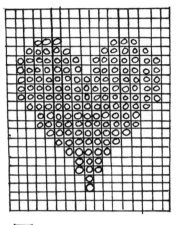

⬭ Pink

Heart

⊡ Red   △ Black

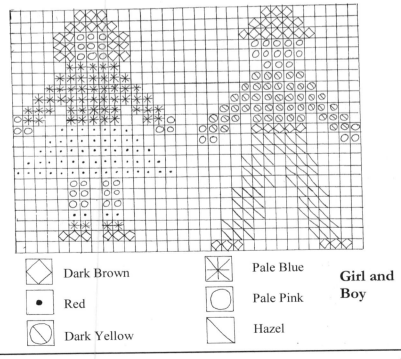

◇ Dark Brown   ✳ Pale Blue   **Girl and**
                                      Boy
• Red   ○ Pale Pink

⊘ Dark Yellow   ◿ Hazel

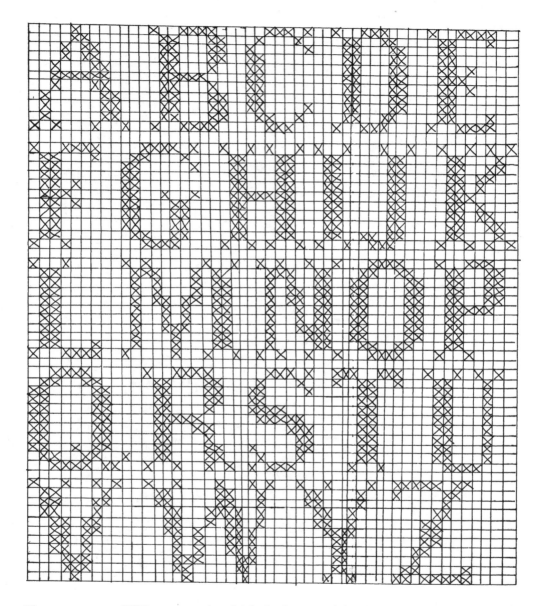

There are many different ways in which the letters of the alphabet can be made from cross stitch. This pattern gives simple, clear letters suitable for a beginner.

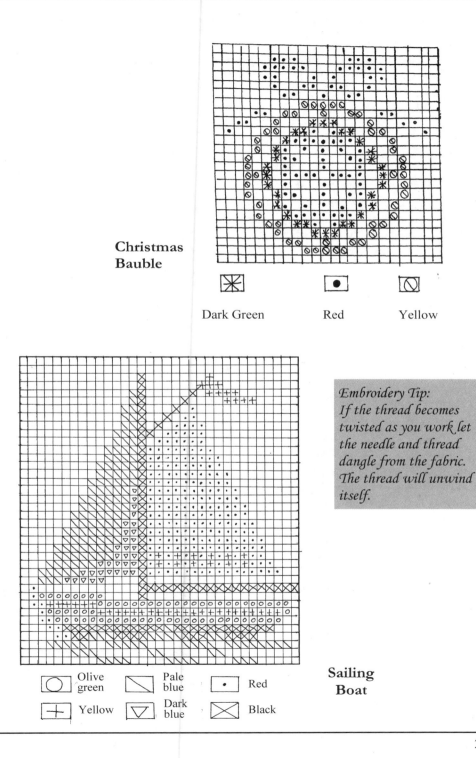

Christmas Bauble

Dark Green   Red   Yellow

Embroidery Tip:
If the thread becomes twisted as you work let the needle and thread dangle from the fabric. The thread will unwind itself.

Sailing Boat

Olive green   Pale blue   Red

Yellow   Dark blue   Black

Candle Making 🏃🏃🏃

There are two basic techniques of candle making: one involves dipping a wick alternately in hot wax and cold water, the second involves using a mould.

Candle dipping is fun but messy and it requires a lot of wax. As a result it is probably better to use moulds at first.

A good craft shop should sell everything that you need to get started as a candle maker.

You will need:

Diagram 1

- **Wick**. Wax-covered wick in a wick-holder (obtainable from craft shops) is best for beginners (*Diagram 1*). Later on you can dip plain wick into wax and reuse the wick holders of burnt-out candles to make your own wicks.

- **Wax**. A block (225 gm, 5 oz) of paraffin wax is the cheapest source of suitable wax (*Diagram 2*). Granulated paraffin wax is easier to melt but may be a little more expensive. You can also use beeswax.

Diagram 2

- **Stearine**. You have to add stearine to the melted wax to stop the candle from sticking to the mould.

- **Perfume**. A few drops of an essential oil added to the molten wax will give your candles a distinctive smell.

- **Dye sticks**. Red, yellow and blue wax dye sticks (*Diagram 3*) will allow you to make candles in whatever colour you want.

Diagram 3

- **Little sticks**. You will need some little sticks (*Diagram 4*) (lollipop sticks or cocktail sticks with the ends chopped off) to prop up the wicks and stop them from falling into the molten candle wax.

Diagram 4

- **Moulds**. It may be better to make several small candles at first, rather than one big one. If you cannot find suitable moulds in the shops, then you can use a plastic biscuit tray like the one shown here (*Diagram 5*).

- **An old plastic or glass bowl**
- **A small pan**
- **A spoon or small ladle**

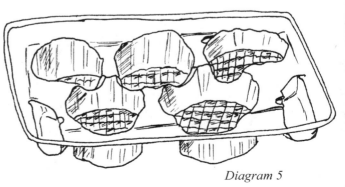
Diagram 5

Instructions:

1. Put enough wax into a bowl to fill the moulds that you intend to use.

2. Add a little stearine (about ¼ teaspoon for each candle).

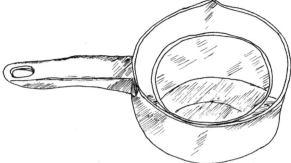

3. To melt the wax, place the bowl in the little pan, which should have about 2½ cm (1″) of water boiling in the bottom (*Diagram 6*). Keep the pan on a *low heat* and stir the wax gently: this will make it melt quicker.

Diagram 6

4. To add a little colour, carefully dip the dye stick into the hot wax. Test the colour by putting a drop of the wax onto a white saucer.

5. Pour ½ cm (¼″) of wax into each mould. (Sealing the base of each candle in this way means that you can float them without the wicks absorbing water through the base.)

Diagram 7

6. As the wax hardens carefully position the wicks in the moulds (*Diagram 7*).

7. Pour a few drops of essential oil into the molten wax.

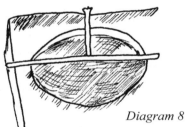

8. Pour the wax into the moulds. Support the wicks with the little sticks so that they don't fall over. (*Diagram 8*).

Diagram 8

9. Wait an hour or two for the wax to harden and then carefully take the candles out of the moulds.

Short, squat candles will float well. Put them in a glass bowl full of water in the centre of the table and watch them float serenely while you eat your meal.

Papier Mâché

Papier mâché is a versatile modelling material that allows children to make beautiful, highly-durable objects.

You will need:
- 5 or 6 sheets of newspaper
- Wood glue (this is better and less toxic than wallpaper paste)
- Vaseline
- A liquidiser
- Water
- A jam jar with a screw top lid
- A small plate (a plain plate is preferable. You may damage the pattern on a painted plate)
- Sandpaper
- Paint
- Varnish

Instructions:

1. Tear the newspaper into strips.

2. Put the strips into the liquidiser with some water (about 1 cup) and some glue (about 1 tablespoon).

3. Liquidise the mixture until it is a smooth paste.

4. Store the paste in the airtight jam jar. It can be kept in this way for several weeks.

5. Liberally cover the top side of the plate with Vaseline. (This will stop the papier mâché from sticking to it.)

6. Cover the plate with a layer of your papier mâché paste.

7. Leave it to dry for a day or two. You can dry it in a warm place or outdoors, but if you put it too close to a fire or in the oven the Vaseline will melt and the papier mâché will stick to the plate.

8. Apply another layer of papier mâché paste.

9. Let it dry.

10. Continue this process in order to build up several layers of papier mâché. You are unlikely to make the plate too thick.

Easy   *Medium*   *Advanced*

11. Leave the plate to dry thoroughly.

12. Gently prise the papier mâché away from the plate, being careful not to distort it too much. (If you have a problem, it may be because the papier mâché is not sufficiently dry. The solution is to apply another layer and to leave it for a few more days.)

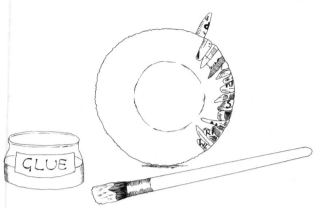

13. Trim the edge of your papier mâché plate with scissors.

14. The cut edge will probably need some attention. Dilute some wood glue and use it to stick strips of newspaper over the edge. You may need to do this a few times to build up a smooth rim around your plate.

15. When the edge is completely dry, sand the plate to remove bumps and traces of Vaseline.

16. 'Prime' the plate with white undercoat, vinyl emulsion or acrylic paint.

17. You can now paint the plate. Acrylic paints are best, but you can use any paints that you happen to have.

18. Allow the paint to dry and then varnish the plate to protect your work. Clear varnish from art shops is better than wood varnish, which usually has a yellow tinge.

This method of making papier mâché is quicker and easier than using strips of newspaper.
It can also be used for making jewellery, boxes, models etc.

Working With Your Child

Lessons

A major difficulty that parents encounter when working with their children at home is that they do not know how to behave in relation to work done in books.

They soon discover that techniques used in schools cannot be transferred to the home. It is not possible, or desirable, for parents and children to adopt the role of 'teacher' and 'pupil', and parents who are too rigid in their approach to lessons will find that it creates a very bad atmosphere in the home, against which a child will soon rebel. The home has to be a haven from the sort of activities that take place in schools.

If you want to work with your child on subjects such as reading, writing, arithmetic and other 'school' subjects, you must find a way of doing so that fits in with your normal family life.

Generally speaking, the best way to get started is for you to sit at a table with your child, or children, in the morning when everyone is at their most alert, and to have a one or two hour session during which you work together. Initially this 'work' should involve drawing pictures.

While you are working you can talk. If your child is young, you can tell them fairy stories, myths and legends and then you can both draw pictures from the story. If your child is older you can wait to see what direction the conversation takes and eventually come to an agreement about what particular area you would like to study on future days – poetry, literature, history, etc.

In this way you develop a system that allows you to work together, and creates an atmosphere in which you can talk to each other without slipping into teacher/pupil roles.

You can call this situation 'lessons,' which gives pleasant connotations to a word that often conjures up painful memories of school.

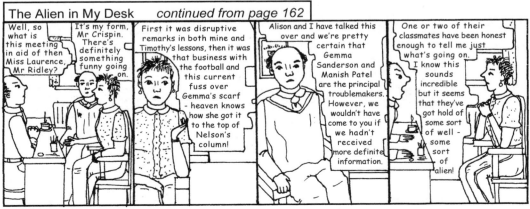

The Alien in My Desk   *continued from page 162*

Natural Learning

Parents who teach their children at home have become aware of a phenomenon that is not readily observed in schoolchildren. They have coined the phrase 'natural learning' to describe it, and it refers to the fact that children, when left to themselves, have an insatiable desire to learn.

'Home-schooling' families in countries around the world have found that it is not necessary to devise a detailed curriculum and programme of study for their children. If children have access to sources of information their own desire to understand the world about them will lead them to 'study' on their own. This 'study' is much more efficient in terms of what children can learn in a given amount of time than a programme of education imposed upon them by someone else.

'Natural learning' has of course always existed, the thing that is different today is the amount of information that is available. Whereas at one time children would have been restricted to learning about people and places in their immediate vicinity, they can now find out about countries and cultures from all over the world.

Books, magazines, television and the Internet provide an almost unlimited amount of information, and one of the effects of this is that schools can no longer match the home as a learning environment. The narrowness of a school curriculum does not help or encourage a child to develop the skills required to deal with all this information.

Children who do not go to school, but who are left to pursue non-academic studies for as long as they want, are well equipped to deal with all this information, once it does start to attract their interest. They apply the same enthusiasm to their studies as they have done to their play and consequently are able to deal successfully with whatever subject areas they choose to tackle.

This does not make the role of the teacher redundant, it simply means that the child's parent will be the person best qualified to fill the role of teacher, and that this role will principally involve relatively small amounts of one-to-one teaching at appropriate times.

Books

Books are still the best educational resource that exists – they present information in a way that is particularly accessible, especially to children.

If you want your children to feel confident about learning at home you have to have books in your house.

In fact, books are much more important at home than they are in school. At home your child is able to ask questions at any time on any subject, and you need to have books in which they can look up the answers and read about the subjects that interest them.

Even more importantly, books contain high-quality illustrations that allow children to form their own impressions about people, places and things that they have heard about.

Books are also the best source of pictures from which to copy (whether it be works of art, people or places) because the quality of printed images that they contain is much higher than those found on the Internet or in newspapers.

Libraries

For most people libraries provide the natural starting point when they want information on a specific subject. The books are not always in the best condition, and having to return the ones that you really like can be annoying, but libraries do provide an opportunity to discover the real value of a book before you go out and buy it.

Second-Hand Book Shops and Jumble Sales

Building up a good collection of books does not necessarily involve vast expenditure. Second-hand books are very good value for money and one often finds old copies of a book that are superior to the modern edition, as well as being cheaper.

New Books

There are certain books that one finds oneself turning to again and again, and these are worth buying new. They include, amongst others, guides to wild flowers, trees, birds and wildlife, history books, mythology books, a good geography book, books of poetry, classic novels, and the great scriptures of the world.

Computers

The long-term impact that computer technology will have on education is still unclear. It seems unlikely to fulfil some of the wilder predictions that were made for it a few years ago, which suggested that computers may one day make all teachers obsolete. Children will probably always learn principally from other people: even children who are self-motivated enough to read and study on their own need someone with whom they can talk over what they have learnt.

Nevertheless, the way in which computers make information more accessible is having a profound effect upon the way in which children learn.

In particular, encyclopaedias on CD-ROM are much cheaper than their printed equivalents and are more interesting because they contain sound clips, video clips and thousands of colour pictures.

This makes it very easy for children to find out about subjects that interest them, and greatly encourages them in the process of studying on their own.

The Internet has the potential of making even more information available to children, but it may not ever become a technology that can be adapted to the needs of people under the age of ten or eleven.

It is not an easy medium to use and children tend to get frustrated, even when assisted by an adult, when they have to make their way through a maze of information that they do not understand, before they can find what they are looking for.

This does not negate the fact that the Internet is already an invaluable resource for parents who want to teach their children at home. It makes it possible to find information on virtually any subject and this opens up new possibilities for working at home with a child.

As an example, if you are working on Africa with your child it is quite likely that they will ask you about the languages spoken in Africa. A few years ago it would have been difficult to find information on the subject, now you can download sound clips of people speaking all the major African languages; you can download African songs and you can download facts and figures about what is spoken where. It is little things like this that radically change a child's view of education.

Social Interaction

One of the most commonly-cited reasons for sending children to school is that it allows them to make friends of their own age. Whilst this may have its advantages, the issue is not as clear-cut as it seems. Schoolchildren do interact with a great number of other people, but it is not a very healthy form of interaction.

They are forced, too much, into the company of their peers (with all the detrimental effects that that can have) and do not have sufficient contact with people of other age groups. The contact that they do have with adults has the effect of alienating them from other generations because school creates a barrier between teachers and pupils.

Schoolchildren can even find it difficult to have a normal relationship with their own brothers and sisters and this alone can cause serious problems within a family, and should cause parents to question the value of the social interaction that takes place in school.

In comparison, children who do not go to school tend not to have social problems. They may be restricted to a smaller circle of acquaintances, but this circle is usually made up of a reasonable cross-section of society and includes people both older and younger than themselves.

If you send your children to school, you could consider:

- not encouraging your children to spend too much time in the evenings and at weekends with their school friends. It is important to have a life outside school.

- making sure that your children are able to spend time with adults, other than yourself, when they are not at school. If they have a chance to get to know your friends they will see that not all adults behave like their teachers.

- giving your child a chance to help look after, and play with, younger brothers and sisters, or other young children of your acquaintance. Remember that no one really outgrows the desire to play with simple toys, and playing with babies and toddlers gives a child a chance to be young again – even though they are grown-up and go to school.

Religion

At one time, religious education was placed at the heart of every educational programme. Church and State worked hand in hand to ensure that children were brought up as confirmed members of a particular faith.

As the influence of religion has declined in society as a whole, the prominence that it is given in the school curriculum has been gradually eroded. This has left a situation in which no one is really sure how religion should be taught to young children.

Consequently, religious education that does still happen in schools varies in quality from place to place and from teacher to teacher. Many children receive next to no religious education at all and grow up without having even heard the stories from the Bible or any other scripture.

This means that religious education is another area in which parents have to consider what contribution they are able to make themselves.

It should not equate with an attempt to indoctrinate a child into accepting a certain set of religious principles. Such an attempt would probably fail in our multi-faith/no-faith society, even if it were desirable: children are able to see how other people live, and become uncomfortable when they feel that their parents are restricting them to a set of beliefs that are only held by a minority of the population and which are at divergence with the mainstream of popular thought. This is something that has frequently led young people to reject their parents' religious beliefs, thereby causing serious family rifts.

A more enlightened approach is to view the world's scriptures as the greatest cultural heritage that we possess. As a parent you have the opportunity to introduce them to your child by reading aloud and by telling stories from them. You will find that you do not need to place interpretations upon what you read – it speaks for itself. Children appreciate the opportunity to reflect upon stories that contain genuine wisdom and welcome the chance to draw their own conclusions.

The ability that children have to understand these stories shows us that we have at least as much to learn from them as they have from us.

Morals

Adults are often appalled by the bad behaviour displayed by many young people and children today, and think that schools should make more effort to instil good morals into their pupils.

There is of course a flaw in this argument. Morals, or a sense of right and wrong, are formed by people's own good sense combined with what they see happening around them.

It is an unfortunate fact that however much someone knows something to be wrong, if they see other people getting away with it they will be tempted to follow suit.

Thus if schools were to have any success in instructing people in good morals, they would themselves have to be run on moral principles.

Even children who are quite happy to go to school would never say that they were run on moral principles and children are confronted by daily examples of injustice: bullies prosper, rich children get the best facilities and are always top of the class, people are punished for things that they did not do and children have little freedom to make their own decisions. In these circumstances, when a teacher stands up and gives a talk about morals, it is treated with derision.

Bad language, drugs, violence and crime are part of school life. They are the inevitable result of a system that does not allow mutual respect to develop between teachers and pupils. Schools have always been a breeding ground for bad behaviour and this provides another reason why school hours should be restricted.

In most homes, on the other hand, people have to learn to get along with each other on a fairly equal footing and to show respect for each other's idiosyncrasies. Children who feel well grounded in a strong family atmosphere are much less likely to indulge in seriously antisocial behaviour of any sort, for fear of incurring the disapproval of other members of their family.

The more time that your children are able to spend in the home environment, the more likely they are to grow up with a good understanding of their moral responsibilities.

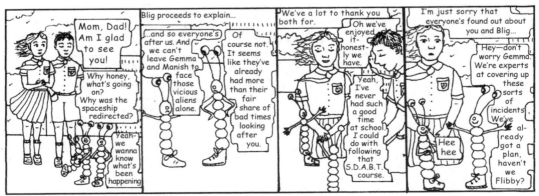

The Curriculum

Not so long ago the primary school curriculum consisted simply of reading, writing and arithmetic. Over recent years, however, it has become much more sophisticated and there is now a National Curriculum that lays out what every child in a state school is meant to learn in every subject in each year.

It must be apparent to everyone who has any understanding of children that a system of this sort cannot work. Each child is an individual who should be treated with respect. As far as possible, each child should be given a programme of education that is suited to their particular needs and interests.

If it was based upon sound educational principles a National Curriculum could, perhaps, offer some help by giving parents and teachers ideas about how to approach the difficult task of providing individual children with a worthwhile education.

Unfortunately, the National Curriculum that we have is not based on sound principles and cannot offer even this advantage. It is built on the false premise that children should be launched into a programme of primary education when they are only five years old, and all its other ills flow naturally from there.

To make matters even worse, a programme of testing has been introduced to back up the National Curriculum. Testing has no place in the education of young children and its effects are universally harmful.

As well as undermining the self-confidence of many children, testing has the effect of preventing them from studying subjects that they find interesting and teachers direct them to learn only those things that are included in the tests. This results in the process of education being thwarted before it has had a proper chance to begin: children develop a dislike for subjects that they know hardly anything about.

This presents parents, who want to keep their children on the right track, with a considerable challenge: they have to find a means of making subjects, such as history, geography, science, music and languages, interesting even though their children may have already lost interest in them at school.

In order to succeed in this, parents need to show more sensitivity than would be the case if their children had never been to school.

It is easy to make mistakes. For example, parents often think that if they help their children with their homework this will stimulate their child's interest in the subject concerned. It is more likely to have the opposite effect.

Another common mistake is expecting your child to share your own interests and passions. In normal circumstances perhaps they would, but if it is something that they have done in school, they may already have developed an aversion to it.

The answer is to not have fixed ideas about what your child should be doing and to not push them into pursuing particular activities. Instead, make sure that they have space in their lives in which they can develop and follow their own interests independently of the pressure placed on them at school. Be ready to help when you are needed.

Even though to you they may be pointless, it is better to encourage children to pursue activities that do interest them, rather than trying to direct them towards pursuits which you consider to be worthwhile.

No one really knows what knowledge will be useful to today's children when they grow up, because so many aspects of modern life are in a state of flux. This makes the idea that it is appropriate to set children a fixed curriculum particularly anachronistic. It is far better to encourage a child to develop skills that allow them to learn, than to make them study specific things.

Music

Sport and Exercise

Japanese in
Three months
German: The Basics
Essential Lat-in
GREEK Phrase Book
Teach yourself Urdu

Learning a Language

Science

History

Geography

Music

It is when we consider the subject of music that we realise how little we really understand about life and what it is to be a human being. The scientific achievements, of which we are so proud, have given us no insight into why music should be important to us. In fact, it is even difficult to define what we mean by music, but everyone recognises it when they hear it and everyone is saddened when they are deprived of it. We all need to have music in our lives and this applies at least as much to children as it does to adults.

Ideally, all the sounds that children hear should be harmonious and musical. Perhaps this would be the case if they grew up surrounded by nature. The sounds of the birds singing, the wind in the trees and the murmuring of a brook are all the sweetest forms of music and it is difficult to imagine the effect that they must have on children who hear nothing else from the moment that they wake up in the morning to the time when they fall asleep at night.

Few children, in the West at least, are lucky enough to grow up in this sort of atmosphere. Instead they are subjected to the raucous and grating sounds that characterise man's contribution to the environment. The sounds of cars and lorries are seldom far away, aeroplanes fly overhead and washing machines, vacuum cleaners, radios and televisions fill the air in their homes. (The noise in schools, playgroups etc. is often even worse: the din can become almost unbearable as children compete with each other to make themselves heard.)

It is easy to see how children lose their ability to appreciate simple music in this cacophony of sound – but it is impossible to tell what effect this has upon them.

The first thing that a parent can do to help their child in the realm of music is to provide them with an environment, when they are young, that is as full of musical sounds as is practicable. This does not mean that parents need to sit and play musical instruments to their children from dawn till dusk (although this might be a good idea), but it does mean taking a few practical steps such as the following:

- Sing to your children as much as you can.

- Do not fill the house with the sound of the radio and television.

- Do not put children into situations, such as playgroups, where noise levels get out of control.

- Do not play too much recorded music (CDs, tapes, etc). There is a subtle difference between live music and recorded music and children do not respond in the same way to the latter as they do to the former.

- Spend time out of doors, in nature, where the air is full of natural sounds.

When is the best time to learn to play a musical instrument?

When people think about children and music they tend to think about children learning to play a musical instrument. This is a particularly peculiar aspect of western life: we live in a society in which relatively few adults play a musical instrument with any degree of regularity, but it is common to make children learn how to play very difficult instruments – often against their will.

There is no discernable logic in this arrangement and, as a general principle, parents should try to reverse it: that is, they should learn to play a musical instrument themselves, they should play it regularly and they should put no pressure at all on their children to learn.

It is impossible to make an objective assessment of when a child should learn to play a musical instrument but certain facts are self-evident:

- Most musical instruments are easier to play when one is older.
- It is easier to read music and to understand musical notation when one is older.
- In order to master an instrument you have to practise. Motivation to practise must come from within.

Taking all these points into account, it is clear that most children will not develop a real interest in learning to play a musical instrument until they are at least ten or eleven years old.

This is older than some parents might expect, but it is an area in which it is very important (even more so than in reading and maths) that children should be allowed to make their own choices.

For most people there is no financial or economic benefit to be gained from playing a musical instrument: it is something that is done for pleasure and there is no sensible reason why anyone should wish to force a child to learn to play a musical instrument against their natural inclination.

Instruments

Of course, children can only decide that they want to play a musical instrument if they are aware that such things exist, and parents do have a responsibility to provide children with enough experience of music for them to be aware of the opportunities open to them.

Ideally there will be instruments in the house, played regularly by other members of the family. This is by far the best way of opening a child's eyes to the fact that, given a little application on their part, they are capable of playing an instrument themselves.

It does not do any harm to let young children play with musical instruments, providing they do not damage them, so that they become familiar from a young age with how to make them work.

Keyboard Instruments

If you have a piano in the house and you play it yourself, then your child is bound to want to play it as well.

Traditional pianos are still preferable to electric keyboards, and second-hand pianos are not expensive. They have to be tuned regularly, about three times a year, but apart from that are very easy to maintain.

You do not need to be an accomplished pianist in order to inspire your child to learn. In some ways it is better if they see you working your way through a beginners' course of piano books—it shows them that they can do the same.

The Piano

The piano was invented at the beginning of the 18th century by an Italian called Bartolommeo Cristofori – in principle it closely resembled the harpsichord, but possessed certain modifications which set it apart from the earlier keyboard instruments. Thanks to an improved design, contrast could be made between soft and loud (hence the Italian name pianoforte, literally soft loud) and, over the next hundred years, pedals were added to increase the amount of time notes could be sustained. Although the piano is an extremely mechanical instrument, when played with sensitivity it is capable of great expression and purity of sound.

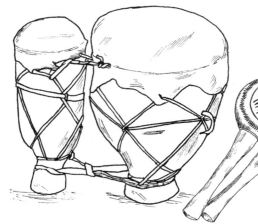

Percussion Instruments

Drums, maracas, castanets, tambourines etc. are traditional instruments that exist in one form or another in most places around the world.

Authentic instruments, often made from simple materials, are now widely available and they allow children to recreate the musical sounds of other cultures in their own homes.

Stringed Instruments

It is physically possible for a young child to learn to play a stringed instrument, but it is a process that requires a greater level of dedication than is reasonable to expect from a young child.

It is a shame when children are alienated from something that could give them enormous pleasure, just because it has been introduced too soon.

The Violin

The origins of the violin go back many thousands of years: tradition maintains that the first stringed instrument played with a bow was invented by a king of Sri Lanka in 5000 BC. However, it was not until the sixteenth century that the violin, as we know it today, came into being. Italian families living in a small town called Cremona perfected the design and instruments made by Amati, Guarneri and Stradivari were the prototypes for all other violins.

The tone of the violin is more high-pitched than its larger relatives, the cello, double bass and viola - perhaps this is why it is so often compared to the human voice.

No other instrument can so ably convey the emotion felt by its player, and its soaring, brilliant notes are as expressive when performing solo pieces as when accompanied by a full orchestra.

Wind Instruments

The recorder is often used to introduce children to playing an instrument because it is affordable and easy to carry around.

Wind instruments are not, however, the easiest instruments to play because they require a level of breath control that does not come easily to young children. When playing instruments with young children the emphasis should be kept on having fun, technique can be worked on when they are older.

The Flute

The flute is a member of a very ancient family of instruments, examples of which have been found in prehistoric dwellings. Although existing in various forms for thousands of years, it took the dedication of a man called Theobald Boehm (1794-1881) to make the flute a truly precise instrument.

Until he devised the modern system of stops and levers, imperfect notes and difficult fingering were problems well known to every flautist, owing to the fact that if the holes were bored in the correct places, they could not be reached. Thanks to Boehm's system the flute has acquired the popularity it deserves. The purity of its notes and the sweetness of sound possess an ethereal beauty unrivalled by other, more mechanical, instruments.

Singing

Singing can offer an introduction to music to every child and it poses none of the problems presented by musical instruments.

All children respond to being sung to. Babies and toddlers are more soothed by someone singing to them than they are by the spoken voice.

The nursery rhymes that parents traditionally sing to very young children provide a good introduction to the world of music. It is often said that the human voice is the most versatile of all musical instruments.

It probably helps if you can sing in tune, but it is better to sing badly than not at all. It is hard to imagine that a child brought up in a home where there is no singing at all could grow up to be a happy child.

You do not have to worry about teaching your child to sing. They will want to express themselves through song and will teach themselves to find the right notes. They will learn to sing in the same way that they learn to talk – through imitation and practice – especially when they are given the peace and quiet that allows them to sing happily to themselves.

The home is the ideal place for a child to develop their musical abilities. They can sing when they want, they can play with whatever musical instruments are available to them and they can be sung to by other members of the family.

CDs, tapes, etc.

Recorded music can never be as stimulating as live music but it does provide an opportunity to experience a range of musical styles that would not otherwise be available.

This has all sorts of benefits: listening to music from other countries gives an insight into their culture and is bound to increase tolerance and open-mindedness. Listening to a wide range of different types of music is stimulating to a developing musician and encourages them to be more adventurous in their own playing.

Music that is marketed directly at children is often, unfortunately, the least appropriate. Pop music has been almost completely absorbed into the global industry that seeks to exploit children's innocence in the pursuit of monetary gain, and it often has little musical merit.

An effective way to counteract the onslaught of pop music is to share your own enthusiasm for different types of music with your children, when they are young: they can then make up their own minds about what sort of music they like themselves, when they are older.

SPORT AND EXERCISE

Children brought up in modern, western countries are generally unfit and the main reason for this is that they spend too much time indoors. They get very little exercise and a growing child needs healthy outdoor exercise every day.

Lack of fitness amongst children, especially when combined with a poor diet, can lead to serious health problems in later life.

Children themselves cannot be blamed for this situation, for neither the town nor the country now offers them the sort of safe, healthy environment that would entice them away from the security of their own homes: urban environments are dominated by the motor car and the countryside has been practically handed over to agribusiness.

Parents, therefore, now have to make a conscious effort to ensure that their children have worthwhile opportunities for exercise.

WALKING

Walking is the best way of keeping fit: it exercises all the different parts of the body without putting undue strain on any of them.

It is also the best way of observing the changes that take place in nature with the rhythm of the seasons. This is very important because children who spend all their time indoors become isolated from the cycles of nature. Compared to the vitality of the natural world, television is very dull indeed and it is a tragedy when children have to grow up spending all their free time in front of a screen instead of being out of doors.

Unfortunately, the predominance of cars and lorries on the roads, and the way in which much of the countryside is managed, means that it is no longer possible to wander freely through country lanes and open woodland and, in addition, people no longer consider it safe to let their children walk around on their own.

This means that walks have to be planned before you set out from the house, and that you have to make the time available to accompany your child on long walks. These are not necessarily disadvantages because walking is an excellent bonding exercise and it enables you and your child to talk things over in a situation in which neither of you feels under any pressure.

The coast is the area that now offers the least spoilt environment, and even if you have to spend an hour travelling there, a day walking beside the sea will amply reward your effort.

Walking must be a top priority and it is worth going to some lengths to experience the pleasure that it can give.

OTHER FORMS OF EXERCISE

Anything that gets a child out of doors will provide them with at least some degree of exercise and, providing that it is not dangerous either to themselves or to other people, it should be encouraged.

Opportunities to go outside are not as abundant as they should be: children who have a garden are the luckiest because they can play in it whenever they want; public parks could offer a similar facility, but no one now lets their child go to the park on their own and this reduces their usefulness.

Cycling is popular but public roads are not safe for young cyclists, even when accompanied by an adult, and you have to research the availability of dedicated cycle routes in your area.

Horse riding combines healthy exercise with working with animals: the only drawback is that it is an expensive hobby.

Swimming is good exercise but it is not necessarily healthy. Public pools tend to be indoors and over used, and it is quite common for children to develop colds or stomach complaints after a trip to the baths.

The more that one considers the question objectively, the clearer it becomes that children are not valued in our society. They have a basic need to be able to walk freely in the area around where they live and this is one thing that is denied to them. Parents have to work hard to patch together a series of different activities – going for walks, cycle riding, riding lessons, gardening, etc. – in an attempt to make up for this basic deficiency in the way our society is organised.

COMPETITIVE SPORT

It is sometimes suggested that sport can atone for the fact that children are no longer free to roam the area around their homes and it is even credited with having distinct virtues of its own. The beneficial effects of sport are probably overrated.

When games such as football, tennis, badminton, etc. are played principally for fun, they are undoubtedly a good thing, but once a more serious, competitive edge is

introduced, the issue becomes more doubtful. It is not good for children to push themselves in a particular sport to the point where they can injure themselves or place too much strain on muscles that are still developing.

The concept of winning and losing is also unhelpful to young children: the idea that special merit should be attached to success in essentially frivolous activities distracts children from those things that *are* important. It is also disheartening for those children who do not win—no one enjoys being branded as a loser in any area, no matter how unimportant the thing is in itself.

RUNNING, JUMPING, ETC.

When pursued in a light-hearted manner – as opposed to making them into competitive sports – running, jumping, hopping, etc. still provide children with an inexhaustible supply of pleasure. It works best with a group of children of mixed ages. If they have a race the older children have to give the younger children a head start and then it does not matter who wins. The emphasis returns to where it should be: on people just experiencing the pleasure of running, hopping, jumping etc.

You do not need to have a lot of children to make this activity worthwhile. Even very young children (who must know that they cannot run as fast as grown-up members of their family) like nothing better than to have race after race with their mother, father or older brothers and sisters.

SKIPPING

Traditional skipping games involve two people holding and turning either end of a stout rope – which should be at least ten feet (3 m) long – while at least one child jumps over it. To enliven the exercise the 'turners' chant a skipping rhyme.

Blue bells, cockle shells

(repeat several times)

Easy ivy over.

This is a skipping rhyme for very young children. Start off by gently swinging the rope backwards and forwards as the child jumps over it.
The rope is swung over the head on 'over' and the rhyme is repeated.

In this rhyme two people skip together. One person, skipping alone, starts the rhyme, then invites someone to join them. The two skip together while the second person repeats the rhyme, and in turn invites someone to skip with them. The first person leaves as the third person joins, and the rhyme continues in this way.

I like coffee, I like tea, I like

(name of a friend)

to come in with me.

When the name of the friend is said, a second skipper should rush into the place vacated by 'Susie'.
The exit and entrance should coincide!

Susie in the kitchen doin' a bit o' stitchin'
Along came *(the name of a friend)*
And chased poor Susie out.

Cowboy Joe lives in Mexico
Hands up, stick 'em up,
Don't forget to pick 'em up
Cowboy Joe lives in Mexico."

On 'pick 'em up' the skipper pretends to pick something up from the ground. The rhyme is repeated to exhaustion!

Teddy bear, teddy bear, turn around,
Teddy bear, teddy bear, touch the ground.
Teddy bear, teddy bear, show your shoe,
Teddy bear, teddy bear, that will do.
Teddy bear, teddy bear, brush your hair,
Teddy bear, teddy bear, climb the stairs.
Teddy bear, teddy bear, turn out the light,
Teddy bear, teddy bear, say goodnight,
G..O..O..D..N..I..G..H..T.

A rhyme for a single skipper. As you skip, perform all teddy bear's actions. At the end, the skipper spells out the word 'goodnight'.

LEARNING A LANGUAGE

It is often said that young children learn languages much more easily than adults. This is true, but in order to learn properly they need to be in the company of someone who can speak the new language fluently. That is how children learn speech, by copying and repetition, they do not learn it from books or by studying grammar, for example. This gives rise to a fundamental difficulty: there are not enough people available who speak a second language with sufficient fluency to give young children a proper language education.

WHERE SCHOOLS GO WRONG

Instead of recognising this fact, schools still teach foreign languages, even though they do not have the proper resources. This can lead to children being given the worst possible introduction to language learning: they acquire a terrible accent, do not learn to make sentences and cannot express themselves in the new language. All that they learn is that languages are difficult and this puts them on making an effort when they are older, when they would have a better chance of being able to learn from books, tapes, etc.

Schools have tried various strategies to try to overcome this problem but they are all based on using audio-visual aids to try to make up for the fact that the teacher in the classroom cannot speak the language being studied. This doesn't work with young children. It has some potential with older children and teenagers, especially if they have a strong personal motivation for learning a language, but younger children need to interact with another human being in order to learn properly.

Machines do not give them the feedback that they need and they soon lose interest. This applies just as much to the most technologically-advanced computer-related products as it does to cassette tapes and videos. Perhaps something will one day be invented that will teach a young child to speak a foreign language, but there is no sign of such a thing happening at the moment.

THE ADVANTAGES

This does not mean that the idea of teaching children a second language should be abandoned.

The advantages of being able to speak two or more languages are considerable. It liberates a person from feeling trapped in one particular culture and opens up the possibility of being able to communicate directly with people in the wider world.

In addition, speaking a second language stimulates the mind and makes someone more articulate in their first language. Bilingual children consistently do better than monolingual children in most assessments of academic abilities, even when they come from similar backgrounds.

HOW CAN PARENTS HELP?

The problem is that there is no easy way to teach a child living in an intensely monolingual society to learn a second language: they are not surrounded by the sights and sounds associated with a second language and their role models only speak one language. There is virtually no incentive and few opportunities for them to take the huge step of learning another language.

This means that you have to be realistic in the goals that you set yourself. Your main objective should be to give your child a positive attitude towards other languages. Encourage them to see languages as enjoyable and do not allow your child to become oppressed by anyone (teachers at school for instance) who may try to force them to learn a particular language against their own inclinations.

Beyond that, there are several practical things that you can do.

BILINGUAL PARENTS

If you speak a second language yourself then this is obviously the one that you should 'teach' your child, and you can introduce it as early as you wish. Parents sometimes worry that teaching their children languages other than those that they encounter at school will somehow disadvantage them, but these fears are unfounded.

Children who speak one language at home and a different one at school usually cope without too much difficulty, and children who spend an hour or two per week learning their parent's mother tongue, or the language for which their parent has a passion, should not have any problems.

रहिमन धगा प्रेम का, मत तोड़ौ छिटकाय ।
टूटे से फिर ना मिलै, मिलै गांठ पड़ि जाय ।

Do not break the string of love suddenly.
The ends will be hard to join, and even when you can there will be a knot.

Hindi proverb

PRIVATE LESSONS

The time-honoured, and still probably the best, way of introducing a child to a new language is with the help of a private tutor or a bilingual friend. The personality of the person involved is more important than their qualifications or even which language they teach.

A few hours spent with a sympathetic teacher, learning the basic sounds of a language, some songs, a few games and perhaps a selection of useful phrases can make a lifelong impression on a child. It can fire their enthusiasm, not only for the language concerned, but also for the idea of being able to speak several languages.

TELEVISION

Television cannot offer the same possibilities as a live teacher and language programmes on the television tend to be frustrating: they do not provide any opportunities for interaction and, as a consequence, children lose interest in them quite rapidly.

Flicking through the satellite channels is probably the best way of using television as an aid to language learning: older children in particular can quickly get a feel for a language by watching a few hours of foreign television. If they are serious about learning a language, watching satellite channels may give them the best opportunity of becoming accustomed to the sound of it being spoken.

L'homme est bien insensé. Il ne saurait forger un ciron, et forge des Dieux à douzaines.

Man is quite insane. He wouldn't know how to create a maggot, and he creates Gods by the dozen.

Montaigne 1533-1592

BOOKS, TAPES AND CD-ROMS

Books, tapes and CD-ROMs should be viewed as means of teaching a child a few words and phrases of a language rather than as a route to becoming fluent in speaking it.

With this in mind, select those that are fun and avoid those that concentrate on grammar. Most language courses are not suitable for children because they are built around situations, such as ordering food in a restaurant, that have little relevance to a child's daily life. Language books written specifically for children, on the other hand, are usually over simplistic and do not say anything interesting at all (a fault that they share with children's books in general).

FOREIGN TRAVEL

Foreign travel has now become part of normal life for many people and it does offer the possibility of being able to hear and to speak a language in its proper setting.

Phrase books can be very useful. You can pick out and learn phrases that you are likely to use while you are abroad.

Even being able to say 'Yes' and 'No' or 'Please' and 'Thank you' in another language, and to be understood, can be quite a wonderful experience and can alter a child's whole attitude towards foreign languages.

A Swahili riddle:

Ninapompiga mwanangu watu hucheza.

When I beat my child, people dance.

(answer page 294)

Siku ya kufa nyani, miti yote huteleza.
The day a baboon is destined to die, all trees become slippery.   *A Swahili saying*

THE INTERNET

The Internet offers access to web sites that provide lists of vocabulary, phrases, background information and pronunciation guides to many different languages, as well as sound-clips so that you can actually hear them being spoken.

As a result, children can now find out about any language that captures their interest. They are not restricted to having to study European languages and the few other world languages that may be represented in their local bookshop.

an hini a vale eeun a gav atao ledan he streat.
He who walks straight will always find the road to be wide.   *Breton proverb*

WHICH LANGUAGES ARE BEST TO LEARN?

Given the number of languages that exist in the world, and given the fact that one cannot know what course a child's life might eventually take, it is difficult to know which language is the most useful.

It is best to follow one's own common sense. If you live in a bilingual area then your children will probably want to be able to speak both languages. If you enjoy foreign holidays in a particular country then it makes sense to learn the language spoken there. If you know someone fluent in a foreign language who will give your child lessons, then that also makes the choice easy.

Die Tat ist alles, nichts der Ruhm.
The deed is all, and not the glory.
Goethe 1749-1832

If none of these possibilities present themselves, you can just wait until your child expresses an interest in a language and then try to give them as much support as you can by way of books, tapes, etc. so that they can start to learn something about it. As with other areas of education, everything becomes much simpler when you realise that you can trust the judgement of your child. They are the ones that are going to have to speak the language that they learn, and it therefore makes sense for them to choose it.

Whichever language they do decide to learn, you will find that there is more to it than lists of words and grammatical constructions.

Bezañ ha Bezañ Bet
n'int ket ur c'hement.
To be and having been are not the same.
Breton saying

Learning a language gives you an insight into another culture which is bound to leave you wiser and with a broader perspective on the world than you can have if you restrict yourself to speaking just one language.

Solution to Swahili riddle (page 293)
Ngoma   a drum

Science

Science is now one of the main subjects in the primary school curriculum, ranking alongside English and maths, but the teaching of science to young children is a fairly new innovation and it is far from clear that it is a good idea.

As far as one can judge, science is taught in primary schools not because it is considered to be appropriate or useful or interesting to children of that age group, but rather as part of a strategy to improve the scientific and technological competence of the population as a whole.

As has been seen in the discussion of maths teaching, simply including a subject in the curriculum does not necessarily result in children becoming more competent in it, in fact the reverse is often the outcome. Trying to develop primary schools away from their original role of teaching reading and writing has not yet met with any success, and science is less likely to lend itself to being taught at this level than any other subject.

Drawbacks to Primary School Science

Pure science is a subject that demands powers of reasoning and analysis that would be inappropriate in a child. Science owes its existence to people not accepting facts that they are told, but questioning them and thereby making new discoveries. Children are not able to understand the mathematics and the reasoning behind scientific theories, they are not able to test them and cannot, therefore, engage in proper science.

Proponents of science teaching would, of course, argue that this is not the point: science is included in the curriculum, not so much to produce scientists, but rather to make people feel more comfortable with using scientific ideas.

This is one thing, however, which the teaching of science in primary schools is not likely to achieve. Young children are taught science at a time when they are incapable of understanding it. Instead of giving them an interest in the subject it gives them the impression that science is too difficult and should be avoided whenever possible.

The fact that schools have trivialised science in an effort to make it palatable to young children does not make the situation any better. One of the defining characteristics of children is that they ask questions – that is how they learn – and when they are introduced to an interesting phenomenon in their science lessons, their response is to ask questions.

It is frightening to observe how quickly teachers get out of their depth when trying to answer these questions and to see how frustrating the situation is for the children concerned.

Primary School Science

The primary school science curriculum is divided into the study of living things (biology), materials and their properties (chemistry) and physical processes (physics), the hope being that introducing children to these subject areas when they are young will prepare them for encountering them at secondary school.

In many ways this does not reflect the way in which science itself is developing. While there are still branches of science that are becoming ever more specialised, there are now very respectable areas of science that require a holistic approach. For example, such pressing issues as climate change, the effectiveness of alternative medicines and the use of organic methods of agriculture cannot be studied by scientists who have limited themselves to the study of one very narrow branch of science. They require people who are able to take a global view and who are able to bring a range of skills to bear upon a subject.

As it stands, the curriculum takes a set of very adult ideas, simplifies them so that they no longer make sense, and then teaches them to children.

This leaves them vaguely confused and does not prepare them either to pursue the route of conventional science (physics, chemistry and biology) or a more modern approach.

What Parents Can Do To Help

Science is an area that intimidates many parents. They do not feel qualified or competent to help their children and they do not understand the science curriculum.

They have to be prepared to put this sense of inadequacy to one side. The science curriculum is inappropriate and parents should not worry that they do not understand it.

Instead they should concentrate on making sure that their children have a fulfilling range of experiences in their daily lives.

Science is fundamentally the study of nature. The best way for a child to study nature is through experience. The more extensive a child's experience of nature, the better their understanding will be.

When children ask questions about something it is not necessary to be able always to give definitive answers. When you think about the questions relating to the natural world, you realise that we do not, and cannot ever, know the answers to them:

we cannot prove whether there is a God or there is not a God; we cannot explain the difference between something that is alive and something that is not; we cannot explain how the material universe could have been created out of nothing.

That is what makes science such an interesting subject.

Children are not frightened by this uncertainty and it does not do them any harm to tell them that we do not know the answers to some of their questions. It gives them a chance to simply enjoy things without having to explain them.

The National Curriculum.

The areas covered by the national curriculum are not in themselves inappropriate for young children. The problem is simply that everyday phenomena are categorised and explained according to scientific ideas.

In their studies of life processes, children are told about the difference between living and non-living things; about plants and animals; parts of the body; things that live and grow in the local area; about the structure of the heart and the skeleton and about micro-organisms. They may also be subjected to a little propaganda about drug abuse at the same time.

In their studies of materials they learn about the difference between wood, metal, glass, plastic etc.; about what happens when you heat things up (especially water, bread, chocolate, and clay); about electrical conductivity; and about separating things by sieving, filtering and evaporating.

In their studies of physical processes, they learn about simple electrical circuits; about magnetism, gravity, friction and elastic bands; about the fact that musical instruments make sounds and that sound can travel through water as well as through air. They also learn a little about light and about the solar system.

A careful consideration of those things that are in the National Curriculum should show parents that it is well within their power to introduce their children to everything that it includes, but to do so in a natural way that does not leave their children thinking that science is something special and unconnected to every other area of life.

Rather than feeling that science done in the home is inferior to that done in schools, parents should be able to see that it is only by being able to experience natural phenomena from within the context of a happy home that children can begin to make sense of the world around them.

Parents do not need to go out of their way to create artificial scenarios for the study of science. It does not need to be treated as a separate subject. For a young child, science is just part of being alive, and providing that their life is fulfilled they will learn everything they need to know about science.

Gardening

It does not take a genius to realise that a child will develop a far better understanding of living things through working in a garden than through any amount of work in a classroom.

They also learn about the seasons, about the lengthening and shortening of the days, about the effects of sun, frosts, rain and drought.

They see the life cycles of butterflies, aphids, ants, wasps, ladybirds, etc. at first hand. They see the bees pollinating the flowers and can see the birds building their nests and raising their young.

By working in a garden children can learn more about nature than they could ever be taught from books and they are learning in the way that they are meant to learn – by doing something that they enjoy.

Cooking

A moment's consideration of the chemistry section of the National Curriculum shows that it does not contain anything that children cannot discover through cooking.

Cooking shows children what happens when you heat food and what happens when you mix different ingredients. It teaches how to weigh things out accurately and how to follow written instructions with a view to getting a desired result.

Crafts

The beauty of crafts is that they allow children to find practical applications for artistic and creative skills. They allow them to explore the potential of different materials for making a wide variety of things.

This is as close to technology as a young child can get and if they learn to make beautiful items out of simple materials such as wool, cotton, wood, papier mâché, paper, cardboard, etc., they will not be intimidated by more complex items when they are older.

Astronomy

The only sensible way of studying astronomy is to look at the stars and, as the stars are not visible during the day, it is not something that can be done at school.

This means that every parent has the opportunity of introducing their children to the night sky themselves.

Before people had street lights, and lived in houses, this would not have been something that required any effort, but it is not now as easy as it ought to be to witness the splendour of a starlit night in all its glory.

However, there is still no substitute to be found for taking a child out on a cloudless night and staring up into the void of infinite space with them. You do not have to offer any explanations, it is just an experience to take your breath away.

Magnetism

You may think that you understand about magnetism until you start to try to explain it to someone. There is, in fact, no simple way in which it can be accounted for, but this does not reduce the fun that you can have playing with magnets.

Experiments

Scientific experiments have been a source of pleasure for children for many years.

The home is the ideal environment for conducting experiments: children can work at their own pace, do not have to finish at the end of the lesson and do not have other people interfering with their work.

'The Usborne Book of Science Fun' contains many experiments that can be done at home and it is very well written.

Technology

Technology now plays a large role in everyone's life and some thought has to be given as to how it can best be introduced to children. The approach of giving children lessons about computers when they are in school is probably not the best way of proceeding.

It may be helpful to consider the reasons why children need to know about technology:

Technology Useful to Children

Most importantly, they may want to use technological devices themselves. When this is the case, the subject does not present any difficulties. They can learn how to use a computer by trial and error, in the same way that children learn about everything else.

A young child does not realise that computers are new inventions. Everything is new to a young child and computers present no more of a problem than anything else in their environment.

This means that if your computer (or any other piece of technology that you have in your house) has any features that are useful or interesting to your child, they will learn how to make use of them without any conscious effort being required from you.

Acquiring Skills for the Future

People sometimes think that it is not sufficient that children know how to visit their favourite Internet site, play some games on a computer and how to send an e-mail. They think that they have a duty to make sure that their children have a certain level of computer literacy.

There is a great deal of concern that society in general and individuals in particular will suffer if skill levels in this area are not dramatically increased. This is especially a source of worry for parents who are themselves intimidated by modern technology, and who find that their own employment prospects are becoming increasingly restricted because they do not have the skills required in the modern workplace. They want to do everything possible to avoid the same thing happening to their children. Whilst this is understandable, the problem can not be solved by instructing children in the use of computers and other machines that we consider to be modern.

In fact, that would be to repeat the mistakes that were made in the past, because the machines that are at the cutting edge of technology today will, in all probability, be obsolete by the time that today's primary school children eventually leave school and enter the work force.

The skills that children have to acquire, in order to have a reasonable chance of success in later life, are not skills relating to a particular technology but rather the ability to adapt to new circumstances.

In the future it is those people who are self-motivated and who see it as their responsibility to keep themselves up to date with new developments in technology who are most likely to do well. This means that it is the way that children learn, rather than what they learn, that will have the greatest long-term effect.

Children who only learn things with a view to passing exams and gaining qualifications do not have a chance to develop an approach to learning that allows them to keep their skills up to date. It is much better if children are encouraged to study only those subjects they find interesting and to view learning as a fulfilling and rewarding experience in itself. They will never then be intimidated by having to learn about new technologies as they become available.

Is it Necessary to Have a Computer?

You are not necessarily putting your child at a disadvantage if you do not have a computer. The lessons that a young child can learn from a computer are very limited when compared to what they learn from other people and from the world of nature.

From a strictly educational point of view it may even be an advantage to them not to have a computer: children had plenty of things to keep them occupied before computers were invented and it does no harm to let a child become acquainted with these things before introducing them to modern technology.

One does, however, have to be sensitive to a child's feelings. If everyone else has a computer and they do not, they are bound to feel underprivileged. In effect this means that if everyone in your circle of acquaintance has a computer, you have to buy one yourself. It is then up to your child to come to terms with how to make the best use of it.

Computer Games

Computer games are highly addictive and when you buy a new game it is difficult to think about anything else until you have mastered it.

This is a feature of the technology and no one seems to be immune to it.

However, any reasonably well-adjusted person soon becomes bored with the process and stops buying new games. This means that there is little point in trying to stop your child playing computer games – they will probably lose interest in them of their own accord.

History

It is impossible to understand anything about the current situation of the world without making a study of history.

This applies to the current political situation; the wars that constantly take place; the system of world trade; social and cultural differences that exist around the world; the distribution of wealth; the development of industry; etc.

Whatever subject you discuss with your child you will find that it makes more sense when you put it into a historical perspective.

However, many of these issues are not of particular interest to children up to the age of eleven, and a really comprehensive study of this subject can be left until a child is able to appreciate the reasons why people have behaved in the way that they have throughout recorded history. History need not play a major part in primary education – it comes into its own in secondary education, where it ought to be the principal subject.

History that you study with young children should be based around drawing pictures and telling interesting stories about people and places from the past.

There is no clear line between mythology and ancient history, which makes stories from bygone civilisations a good starting point – especially if your child enjoys hearing about the ancient gods and goddesses.

The civilization of ancient Egypt goes back far beyond recorded history. No one knows when people first settled on the banks of the Nile, nor where they came from. One thing is certain however: by about 3000 BC a complex, highly developed civilization was in place.
It was so successful that it remained one of the world's foremost nations for millennia.

The ancient Egyptians invented their own systems of writing, and were skilled mathematicians – in fact it was they who first divided the year into 365 ¼ days. From articles found buried in tombs we can also see that they were master jewellers, artists and sculptors.

QIN SHIHUANGDI

'He has the proboscis of a hornet and large all-seeing eyes. His chest is like that of a bird of prey and his voice like that of a jackal. He is merciless, with the heart of a tiger or wolf.'

This is how the first emperor of China was described by Wei Liao, one his advisors, before he fled the court.

Qin Shihuangdi ruled China from 221 to 210 BC after unifying it with the help of a ferocious army.

Once in power he established a system of government that was to last for two thousand years. He also standardised weights and measures, introduced a standard form of writing, built roads, ordered complete disarmament, melted down weapons to make bells and statues and extended the Great Wall so that it covered 2,500 miles (4,000 km).

ANNE BOLEYN

The six wives of Henry VIII are as famous as the King himself, but it is easy to forget that each one of these women had her own thoughts and feelings and was, for a time, the undisputed Queen of England.

Anne Boleyn (c. 1507-1536), was courted by Henry at her father's house, Hever Castle, and they were secretly married in 1533 when Ann was 26 and Henry 41 years old.

Possessed of a lively, playful disposition she was not, however, reckoned much of a beauty. A contempory writer describes her as having a "swarthy complexion, long neck and wide mouth".

She rapidly fell out of favour and after only three years of marriage found herself being tried for unfaithfulness. She protested her innocence but the execution went ahead, and the next day Henry was betrothed to Jane Seymour.

Geography

At the primary school level, history and geography are often lumped together, but they are really quite different subjects. Geography is more analytical than history and does not lend itself to being used as a vehicle for telling stories. It gives a child an understanding of their place in the world, but it can become boring if one is not careful.

One aspect of geography that most children enjoy is the drawing of maps. Maps that show the different countries of the world are the most enjoyable and you can combine this with a study of flags.

Learning a few facts about various countries can also be interesting and you can give each other quizzes about capital cities, major rivers, mountain ranges etc.

Local geography will be of interest to your child. The simplest way to introduce it is for *you* to read all the available books on the subject and to then point out interesting landmarks to your child when you are out walking together. This will enable you to explain how the physical geography of your area has determined the development of roads, bridges, towns and villages etc. in a way that stimulates, rather than stifles, your child's interest.

A proper study of geography is best left until a child is a little older.

- The Sahara is the largest desert in the world and covers much of North Africa.

- Mali is the hottest place on Earth.

- There are more than 600 ethnic groups in Africa.

- Africa is larger than China, India, U. S. A., Argentina and Europe combined.

- Lake Victoria is the second-largest lake in the world (Lake Superior, in N. America, is the biggest).

The Nile is the longest river in the world. Starting from Lake Victoria in Uganda and Lake Tana in Ethiopia, the two main tributaries come together to form the single River Nile which finally comes out in the Mediterranean Sea.

There are 49 countries in mainland Africa, including Madagascar.

Sudan is the largest country in Africa.

West Africa is the world's largest producer of cocoa beans.

More than half of the world's gold comes from South Africa.

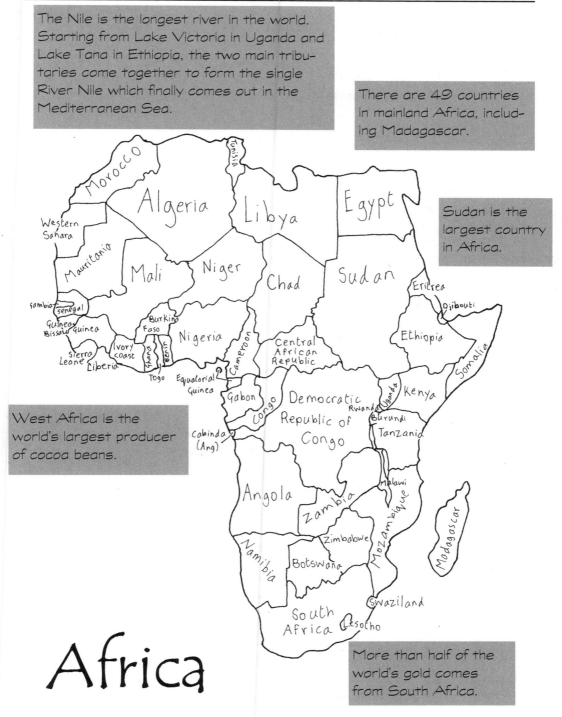

Africa

Conclusion

The purpose of this book has been to illustrate that children do not need to be forced down a particular path of learning and that they do not need to have their childhood blighted by being made to go to school to study things that do not interest them.

Education is difficult and problematic, not because children are incapable of acquiring the skills that are necessary to succeed in life, but because these skills are presented to them in an inappropriate way.

In particular, the school system teaches everything too early, thereby depriving children of the chance to discover things for themselves and putting them in a situation in which they are always trying to come to terms with information that they do not quite understand.

The consequence of this approach is that many children lose their enthusiasm for education while they are still young, even before they leave primary school. As a result, it is almost impossible for secondary schools to achieve their goal of equipping children for life in the outside world.

The solution lies with parents. Parents should not try to back-up the work that takes place in school but should pursue an alternative curriculum with their children. At first this curriculum will lag several years behind the work being done in school: children need not be made to read when they are five; they need not be made to do sums; they need not be made to study science; etc. but at some point, providing parents have been successful in keeping their child's interest in learning alive, it will overtake the school curriculum and leave it far behind.

There is virtually no limit to what a self-motivated child is capable of learning and, when this enthusiasm is coupled with the sources of information that are now available through books, computers and the Internet, children can study any subject that captures their interest without being hindered by not being able to get hold of accurate reference material.

This process of acquiring knowledge is something that occurs naturally when a child is in the secondary stage of their education i.e. from eleven years of age and upwards. It is not something of which people now have a wide experience because most children have been through the primary school system and have consequently lost much of their motivation by the time they enter secondary school. The natural state, however, is for people of this age group to be highly motivated and very keen to learn in detail about everything that relates to the adult world they are about to enter.

The main objective of parents of young children should be to nurse them through the early years of their education so that when they are eleven years old they can read and write, understand simple arithmetic, have a profound understanding of nature, know a little about looking after themselves (cooking, housework, crafts, etc.) and, above all, have retained the full force of their enthusiasm for life and for living.

Last Lines

No coward soul is mine,
No trembler in the world's storm-troubled sphere:
I see Heaven's glories shine,
And faith shines equal, arming me from fear.

O God within my breast,
Almighty, ever-present Deity!
Life—that in me has rest,
As I—undying Life—have power in Thee!

Vain are the thousand creeds
That move men's hearts: unutterably vain;
Worthless as wither'd weeds,
Or idlest froth amid the boundless main,

To waken doubt in one
Holding so fast by Thine Infinity;
So surely anchor'd on
The steadfast rock of immortality.

With wide-embracing love
Thy Spirit animates eternal years,
Pervades and broods above,
Changes, sustains, dissolves, creates, and rears.

Though earth and man were gone,
And suns and universes ceased to be,
And Thou were left alone,
Every existence would exist in Thee.

There is not room for Death,
Nor atom that his might could render void:
Thou—Thou art Being and Breath,
And what Thou art may never be destroyed.

Emily Brontë

Sewing Glossary

Back Stitch
(Diagram 1)

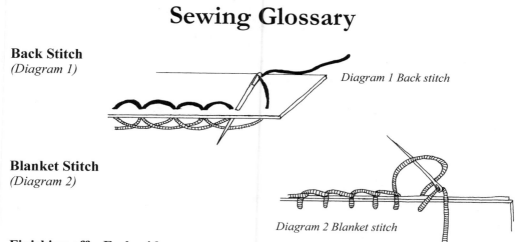

Diagram 1 Back stitch

Blanket Stitch
(Diagram 2)

Diagram 2 Blanket stitch

Finishing off – Embroidery
Go to the wrong side of the work and thread the needle through the backs of several stitches.

Finishing off – General Sewing
Make 3 small stitches where you want to finish. Take the needle to the other side of the work, and cut off the thread.

Over and Over Stitch
(Diagram 3)

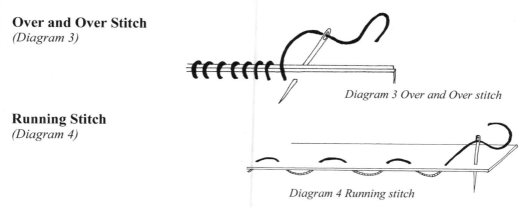

Diagram 3 Over and Over stitch

Running Stitch
(Diagram 4)

Diagram 4 Running stitch

Starting off / joining in – Embroidery
Wherever possible avoid making knots at the back of your embroidery.
Leave about 4 cm (1½″) of thread on the wrong side of the fabric and cover this end by working several stitches over it as you proceed with the embroidery.

Starting off / joining in – General sewing
Wherever possible avoid making knots at the back of your work.
Leaving a short end of threaded cotton on the underside of the fabric, make 3 small stitches in the same place and then begin sewing.

Conversion Tables

Knitting Needle Conversion Table		
English	**American**	**European (mm)**
000	15	9
00	13	8½
0	12	8
1	11	7½
2	10½	7
4	10	6
5	9	5½
6	8	5
7	7	4½
8	6	4
9	4	3½
11	3	3
12	1	2½
14	00	2

Oven Temperature		
Gas Mark	**°C**	**°F**
1		
2	120	250
3	160	325
4	180	350
5	190	375
6	200	400
7	220	425
8	230	450

Weights	
ounces (oz)	**grams (gm)**
⅓	10
½	15
1	25
1½	40
2	50
2½	65
3	75
4	125
5	150
6	175
7	200
8	225
9	250
10	300
11	325
12	350
13	375
14	400
15	425
16 or 1 lb	450
2 lbs	900
2 lbs	1000 or 1 kg

Measures	
teaspoons	**ml**
½	2½
1	5
2	10
3	15
tablespoons	
1	15
2	30
3	45
pints	
¼ pint	150
½ pint	275
¾ pint	425
1 pint	600
1¾ pints	1 litre

Note:
It is difficult to make accurate conversions between the metric and imperial systems of weights and measures and it is strongly advised that you follow either one system or the other throughout a particular recipe.

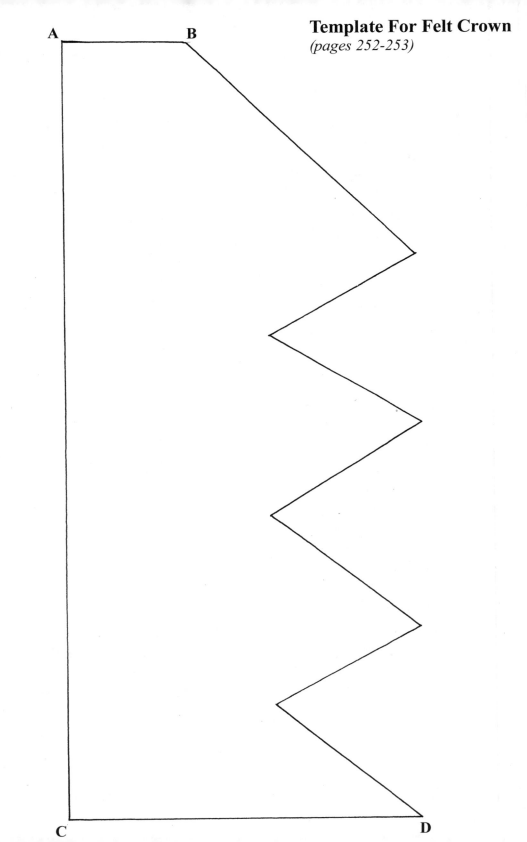

Template For Felt Crown
(pages 252-253)

A B

C D

Recommended books

The Usborne Illustrated World History series

DK Pocket Encyclopaedias: Organic Gardening, Dorling Kindersley, Geoff Hamilton (Editor)

Pan Book of Card Games, Hubert Phillips

The Doll Book, Karin Neuschütz, Floris Books

The Nature Corner, M. Van Leeuwen (Editor), J. Moeskops, Floris Books

John W. Schaum Piano Course Books for the beginner to the virtuoso

The Usborne Book of Easy Flute tunes.

The Usborne Book of Science Fun by M. Johnson et al.

Useful Addresses

Chase Organics
Riverdene Estate, Molesey Road, Hersham, Surrey KT12 4RG
Tel: (00 44) (0)1932 253666
E mail (to order catalogue): chaseorg@aol.com
www.organiccatalog.com

Centre of Alternative Technology
Machynlleth, Powys SY20 9AZ
Tel: +44 (0) 1654 702400
www.cat.org.uk/

Floris Books
15 Harrison Gardens, Edinburgh, EH11 1SH, Scotland, UK
www.florisbooks.co.uk

Education Otherwise
P.O. Box 7420, London N9 9SG, UK
www.education-otherwise.org

Freedom in Educatiom
www.freedom-in-education.co.uk

Index

Freedom in Education Magazine

Started in January 2003, the Freedom in Education Magazine is a monthly, independent journal that supports home education and new educational initiatives.

- Articles
- Cartoons
- Quizzes and Puzzles
- Recipes and Gardening tips
- News and Information
- Stories from History
- Mathematics
- Letters

For more information, visit our websites:

www.freedom-in-education.co.uk - a popular, comprehensive site, featuring articles that have attracted attention from around the world.

www.jamboree.freedom-in-education.co.uk - an internet site for parents and children, featuring original cartoons, recipes, crafts and much more.

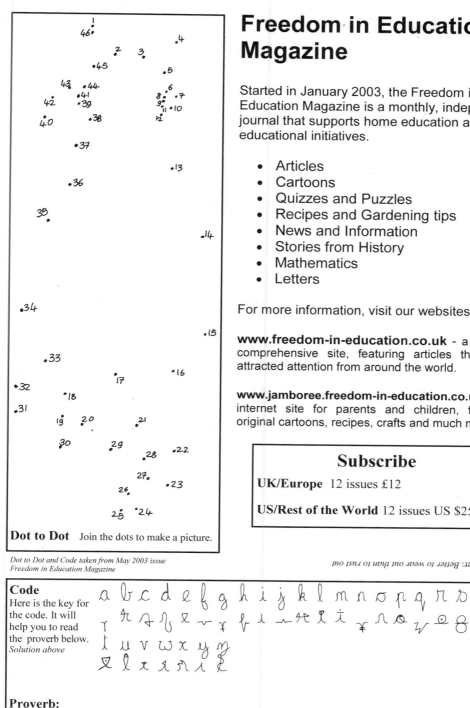

Dot to Dot Join the dots to make a picture.

Dot to Dot and Code taken from May 2003 issue
Freedom in Education Magazine

Subscribe

UK/Europe 12 issues £12

US/Rest of the World 12 issues US $25

Code
Here is the key for the code. It will help you to read the proverb below.
Solution above

Proverb:

Set of Maths Books

Written by Gareth Lewis, this set of maths books provides a simple introduction to the world of arithmetic:

500 Adding-Up Sums

500 Taking-Away Sums

500 Multiplication Sums

500 Division Sums

A total of 2000 carefully-graded sums guide the learner through the basics of simple addition and on to long division and long multiplication.

These four books will make a lasting impression and are guaranteed to restore anyone's fascination for the magical world of numbers.

Each book comes complete with answers and detailed instructions.

Special offer

Set of four books **£12.50**
including postage and packing.

(Normal retail cost £4.50 per title.)

Suitable for people of all ages and all abilities.
Illustrated with original cartoons and drawings.

Published by Nezert Books,
Nezert, 22160 Duault, France

Nezert Books

If you would like to be kept informed about future publications from Nezert Books please write to Nezert Books, Nezert, 22160 Duault, France.

For more information, visit our website: **www.nezertbooks.net**

<table>
<tr><th colspan="4" style="text-align:center">Special Offer – Order Form</th></tr>
<tr><td></td><td>Price</td><td>Quantity</td><td>Total</td></tr>
<tr><td>Freedom in Education Magazine (12 issues)</td><td>£12.00</td><td></td><td></td></tr>
<tr><td>Set of Four—500 Adding-Up Sums, 500 Taking-Away Sums, 500 Multiplication Sums, 500 Division Sums.</td><td>£12.50</td><td></td><td></td></tr>
<tr><td>One-to-One
A Practical Guide to Learning at Home Age 0 - 11</td><td>£12.50</td><td></td><td></td></tr>
<tr><td>Postage and packing—postage and packing free for customers using this form. Please allow ten days for delivery.</td><td colspan="2"></td><td>0.00</td></tr>
<tr><td>Please return this form, with a cheque made payable to Nezert Books to:
Nezert Books, Nezert, 22160 Duault, France.</td><td colspan="2" style="text-align:center">Total</td><td></td></tr>
</table>

Name: ....

Address: ....

....

....

E-mail (if you wish to be informed of despatch of order):

Telephone (optional):

Customers outside the UK, please contact us directly regarding prices and methods of payment. Please mention that you are enquiring about the Special Offer available to purchasers of One-to-One:

Nezert Books, Nezert, 22160 Duault, France
Tel: 0033 296 215597
E-mail: info@nezertbooks.net

For news and information about alternatives to school-based education:

www.freedom-in-education.co.uk